# RENAISSANCE DRAMA

*New Series* X 🙰 1979

# Renaissance Drama

NEW SERIES X

*Comedy*

Edited by Leonard Barkan

*Northwestern University Press*

EVANSTON 1979

81-1210

The illustrations on the front cover are from Jacques Callot's etchings for *Balli di Sfessania*. Reproduced by courtesy of the National Gallery of Art.

The illustration on the back cover is from the title page of the 1616 Folio of Ben Jonson's *Works*. Reproduced by courtesy of the Folger Library.

Publication of this volume was made possible by a grant from the College of Arts and Sciences, Northwestern University.

# *Editorial Note*

RENAISSANCE DRAMA, an annual publication, provides a forum for scholars in various parts of the globe: wherever the drama of the Renaissance is studied. Coverage, so far as subject matter is concerned, is not restricted to any single national theater. The chronological limits of the Renaissance are interpreted liberally, and space is available for essays on precursors, as well as on the use of Renaissance themes by later writers. Editorial policy favors articles of some scope. Essays that are exploratory in nature, that are concerned with critical or scholarly methodology, that raise new questions or embody fresh approaches to perennial problems are particularly appropriate for a publication that originated from the proceedings of the Modern Language Association Conference on Research Opportunities in Renaissance Drama.

The Editor gratefully acknowledges his debt to the members of the Editorial Committee, and similar warm thanks are due to the editorial assistant, Mary Ann Creadon, and to our administrative assistant, Marjorie Weiner. The efficient and expert help of the assistant editor, Janice Feldstein, has been absolutely indispensable.

The topic of Volume XI is "Tragedy," edited by Douglas Cole. Guest editor for Volume XII, "Dramatic Technique," is Professor Alan Dessen of the University of North Carolina.

# Contents

vii

# RENAISSANCE DRAMA

*New Series* X ❧ 1979

# Bernardo Accolti's Virginia:
# The Uniqueness of Unico Aretino

## HOWARD C. COLE

Nè altrimenti che nei dì festivi si serravano le botteghe, correndo ognuno in Castello tosto che si sapeva che il celeste Bernardo Accolti doveva recitare al conspetto d'infiniti gran Maestri, e Prelati, con solenne luminario di torchi, ed accompagnato dalla molta guardia degli Svizzeri. . . . [N]è prima apparve nelle reverende Sale di Pietro che il buon Vicario di Cristo [Leo X] gridò: aprite quante porte vi sono, e vengano le turbe drento . . . [e] lo ammirando ed Unico . . . fece in modo restare le genti attonite con il dove dice . . . che sentissi esclamare dalla pubblica voce d'ognuno: viva in eterno un sì divino spirito, e sì solo.

*Lettere di Pietro Aretino*[1]

NO ONE COULD HAVE ENJOYED the Papacy God gave Leo more than Bernardo Accolti, who stood out among the swarms of poets lured to Rome by the prodigal liberality of the man "who boasted that he had been born in a library."[2] While Machiavelli and Castiglione wrote their

1. An undated letter, cited by Giammaria Mazzuchelli, *Gli Scrittori D'Italia* (Brescia, 1753), I, 66.
2. Ralph Roeder, *The Man of the Renaissance*, 2d ed. (1933; rpt. New York, 1958), p. 318.

classics in enforced retirement, the spirit so divine and so unique extemporized ephemeras before throngs of admirers and gained honors denied to Petrarch.[3] Part of Pietro's praise of his countryman—both came from Arezzo, hence "Aretino"—may reflect their age's common currency of acclaim, epithets that eventually inflated Ariosto's "il flagello / de' principi, il divin Pietro Aretino"[4] into *divinissimo, precellentissimo, omnipotente* and inspired one imperial general to declare "that the Divine Aretino was 'absolutely necessary to human life'."[5] But the era's commonplace hyperbole does not quite explain the singular plaudits given Bernardo, who leads Ariosto's list of over five dozen luminaries, the only man not to share a stanza with others (XLVI, 10–19). Is it not odd that a poet so often ignored in modern histories of Italian literature should appear first among Ariosto's examples of "sublimi e soprumani ingegni," even odder that contemporary celebrations of Arezzo's famous sons[6] should omit the "gran lume aretin, l' Unico Accolti"? We may well wonder how a writer so generally forgotten in our time could have been so widely heralded as unique in his own.

It is another irony of history that Accolti's closest brush with true uniqueness, his comedy of *Virginia*, was evidently unmarked by his contemporaries. They praised him instead as the god of *improvvisatori*, a "nuovo Orfeo" attracting Apollo's envy for creating "All' improviso un stil tanto divino."[7] And the same ready wit, facile learning, and ingratiating mannerisms that went into Accolti's public performances must have also characterized his displays in politer circles, where other Orpheuses were on the make and working just as hard at their own varieties of *sprezzatura*. The documents make it clear that whereas Accolti was occasionally an extemporaneous versifier, he was always a courtier, more typical than unique in his bowing and pushing, flattering and intriguing, a realistic gloss upon the perfect creature Castiglione was in the process of fashioning. In this respect Accolti's life was much like his nondramatic

3. Francesco De Sanctis, *History of Italian Literature*, trans. Joan Redfern (New York, 1959), I, 432.

4. *Orlando Furioso*, ed. Lanfranco Caretti (Milan, 1954), XLVI, 14.

5. Roeder, p. 532.

6. See, for example, the *Enciclopedia Italiana* (Milan, 1929), IV, 171.

7. Cassio da Narni, *Morte del Danese* (1521), II, iv, 126 as cited in Mazzuchelli, I, 67, n. 12.

poetry, generally colorful, sometimes spectacular, but almost invariably conventional.

A third and final irony concerning Accolti's significance is less a matter of history than of historical criticism, of our own failure to use the playwright to gloss the greater artists who came before and after him. It is in fact easier to understand the neglect of the *Virginia* in its own time than in ours. Firsthand witnesses can be excused by the excitement of the moment, in which flashy imitations are often mistaken for true originality. From our vantage point, however, we know that Accolti's nondramatic poetry merely advanced that tradition D'Ancona vilified as *"secentismo,"* helping to link the affected metaphors and strained conceits of Tebaldeo and Serafino with those of Marino and Góngora,[8] whereas the *Virginia*, as the first dramatization of the *All's Well* story and one of Italy's earliest high comedies, brings together and comments upon the narrative and dramatic artistries of Boccaccio and Shakespeare.

But neither the *Virginia*'s intrinsic worth nor its value in defining its illustrious tradition has inspired serious consideration. W. W. Lawrence, for example, spends five pages outlining Oriental fairy tales and Scandinavian sagas "from which instructive conclusions may be drawn as to the general significance of the story as told by Boccaccio and by Shakespeare," but the *Virginia* is sloughed off in a footnote merely because Shakespeare's dependence upon Accolti has not been proved.[9] Curiously enough, the only provocative comment on this neglected play, one that emphasizes its unconventionality, appears not in a study of Accolti but in a comparison of his source, the *Decameron*, III, 9, to *All's Well*. To support his contention that both Boccaccio's Giletta and Shakespeare's Helena were meant to elicit our admiration, Herbert G. Wright glances disapprovingly at the "excessive astuteness" and "grovelling self-abasement of Accolti's Virginia."[10] A play centered in the exploits of this kind of heroine certainly suggests that something new, if not unique, is afoot, whether it be a straightforward extension of the medieval virtue story's traditional boundaries or something in a satiric, ironic, or cynical vein, the theme of

8. Alessandro D'Ancona, *Studi sulla Letteratura Italiana de' Primi Secoli* (Milan, 1891), pp. 151–237, esp. p. 218.

9. *Shakespeare's Problem Comedies* (1931; rpt. New York, 1960), pp. 41, 237–238.

10. Herbert G. Wright, *Boccaccio in England from Chaucer to Tennyson* (London, 1957), pp. 215–216.

designing humility. Such a heroine, moreover, implies that a writer close to Boccaccio did not see Giletta as simply and sentimentally as recent critics, though she does lend some encouragement to moderns who have trouble with Helena. Since our view of the whole of the *All's Well* story, not just Accolti's contribution, will be affected by our view of Virginia's character, we must be cautious in speaking of satire, irony, or cynicism. An enthusiasm for discovering the original must be disciplined by a knowledge of what was common, and speculations about Accolti's interests and attitudes should be guided by the facts of his biography. Before examining the *Virginia*, therefore, a brief survey of the traditional aspects of Accolti's life and work seems in order.

## I

Accolti must have thrown in his lot with the courts of central and northern Italy soon after coming of age. Born in Arezzo in 1458 and raised in Florence (where his father, the jurist and historian Benedetto, apparently saw better opportunities), by 1480 he was already in Rome, whence he began what Emilio Santini terms "una specie di vagabondaggio poetico e un po' anche ciarlatanesco" that eventually led to his being "accarezzato e applaudito" at the courts of Urbino, Mantua, and Naples and by the whole city of Rome.[11] Accolti attracted unsought attention in 1489 for "atti molesti compiuti ai danni di un fiorentino," but by 1494 he had gained the office of Papal Scriptor and Abbreviator.[12] Drawing up briefs for his unsanctified Holiness, Roderigo Borgia, did not prevent Bernardo from currying favor elsewhere. Since the *Virginia* is a piece of occasional drama, a comedy to honor the wedding of the Sienese magnifico, Antonio Spannocchi, in January, 1494, it is unlikely that the playwright would have missed the performance. He also found time to get into trouble again with the Florentine authorities. He was banished for some unexplained wrongdoings that same year, and the peace he later made with the Signoria was forfeited in 1497, when he became involved in Piero de'

---

11. Emilio Santini, in *Enciclopedia Italiana*, I, 267. Cf. Lilia Mantovani's biographical comments in *Dizionario Biografico Degli Italiani*, I (Rome, 1960), 103–104.

12. Mantovani, I, 103; also see Mazzuchelli, I, 66.

Medici's attempt to regain the Republic.[13] Among the conspirators be-
headed that summer was Lorenzo Tornabuoni, the "thesor de la na-
tura,"[14] according to the sonnet in which Accolti mourns his pathetic
death. Bernardo himself was again merely banished and returned to
Rome, where the Pope, having just excommunicated Savonarola, was also
in mourning. His eldest son Juan, Duke of Gandia, had been assassinated,
and among the leading suspects was Juan's younger brother, Cardinal
Cesare.

The equally glittering and equally dangerous courts to which Accolti
was invited over the next two decades—Milan, Urbino, Mantua, and
Naples—are reflected in his sonnets and *strambotti* or folk lyrics. For he not
only celebrated the virtues of the Borgias with courtly poems to chaste
Lucrezia, resolute Cesare, and their devoted father; he also sang for a
future Pope, Cardinal Farnese, for a recently widowed Neapolitan
princess, Isabella of Aragon, for her ambitious adversary, Ludovico
Sforza,[15] and for her brother, Ferdinand II, King of Naples, who is given
sole credit for expelling the "furor Barbarico" of the French invasion of
Italy in 1494 ("Epitaphio del Re di Napoli," sig. F5$^r$). But it was usually
love, not war or politics, that Accolti treated, even in his sonnets to a
statue and an artichoke. Like his cruel lady, for example, the artichoke she
has sent conceals its essence within a thousand deceptions, thrives amid
ruins, allows one fleeting favor among so many disappointments (sig.
F7$^r$). Similarly, both the Duchess of Urbino and her statue smile but do
not answer, quicken the blood only to defraud the desire (sig. F4$^v$).

Given the different kinds of women Accolti worshiped, it is not surprising that the mood and tone of his poetry vary a great deal. Recognizable
contemporaries are of course treated respectfully: the two sonnets to Lucrezia contain not a hint of the affair Accolti was alleged to have had with
her; several others to the Countess Costanza Vittoria d'Avalos are similarly
appreciative yet respectful.[16] And Accolti's muse is most chaste in honor-

13. Mantovani, I, 103.

14. *Verginia. Comedia di M. Bernardo Accolti Aretino intitolata la Verginia, con un Capitolo
della Madonna, nuovamente corretta, & con somma diligentia ristampata* (Venice, 1535), sig.
F5$^r$. All citations to Accolti's work are to this edition, which probably appeared shortly
after his death on 1 March 1535; *u, v* and long *s* are normalized throughout.

15. See Mantovani, I, 103.

16. *Ibid.*

ing the grandest of ladies, the Mother of God. In his 172-line "Ternale in laude della gloriosa Virgine Maria" (sigs. G4$^v$-G7$^v$), the poet is unquestionably reverential, even though the sense of wonder he would enhance is not helped by his overingenious wordplay and straining of conceits: Mary, like a prism ("saldo vetro"), remained unbroken in the sun's passage through her, begetting the One by Whom she conceived and bearing the One through Whom she was made. But in treating unidentifiable ladies of the present or well-known women of the past, Accolti is rarely gallant. To a mysterious Lidia of Florence and an even crueler Giulia there are dozens of despairing plaints. Constant only in her irresistible and unlovely beauty, Giulia is usually deceitful, haughty, and merciless, often sadistic and vicious, and alternately likened to insatiable Death, to the pestilent Dog Star, to a viper in a golden vase and to the deadliest curse pronounced on any male (sigs. F5$^v$-F6$^v$, G1$^v$-G4$^r$). Equally grim are Accolti's portraits of the ancient world's famous women: hapless Lucretia, Niobe, and Cleopatra; the not so innocent Clytemnestra, shrinking before Orestes; Helen, who calls herself the ruin of Europe and Asia; shameless Semiramis justifying incest on the ground that love is never subject to law; an even more reckless Medea, whose murderous passion neither beauty, station, wealth, nor magical potions were able to subdue (sigs. F7$^v$-F8$^v$).

Medea's desperate plight—"ma non vinsi amore"—voices a theme Accolti exploits in all but his few political and religious pieces, the power of love to drive, delude, frustrate, and often destroy. The most complex articulation of this theme is of course in the *Virginia*, where the hero's outcries against the destructive heroine are repeatedly followed by the heroine's protests against destructive love. The extent to which Accolti actually experienced those passions he never tired of celebrating is impossible to determine, though the scanty biographical evidence available has not prevented critics from inferring relationships between the poet's life and his art. Mazzuchelli long ago noted, for example, that Accolti had two children by one of his domestics—Alfonso, who succeeded him as Duke of Nepi, and Virginia, whom he married off to Count Giambatista Malatesta with an exceptionally large dowry.[17] But if the amount of the dowry argues Accolti's love for his natural child rather than his own social

17. Mazzuchelli, I, 66–67. Alfonso did not succeed his father as Duke of Nepi according to Mantovani, I, 104, and Girolamo Tiraboschi, *Storia della Letteratura Italiana* (Milan, 1833), III, 164.

ambitions, that affection does not in turn prove that the *Virginia* was named after or in honor of her, as Mazzuchelli and those who follow him suggest.[18] Surely Accolti's allegedly beloved daughter throws as little light upon the play's designing heroine as does his son, Alfonso, upon his dramatic "namesake," the dying King of Naples.

A more difficult question concerning the relationship between Accolti's life and art arises in his sonnet "Della Duchessa di Urbino sculpita" (sig. F4ᵛ), one of the few poems that imply a passionate involvement with a well-known woman of the present. Accolti's "pazzo amore" for Elisabetta Gonzaga merely amused her sister-in-law, that most intellectual of ladies, Isabella d'Este.[19] Nor does Bembo seem to have taken the affair very seriously when he wrote to Bibbiena about the Duchess being frequently courted by "Signor Unico," who, warmer in his old love than the ever-burning lads of seventeen, hopes finally to achieve his goal by moving that heart of stone or at least making her cry.[20] A similar sense of humor seems to pervade Castiglione's account of "signor Unico" and his beautiful betrayer near the beginning of *The Courtier*. Despite such evidence, the most recent study of Accolti detects a note of sincerity in his urbane bantering and witty protestations, assumes that all the anger and bitterness expressed against Giulia was actually directed at Elisabetta, and suggests that his later dream of having his brother, the Cardinal of Ancona, succeed Pope Julius II was fostered only by his desire to make himself worthy of that lady he spent so much of his life pursuing.[21] Earlier criticism, on the other hand, has seldom accused Accolti of any kind of sincerity other than the earnestness with which he played his elaborate game.[22] Art still reflects life, but only in the sense that the partly sentimental, partly aggressive posing within the poems reflects the actual poses through which Accolti achieved his identity at court. Unrequited love kept him dying for thirty years; the ladies continued to listen with delighted astonishment and their husbands, even the impotent Guidobaldo, with complete equanimity.

It is doubtful that the basically serious, idealistic Castiglione found

18. Cf. Mazzuchelli, I, 67; Santini, I, 267; Mantovani, I, 103.
19. Mantovani, I, 103.
20. This letter of April, 1516, is cited by Tiraboschi, III, 164.
21. Mantovani, I, 103.
22. Eg., Santini, I, 267, and D'Ancona, *Studi*, pp. 216–218.

much to admire in such Petrarchan posturings, but *The Courtier* allows
every person his say and no document illustrates so clearly that Accolti was
actually a player among players, a light turned up and down at the
pleasure of his sophisticated circle. "Unico Aretino" initially appears in
Castiglione's cataloguing of courtiers who "spent most of their time" at
Urbino during its decade of happiness under the protection of Julius II
(1503–1513), a period when "poets, musicians, and all sorts of buffoons,
and the most excellent of every kind of talent that could be found in Italy,
were always gathered there."[23] It is not long, however, before "signor
Unico" is given leave to characterize himself, first as a poet, then as a
buffoon, and finally as a curious composite of each. Although some suspect
that his sonnet on the "letter *s* . . . that the Duchess is wearing on her
forehead" is too "ingenious and polished" to have been improvised, this
initial attempt to dazzle his circle is "praised with merry applause" (pp.
22–23). But during the next two evenings he is less successful. His witty
interruption—Federico's "great burden" is merely to belabor the
obvious—is promptly squelched: "You indulge too much in extremes" (p.
96). Even less heeded is his mischievous misappropriation of Plato's *Republic* (V.3) to counter the view that the Court Lady should not engage in
certain bodily exercises: "With the ancients it was the custom for women
to wrestle naked with men, but we have lost that good practice, along
with many others" (p. 210).

Perhaps the most helpful evidence in interpreting Accolti's interests
and attitudes is provided during the waning moments of the third eve-
ning, when the poet-buffoon makes a last attempt to steal the scene and
matches wits with Emilia Pia. Anticipating Bembo's Platonic rhapsodies
in Book IV, Castiglione has the Duchess compliment Giuliano for teaching the Court Lady what the other men have not yet taught their Courtier,
namely, how to love. By now Unico's interruption is predictable: ladies
need that lesson for they generally ignore desert; men such as I need
instruction not on how to love but on how to be loved (pp. 266–267).
Emilia at once encourages him to enlarge upon so important a point, but
Unico becomes caustically deferential: only a woman is privy to those
"strange things" women take pleasure in. But Emilia defers in turn. Since
Unico enjoys "such universal favor with women," he surely must know
"all the ways" by which he gained it. Emilia's request that he acknowl-

---

23. *The Courtier*, trans. Charles S. Singleton (New York, 1959), p. 17.

edge the tricks of his trade is answered by another trick as the grand poser descends to personal insult: the most useful lesson he could give the lover is to remove Emilia's influence over his lady, for neither his own merits nor "the sincerest love that ever was" has had as much power to make him loved as Emilia has had to make him hated (pp. 267–268).

A good argument for a sonnet, perhaps, but hardly for the unsentimental lady he is pouting at. Affirming Unico's preeminent lovability—to make him hated would be "attempting the impossible"—Emilia questions instead the sincerity of his love. Yet never has a mask been removed so courteously: "being so very lovable," you are loved by many; your "constant lamenting" over ladies' cruelty is, therefore, only a "concealment designed to hide the favors" you have actually received; each woman who has secretly given herself to you is content not only to hear of your unrequited passion but also to watch you "openly show feigned love" to the others. Now if those whom you presently "pretend to love are not so ready to believe you as you could wish, this happens because your art of love is beginning to be understood, and not because I cause you to be hated" (p. 268). Alas, it is "my fate not to be believed," Unico lamely insists. We cannot believe you, replies Emilia, for if your complaints are true, then you obviously wish what your beloved does not, which violates love's law. Nay, answers Unico, grasping desperately, I wish what she wishes and complain because she does not wish what I wish. Unflustered by such special pleading, Emilia calmly distinguishes between wishing rightly and wrongly and underlines self-denial. "Precisely," answers the wily Unico, twisting the thesis he pretends to support, "my highest happiness would be to have a single will govern both our souls." But Emilia has the last word, eminently practical and so relevant to the larger design of that modest man who keeps Accolti silent throughout the remainder of his conversations: "Then it is for you to act accordingly."

While Urbino thus controlled Arezzo's shining light, Leo X's Rome let it blaze unchecked. And yet if Accolti's presence was no more impressive than Castiglione allows and his unrecorded inspirations no better than his extant lyrics, it is difficult to understand the sensation he created. Mazzuchelli and Tiraboschi both attempt charitable evaluations, yet both sooner or later agree with the essentially unsympathetic criticism of Accolti's near contemporary, Benedetto Varchi: after the passing of Dante, Petrarch, and Boccaccio, the Florentine style of writing began to change, and so much went from bad to worse that it became almost unrecogniza-

ble, as one may still see in the compositions of Unico Aretino, Antonio
Tebaldeo, and some others; although their pieces are less disgusting than
those of Sasso, Notturno, and Altissimo, they nevertheless show neither
Dante's learning nor Petrarch's elegance.[24] Varchi's double censure—
Unico's poetry was neither good nor unique in its badness—is most fully
supported by D'Ancona, who ranks Accolti as one of the most mediocre
imitators of Petrarch's wretched imitators and singles out his sonnet to an
artichoke as an example of the depths to which these poets' bad taste
sometimes sank.[25]

Whether we view *secentismo* in D'Ancona's terms, the "tumido e . . .
pettoruto" style that flowered into gongorism, or relate it to that lust for
novelty Dr. Johnson scorned in the English Metaphysicals, or simply call
it "baroque," it is a mannerism shared by Varchi's most and least "disgusting" poets. They all knew Petrarch by heart and relished the analogies
he drew between subjective moods and objective phenomena. But there
were elegant possibilities Petrarch had not fully exploited. So many arrows
have pierced Tebaldeo's heart, for instance, that Cupid uses him as a
quiver; the tears of his popular contemporary, Serafino, water the plains,
relieving the thirsty cattle, but his sighs of unrequited passion scorch the
birds passing above.[26] For the man Castiglione portrays as indulging "too
much in extremes," the desire to turn tropes into facts and analogies into
identities was just as irresistible. "Extremism," in fact, may be the best
word to remember in passing from Accolti's theatrical life and lyrics to his
one literal piece of theater—his melodramatic performances at the courts
of popes and princes, his idealistic-cynical exhibitionism among the
ladies, his choice of heroines as pure as the Blessed Virgin and as shameless
as Helen, his fascination (in both his life and his lines) over love's power to
exalt and destroy.

## II

Even the *Virginia*, Accolti's only claim to greatness, is not entirely
untraditional. From the standpoint of diction, it has a good number of

24. *Ercolano* (1580), as cited by Mazzuchelli, I, 67, n. 10.
25. *Studi*, p. 218.
26. See Jefferson Butler Fletcher, *Literature of the Italian Renaissance* (New York, 1934),
pp. 220–222, and Ernest Hatch Wilkins, *A History of Italian Literature*, rev. Thomas G.
Bergin (Cambridge, Mass., 1974), pp. 174–176.

*secentismo* passages, lengthy declamations that cultivate far-fetched conceits at the temporary expense of dramatic interest. Also reflecting easily identifiable models are its basic plot, major characters, and method of construction, which is probably why recent critics are content to skirt the play with brief notes on its sources. For Mantovani, the *Virginia* is simply a comedy in *ottava rima* divided into five acts, whose plot is taken wholesale ("di peso") from Boccaccio but whose formal construction resembles that of the miracle play (I, 103). Santini is hardly more helpful when he comments that this adaptation of the *Decameron* and sacred drama projects some figures with contemporary appeal (I, 267). Even D'Ancona's three-page discussion of the play's central episodes [27] offers no hint of Accolti's originality. But with or without the heightening of *secentismo*, no heroine in the sources seems to suggest Wright's excessively astute, self-abasing groveler. The story of Giletta, that "savia donna," was designed by Queen Neifile to satisfy her own command that the Third Day treat "di chi alcuna cosa molto desiderata con industria acquistasse, o la perduta recuperasse." [28] Similarly sympathetic, though not nearly so industrious or ingenious, are the long-suffering heroines of the *sacre rappresentazioni*— Santa Guglielma, Stella, Rosana, and Santa Uliva—each a beautiful princess who endures all manner of persecution before being reunited with her beloved through the Blessed Virgin's intervention.

Perhaps one clue to Accolti's reason for first combining and then innovating upon these different traditions lies in his characteristic extremism. To dramatize Boccaccio's brief narrative he could have obliged classical tastes with more than a five-act structure. Except for a few low-comic scenes involving the Prince of Salerno's rascally servant, Ruffo, however, Accolti was not interested in the brisk dialogue and horseplay of Roman comedy. For the *secentismo* sonneteer, it was more natural to associate Giletta's travails with those of her spectacular sisters in the native dramatic tradition. Hence the *Virginia*'s disregard of the unities observed in contemporary learned comedy, its frequent and rapid shifts between Naples, Salerno, and Milan, its romantic insistence that time's passage be determined by each moment's emotive potential. Hence also its use of octaves not to describe events, as the *cantastorie* were doing in their songs

27. Alessandro D'Ancona, *Origini del Teatro Italiano* (Turin, 1891), II, 15–17.

28. *Decameron*, ed. Vittore Branca (Florence, 1951), I, 308. Branca, whose edition is cited throughout, glosses "industria" as "ingegnosità, abilità."

about Roland, but primarily for characters to express their most personal feelings, as in the miracles.[29] Hence, finally, the *Virginia*'s huge cast of characters. As we might expect, almost every person Boccaccio even alludes to is given a speaking part. More important, however, is Accolti's addition of personae never mentioned by Boccaccio but included in at least three of the four miracle plays noted above: the royal couriers, a seneschal, councillors and chancellors, the heroine's mother (or stepmother). There is, in fact, only one major character common to all four plays yet absent from the *Virginia*, the Virgin herself, who always preserves her faithful daughter and usually effects as well a miraculous healing.[30]

In none of these solemn pieces, however, could a poet even as witty and cynical as Unico have found a suggestion of satire or irony, an encouragement to question the heroine's credentials. The tale of Giletta, though, can be read in very different ways. As we have noted, Neifile presents the story as a thoroughly sympathetic illustration of human "industria." To insure our admiration of her heroine's behavior, in fact, she attempts to make Giletta more virtuous than the protagonists of simple virtue stories by investing both the acquiring and recovering of Beltramo with religious sanctions; the resolute girl claims and apparently receives God's help in realizing both goals. But when Neifile's celebration of a divinely sanctioned "industria" is read in the context Boccaccio provides, the other tales told on the Third Day, it becomes an ironic part of a satirical whole that repeatedly unmasks religious rationalizations.[31] Queen Neifile's subjects all make her "alcuna cosa" sexual and her "industria" disingenuous.

29. Accolti's only departures from the octave are three lengthy passages in *terza rima*, exceptions that only confirm the rule about his penchant for melodrama: the Prince's passionate love letter to Camilla (97 lines); Virginia's anguished petition to her husband (112 lines); Virginia's extravagant summation of her sorrows before the Salernese nobility (139 lines).

30. Two of Burgundy's wisest doctors cure Stella's wounds, but her amputated hands are only later restored by the Virgin; Uliva's mutilated members are similarly recovered; Guglielma assumes the Virgin's role when she cures a Hungarian prince of a leprosy beyond his physician's practice. See *Sacre Rappresentazioni del Quattrocento*, ed. Luigi Banfi (Turin, 1963), pp. 565 ff., 602 ff., 634, 770. The Virgin does not appear in *La Rappresentazione di Rosana*, but an angel enters to tell the heroine that the Mother of God has heard her prayers and will grant them (p. 707).

31. This interpretation is supported in greater detail in my article on "Dramatic Interplay in the *Decameron*: Boccaccio, Neifile and Giletta di Nerbona," *MLN*, XC (1975), 38–57.

In at least four of the eight stories preceding her own, sexual desire dons a religious mask; the other tales set their events in a religious (or sacrilegious) perspective. Whereas Neifile emphasizes her heroine's "onesta" means and ends, Boccaccio underlines embarrassing associations: Giletta gains her husband through a "polvere" similar to the guileful abbot's in III, 8 and regains him with a pilgrim's mask like lusty Tedaldo's in III, 7 and by means of a bed trick reminiscent of lecherous Ricciardo's in III, 6. The final associating is left to roguish Dioneo, whose heroine also honestly confuses sexual and divine service; sincerely seeking to worship God, Alibech first obtains a "cosa" she never dreamed she much desired and then, having lost it, recovers it whence she never expected.

The melodramatic, emotionally surcharged worlds of the miracle plays therefore offered Accolti much more than models for *secentismo* flights and a method of constructing Giletta's adventures. They also furnished many elements Neifile had already represented as sublime and Dioneo as ridiculous: a pervasive theme of spiritual and physical healing, an atmosphere at once devoutly religious and extravagantly romantic, a tone affirming the values of sacred and profane love and a strong trust in Providence. Only an examination of the *Virginia* will reveal whether the playwright actually exploited the Dionean perspective, but we may be fairly certain that he noticed and appreciated it. In the first place, Accolti must have been as familiar with Boccaccio's fiction as he was with Petrarch's poetry. Castiglione has his polite circle frequently couple these men as either the only models to imitate slavishly or the best examples to attempt to outdo (e.g., pp. 50, 61–62), and in the course of conversation the characters or events of at least nine scattered stories in the *Decameron* are casually alluded to, including one that shows what "a very great enemy of women" Boccaccio was, Ricciardo's bed trick in III, 6 (p. 193). Second, granting Accolti's familiarity with the tales surrounding Neifile's, the very roles he played to tease and flatter his sophisticated audiences indicate an intellect lively enough to have grasped Boccaccio's implications concerning disingenuous ingenuity, an ear quick to catch his mischievous master's refrain about that odd divinity which shapes our sexual ends.

Finally, if Accolti sought to dramatize Giletta's exploits in the spirit of his direct source's larger context, his heroine would have to become as unconventional and enigmatic as Wright apparently finds her. The *Virginia*'s importance, then, would not be based only upon its value in defining its tradition, the significance it assumed mainly by virtue of *All's*

*Well*. Granted, Accolti was not the first to dramatize a *novella*, probably not even the first to borrow from the *Decameron*.[32] And for hints as to how the miracle play could be used to stage a profane tale, he could have turned to Poliziano's fairly recent *Orfeo* (1480), the first secular play in Italian, which replaces the angel-prologue with Mercury and Paradise with Olympus.[33] Accolti's originality would rather depend on how well he could realize Boccaccio's narrative relationships in dramatic terms, on finding theatrical equivalents for the interplay between tales and tellers like Dioneo's upending of Neifile's naïve glosses.

Sensing the motive behind those bawdy, ethereal, and ironic responses to the announced topic's "industria" was, of course, a far simpler matter than finding a new way to convey the same point within a single staged piece. Unlike Accolti's low-comic scenes, which resemble earlier fifteenth-century imitations of Plautus and Terence, his main plot therefore employs a method of his own devising, less broad but wittier, a continuous and often whimsical alternation of scenes and sentiments sublime and mundane. Perhaps such a method was partly inspired by the *Decameron*'s juxtaposition of sexual and divine service; it also resembles the sentimental-cynical mask worn by Accolti the courtier-poet extremist. But if the courts of the time offered numerous instances of the detached, high-comic spirit, its theaters rarely reflected anything approximating the spirit of high comedy. Back of the *Virginia* lay a century of Latin humanistic comedy, the sacred drama, the rustic *maggio*, but nothing like the deft exposures of social affectations and moral posturings that we find first in Accolti and shortly thereafter in Ariosto, Bibbiena, Machiavelli, and Pietro Aretino. Surely one measure of a writer's greatness, if not his uniqueness, is what he makes of materials on hand.

## III

The first indication of the Dionean perspective appears in the Prologue's five-octave greeting. Neither Christian angel nor pagan god, this courtly

32. See Vittorio Rossi, *Il Quattrocento*, rev. Aldo Vallone (Milan, 1964), pp. 502, 508; and Madeleine Doran, *Endeavors of Art: A Study of Form in Elizabethan Drama* (1954; rpt. Madison, Wis., 1964), pp. 103, 191.

33. Joseph Spencer Kennard, *The Italian Theatre* (New York, 1932), I, 89, 158; cf. Wilkins, p. 154.

fellow both invokes and banishes commercial considerations, employs flattery only to condemn .it. Although decrying "La voglia e sitial d'argento & oro, / Vil mercatura, ingrata adulatione," for example, he assures his audience—nothing less than "dei in carne humana"—that the play will show how "ardir, tempo, ingegno, oro, & parole / Fanno ottenere al fin cio che l'huom vuole" (sigs. A2$^r$-A2$^v$). A similar juxtaposition of opposites occurs immediately thereafter with Virginia's entrance: a heroine whose name suggests purity and innocence at once confesses to passions far stronger than Giletta's and an ambition "horrenda impia & proterva"; a "semplice, & in esperta damigella" files a quasi-Petrarchan inventory of her Prince's charms and "prove" that "Havren forza a levar sua sposa a Giove" (sigs. A3$^r$-A3$^v$).

Throughout the early scenes, in fact, Accolti continually strives for such heightened, usually melodramatic effects. Through his heroine's lengthy agonizing in *ottava rima*, her claim of being persecuted by "ogni stella," and her association with physical healing—"Io d'Hippocrate fisico figliuola"—he encourages us to think of the miracle plays. But these similarities between Virginia and the Virgin's faithful daughters only make their great differences more noticeable. Whereas they are sometimes the objects of other characters' illicit desires, sexual passion here resides in the protagonist; whereas they are all of royal blood, Virginia is socially far inferior to the man she craves and pursues, the Prince of Salerno. If her admission "Che s'accenda del suo signor la serva" reminds us of the *Decameron*, on the other hand, we should realize that Accolti has ignored the less sensational aspects of Giletta's situation: the wealthy young heiress rejecting each suitor proposed by her guardians is now the isolated, distraught victim of a blind and deadly passion—"tanto è cieco amor tanto è mortale / Ch'io vedo & lodo el meglio, & seguo el peggio" (sig. A3$^r$). Even the Prologue's passing reference to "Salernitana" seems designed to raise our expectations of the extraordinary. While Boccaccio's story contains no characters that are remotely historical,[34] and while there is therefore no special significance in Giletta's being from Nerbona, Virginia's origin was a city so famous for its medical school that it was called *Civitas Hippocratica* throughout Europe.[35]

For all Accolti's improvements on Boccaccio, however, the original

---

34. *Decameron*, ed. Branca, I, 419, n. 2.
35. Kennard, I, 95; Wright, p. 187.

audience must have been at least as surprised by his improvement upon recent history, political relationships that are first implied in Virginia's relatively prosaic conclusion: "e sta mia stella / Col Rè Alphonso in Parthenope bella" (sig. A3ᵛ). We may be fairly certain that most of the Sienese who watched the play in January, 1494, knew a great deal about King Alphonso, the House of Aragon which had ruled Parthenope or Naples since 1442, and the troubles it had experienced with Ferrante Sanseverino, Prince of Salerno. When Alphonso I died in 1458, bequeathing the Kingdom of Naples to his bastard son, Ferdinand I, the most powerful of his barons declared for Ferdinand's rival, John of Anjou, and only after six years of desolating warfare did the son possess in fact what he had been left in theory.[36] And though Ferdinand reigned for thirty-five years—he died toward the end of the same month the *Virginia* was first performed—he was rarely at peace with his proud nobles, especially the Sanseverini, the family that usually headed the Angevin faction. The barons' most extensive uprising, what Benedetto Croce terms the "Great Conspiracy" of 1485–1486, was of cource subsidized by the French court, whence many of them fled for refuge.[37] Their pleas that Charles VIII assert his claim to Naples were eventually seconded by Lodovico Sforza, between whom and the dukedom of Milan stood his nephew's Aragonese wife. Although the French armies did not move south until August, 1494, most Italians must have foreseen dark days for the House of Aragon earlier that year when its old fox, Ferdinand, left the throne to his less talented son, Alphonso II.

Given the repeated rebellions within and the proposed invasion from without, any suggestion of Parthenope's political harmony must have seemed as ironic as the news of the "Corriere adorno," who now enters to announce that Alphonso's days may be numbered (sig. A3ᵛ). And as Accolti approaches the first of his play's grand confrontations, Virginia's interview with the King, he continues to shape our responses with ironic allusions. Learning of Alphonso's deadly fistula, Virginia immediately determines upon a cure, then pauses to consider some cautionary proverbs, and is finally resolved "far del mio Principe acquisto" only after remem-

36. Alfred de Reumont, *The Carafas of Maddaloni: Naples under Spanish Dominion*, trans. anon. (London, 1854), pp. 6–7.

37. Benedetto Croce, *History of the Kingdom of Naples*, trans. Frances Frenaye (Chicago, 1970), p. 92.

bering the amorous achievements (but not the eventual miseries) of
Ariadne, Semele, and Callisto. The scene now shifts to Naples where the
sickly Alphonso describes the vast regions of Parthenope, his possession of
whose "regno & thesor" is threatened only (so he believes) by his own
malady (sig. A5$^r$). Finally, just before Virginia enters with her dual
remedy ("Ch'al Re guarira el braccio, & a me el core"), the Prince ironically exhorts his liege to show wisdom in adversity, patience in sickness,
and hope for a cure "Con arte, ingegno o vecchia esperientia" (sig. A5$^r$).
"Ingegno" is the first word the Prologue uses to describe Virginia and one
of the three words Virginia uses to describe what Love demands of his
servants (sigs. A2$^r$, A4$^v$). And since we know that the heroine's "famoso
licore" is a "vecchia esperientia"—with it her father once cured a queen's
"fistola infetta"—we are prepared for an ingenious healing, a healthy
King, and an afflicted Prince who is neither wise in adversity nor patient
in "sickness."

But none of Accolti's melodramatic or ironic elaborations is quite so
startling as his addition of an incident Boccaccio never even faintly
suggests. We should recall that Giletta's entrance into the royal presence
is described very matter-of-factly: "e appresso nel cospetto del re venuta,
di grazia chiese che la sua infermità gli mostrasse" (I, 420). Since the king
has already refused further medical attention, his granting of her request
on the not very logical ground that she is "bella giovane e avvenente"
indicates an amused, possibly skeptical point of view. In Accolti, however, the mischievous smile at an arbitrary French king becomes a cynical
smirk at a vicious Neapolitan court. Among the "molta gente in questo
loco" that Virginia now enters are two characters Accolti must have
invented for the sake of mood and theme since they do nothing for the
plot. The first is a surly guardsman who blocks her approach to Alphonso;
the second is a gallant who comes to her aid: "Come prosumi o pien di
vino & stolto / Voler tal donna a torto ingiuriare?" (sig. A6$^r$). Virginia's
"pietoso volto" alone should move him, contends her champion, but the
guardsman stands his ground :"Io non mi curo de le donne molto. / Che
una gia mi stratiò." Compared to such thoughtless misogyny, the courtesy
of this courtier—"servo di donne nato sono"—at first seems attractive.
His introduction of her as a "gemma in oro, & fresco giglio in horto"
apparently reflects the idealism of any "Giovin benigno," and even the
solace he promises the King—"Ne veder la potrai senza conforto"—need

not follow Boccaccio's sexual implications. It is rather in the King's response that we first find the source's comedy—"Se è bella, io son contento che la chiami"—as well as a new and sadder smile: "Ma guarda non sia quella che tu ami / Che rotta & fredda è stata tua proposta" (sig. A6ʳ). We hear no more about that unpleasant incident involving the young man's mistress, but enough has been said to undermine his gentility and to make us wonder about the health of the diseased King's court.

Virginia's greeting to Alphonso, "Te salvi el ciel," and her consequent explanation of what "al ciel cosi piacque" (sig. A6ᵛ) once more supplant the cynical with the sublime, bringing us close to Neifile's self-appointed agent of the Almighty. But Giletta's claim that she heals "collo aiuto d'Iddio e colla scienzia del . . . mio padre" (I, 421) must be heightened to Virginia's "di mie prove / Tu stupirai in terra, & nel ciel Giove," and it is probably Accolti's own penchant for *secentismo* that makes his heroine appear smug or flippant rather than brave in the face of adversity. The King's threat to have her "membri adorni" burned if she fails is not weighed "una dramma"; she is, after all, already "nutrita di fiamma, esca di fiamma / . . . in terra elemento del foco" (sig. A7ʳ).

Within the week (whose passage is signified by eight "molto mi muove" octaves) we hear that the recovered King now "per dea l'adora" (sig. A8ᵛ). Such adoration may point back to the source, the French king's willingness to test Giletta's divinity—"Forse m' è costei mandata da Dio" (I, 421)—and it certainly supports a reading of "pious" rather than merely "merciful" in the "fanciulla pia" (sig. B1ʳ) by which the King now identifies his preserver. Quite ignorant of what the "ingegno grato" (cf. the Prologue's "mirabil ingegno") of the King's goddess has contrived, the Prince enters with a wish for heaven's direction—"Te salvi o Re el ciel sommo & superno"—but he is shortly railing against "questa donna, che con falsità" and "inganno" vanquished his will and hoping that he may "l' ingannatrice inganni" (sigs. B3ʳ-B3ᵛ). But Virginia is not the only party responsible for the Prince's bitter redefining of "ingegno" as "inganno." Like Boccaccio's arbitrary sovereign, not to mention Shakespeare's, Alphonso would remain true to his bargain at another's expense. None of the "giustitia, & . . . pietate" he directs the Prince to rule by is found in his own sudden display of power, and his own naïve conclusion that this festive night "veramente è felice & serena" (sig. B2ᵛ) seems to represent Accolti's way of deceiving the deceiver.

Another means Accolti employs to relate "inganno" and "ingegno" are the escapades of the Prince's wily servant, Ruffo, a scrambling, snatching, bullying, thieving pander—everything, in short, that the modern *ruffa, raffa, riffa*, and *ruffiano* suggest and quite close to John Florio's sense of *rúffo*, "a ruffian, a swagrer, or a ruffling roister."[38] Partly the classical parasite, partly the clever slave and braggart soldier, Ruffo devotes his wicked wit and boundless energy to lusting after or theologizing over womankind, created by the devil when God was out for a stroll ("Quando nacquero il Dio andava a spasso / Et credo la facessi sathanasso," sig. B6r). At first confident that neither the Prince's love, Camilla, nor her mother, Costanza, is a match for his "ingegno & arte"—"preci pie," "volto di Marte," "molte bugie"—he soon concludes that plain gold works better than the fanciest fictions: "Frappa se sai," he cautions, "Senza oro non farai cosa che vogli" (sig. C1v). Even his most sincere pose—hair combed, face shaved, stomach corseted, thick lips sucked in, and eyes overflowing with what will pass for tears, his own saliva—does not impress constant Costanza, that "Vecchia ribalda d'antichristo madre" (sig. C2r).

But the clearest evidence of Accolti's desire to puncture social pretensions by mingling the ethereal and earthy lies in his having the play's most idealistic sentiments, the Prince's love letter to Camilla, declaimed by its dirtiest character. For ninety-seven lines it is Ruffo who weeps and wastes away, whose soul burns, who protests that "in nobil cor mai non alberga inganno" (sig. C1r). Given Ruffo's self-serving nature, we are not surprised to see him open and read the letter his master entrusts him with. Since Accolti has him read it *aloud* (when it would have been as easy and surely more romantic first to let the Prince himself rehearse his Petrarchan passion and then allow the cynical servant to scan the lines silently), it appears that irony is controlling melodrama and *secentismo* being forced to fuel comedy.

Even as Accolti allows Ruffo to ridicule the sublime, another amorous epistle, no less farfetched, is delivered by the Salernese chancellors, Callimaco and Domitio, who beg the Prince's hearing "perche tutte le gratie divine / Ti conceda el signor del sommo chiostro" (sig. C3v). Because Salerno agrees only to hear Domitio read Virginia's letter, not to

38. *Queen Anna's New World of Words* (1611; rpt. Menston, Eng., 1968), p. 455.

peruse it himself, the play's second passionate address, like the first, must be declaimed by a third party. The petition itself is remarkable not for its conventional anguish—the left hand holding "ferro, & veneno" while the right falters with a pen dipped in "lagrime & sangue"—but for its curious reasoning, the rhetoric with which Virginia moves from self-condemnation to self-justification, from "mio fallo insano / E . . . tuo giusto sdegno" in the opening lines to her closing concession, "Ben ch'a torto da te stratiata sia, / Non cerco el morir tuo" (sigs. C3ᵛ-C5ᵛ). It is impossible to pinpoint where "ingegno" becomes purely "inganno," but by tercets ten through thirteen we are reminded of Wright's comments concerning Virginia's astute self-abasement as well as of Boccaccio's exposure of religious rationalizing:

> Che dove offender puoi è gran vendetta,
>     El perdonare, ch'a ogni humano eccesso
>     Non lascia sempre Giove ir sua saetta:
> A piedi tuoi mi stendo, & io confesso
>     Essere incolpa, riguarda al Leone
>     Che non è crudo a l'huom ch'è genuflesso:
> Habbi di me qualche compassione,
>     Pietà mi impetri l'infinito amore
>     Che merta gratia & non desperatione.
> Che s'io errai, ha purgato ogni errore
>     La stanca faccia di lagrime piena,
>     Et ogni pena è vinta dal dolore.
>
>                               (Sigs. C4ʳ-C4ᵛ)

*Since* Virginia has sinned, the Prince is obliged to follow the examples of the kings of gods and beasts; *if* she has sinned, her own suffering obviates the need for such forgiveness. And between these contradictory assertions is an equally illogical mercy that obtains a love that *merits grace*.

But the Prince only scorns "tanto inganno," even after Callimaco insists "cha'ngannarti la constrinse amore" (sig. C5ᵛ). The "dura impossibil conditione" he immediately sets bespeak Boccaccio's plot, but the ironies developed in the next few episodes indicate just as surely the Dionean perspective. At first Accolti apparently strives to elicit sympathy for his heroine: Domitio has "gran compassione" for this lady; Callimaco calls the Prince "crudo, et pien d'orgoglio"; Virginia, quite "innocente," calls on Death, and her maids rush about to relieve "queste membra tribolate &

frante" (sigs. C6^r-C6^v). The same pathos characterizes Virginia's eighty-line farewell to her subjects, during which she forgives Salerno for "l'immerite doglie, / El morir mio d'ogni ingiustitia pieno" and vows to spend her last moments wandering in the wilderness, "Poi che non piace al ciel ch'io sia felice" (sig. C7^v-C8^r). But no sooner have her tearful subjects departed than she shatters this sublime mood (and what she professed to be Heaven's will) with the frankest of confessions: "Sol per venir del mio disegno al fine / Celato ho el vero," the truth of making straightway for Milan, and "le bellezze divine / Del Principe" (sig. C8^v).

In emphasizing the heroine's attention to appearances—the word "honesto" is used three times in one stanza—Accolti is merely following his source ("onesto" is one of Neifile's favorite words; cf. I, 425–428, where she uses it or "onestamente" or "onestissima" five times). But Giletta's shifts take shape slowly, calmly, and methodically, whereas Accolti prefers to startle his audience, using every possible melodramatic device to convince us of Virginia's helplessness before abruptly revealing her strength. And though she is more often off than on stage during the rest of the play, we are never allowed to forget that she is directing the action, seducing the would-be seducer with plots beyond the depth of his designing servant. To enforce the irony of the pursuer pursued, Accolti has one party unknowingly echo or describe another. "Andiamo," cries Virginia, hurrying her maids off to Sabina's inn; "Andiam," cries the Prince in the very next line, as he hurries Ruffo back to Camilla's (sig. D1^r). Although Ruffo knows much about the game of love—"Scaccian chi viene & chiaman quel che fugge / Queste donne"—he is woefully ignorant of its most important player.

Far more subtle and clear-sighted is Ruffo's chief adversary, the widow Costanza, whose moral-commercial dialogues with Virginia add a mischievous note found not in Neifile's story but in the tales that surround it. Having heard from Sabina of the Prince's passion for Camilla, Virginia immediately (and characteristically) senses some higher power at work: "Forse dopo un mio lungo lagrimare / Sarò da qualche stella pia riscossa" (sig. D1^v). This compassionate star, however, requires that Costanza be "prudente" as well as "casta" and a "poveretta," for "la forza dell'or troppo è possente." Virginia's overtures naturally ignore such prudent concerns, though the bed trick is introduced as a means of employing "prudentia e ingegno" (sig. D2^v). The widow is rather asked to accept the heroine's shaping divinity: "Et co'l Principe me come el ciel mostra / Poniate in cambio della figlia vostra." Although understandably anxious about her reputation, Costanza eventually skirts another issue, something akin to Virginia's earlier reflection on the power of gold: "Chi va a l'util dietro non s'accorge / Che in un continuo mal tale util torna" (sig. D3$^r$).

Just as Sabina said nothing to encourage Virginia's faith in Costanza's prudence, so Virginia has said nothing to inspire Costanza's comments on those who pursue profit. Virginia replies in kind, however, with a model of euphemistic casuistry, first allaying Costanza's explicit fears by promising that "Quando si sappi un si piatoso inganno / Ne sarai commendata in infinito," then acknowledging the "util" she hinted at by repeatedly promising a handsome dowry for Camilla, and finally glancing darkly at the risks "Se tua figlia non sposi presto & bene" (sig. D3$^v$). Dioneo could not have done a wittier job of questioning Neifile's earnest efforts to sanctify deceit. Following so many narrators who have stressed hypocritical means to selfish ends, it behooves the Queen to emphasize how "la gentil donna" desires nothing more than "consolarsi onestamente"; avendo l'animo gentil," the woman need only be convinced that her role in the assignation would be an "onesta cosa" leading to an "onesto fine" (I, 426–428). But the lady-narrator doth protest too much her characters' innocence, and the smiles Boccaccio encourages probably influenced Accolti's repeated use of euphemisms.

Another method Neifile employs to idealize her heroine's trickery may have suggested some of the *Virginia*'s most humorous low-comic scenes. To make her agent's part in the bed switch more palatable, Giletta offers a pious hope that "Forse mi farà Iddio grazia d'ingravidare" (I, 428). This wish is of course Neifile's first move in sealing her heroine's program with God's approval; in the next paragraph we are offered a sign few would dare gainsay: "Ne' quali primi congiugnimenti . . . come fu piacer di Dio, la donna ingravidò." But blocking Neifile's path is Boccaccio's own ironic interplay. Signs of surety have been and will continue to be whimsically questioned by the Third Day's other storytellers, and it appears that Accolti honors that quizzical spirit with the largely farcical doings of Ruffo and his befuddled master in the rest of Act III. Since Virginia has instructed Costanza to show Ruffo a "faccia pia" (sig. D3$^v$), the bully's third attempt is welcomed with a smile. Still suspicious, he is nevertheless comforted by this omen of success: "Che Volpe è questa vitiata &

maestra / Pur è buon segno haver da lei buon viso." And though Ruffo now prefers to keep God out of the picture—to Costanza's "El cielo salvi e pensier tuoi" he replies, "Tu sola, non el ciel salvar mi puoi" (sig. D4$^v$)—he is soon congratulating himself for his success:

> Questa novella al mio signore arreco,
> Che dormira con lei, & io con teco?

The most ludicrous parts of this interview, however, are the details of so ironic a tryst, procedures odd in their own right and in being devised and discussed with such apparent seriousness. The Prince must arrive "a cinque hore, / Batti le palme, & venga senza gente, / Aspetti d'acqua ch'io versi el romore" (sig. D5$^r$). Possessing such valuable information enables Ruffo to lord it over his proud master—"intendo . . . / Schernirlo alquanto essermi vendicato"—but the teasing subsides before the instructions are given, even though the Prince is now evidently to feel as well as to hear the water: "Che per segno acqua a te gettata fia" (sig. D5$^v$). Was water actually thrown upon or merely toward the Prince? His first response, "Sentito ho l'acqua" (sig. D7$^r$), does not tell us what the audience saw. Neither does his subsequent moralization: "Poca acqua è questa a spegnere el mio foco." Another unanswerable question is what associations Accolti's audience made with this strange sign. Ruffo tells the Prince that if Camilla knew of his reluctance to surrender the ring, "Non ti laveria l'acqua del Danubbio" (sig. D6$^r$). Perhaps the water Costanza pours out also represented some cleansing ritual, the lover's baptism. But if "a cinque hore" refers to the fifth hour after sunset, it is just as possible that the audience thought of another ritual, pouring out the slops at curfew.

In any case, earthly and heavenly considerations continue to alternate in the short scenes that conclude Act III and initiate Act IV. To herself Costanza confesses being motivated by both "Tanta pietà di questa donna" and "la dota ch'io guadagno scorto" (sig. D6$^v$). Virginia then enters to thank her "pia, piatosa, & chara" servant: "In prima Dio ringratio & te da poi." The next stanza ushers in the Prince, the happiest person "sotto el ciel," and ironically grateful: "Io ti ringratio benigna fortuna" (sig. D7$^r$). But he is immediately replaced by Costanza, praying "el ciel non si scopra l'inganno," and he returns only to describe the joys he thinks he has just experienced with Camilla. Still wiser than he realizes, Ruffo closes the Third Act with a question for the audience, "Fidate poi di queste donne

ladre," and Virginia and Costanza open the Fourth with the same
sublime-mundane considerations that characterized their initial bargain-
ing. Having fulfilled the impossible conditions "Per la Dio gratia & tua,"
Virginia bids her agent fix her own reward. To the very same request
Neifile's "gentil donna" simply answers that she has not done a thing "per
alcuna speranza di guiderdone, ma perché le pareva doverlo fare a voler
ben fare" (I, 429). Costanza is even more "gentil" and therefore even less
direct. She requires half a stanza only to express her joy in serving the
"generosa" princess and another half to ask for nothing and hint for much:

> Nulla ti chiederei donna pietosa
> Sol di tua gratia resto, & son contenta,
> Che a cor gentil son parole proterve,
> Et chiede assai chi ben tacendo serve.
>
> (Sig. D8$^r$)

It is these problematical sentiments and ironies never hinted at by Neifile
that remind us most of Boccaccio's framework and, for that matter, of the
darker corners of Shakespeare's comedy. Accolti's own representation of
"our life['s] . . . mingled yarn" allows Ruffo a sudden, Parolles-like
self-knowledge ("A me sta ben se ogni vitio osservo, / Che ignobil son
plebeo, povero & servo") as well as some ironic moralizing, "El fin mostra,
[c]hi ha piu senno fido" (sigs. E2$^r$, E3$^v$). The Prince's melodramatic
mourning for the loss of a woman he actually shunned sounds another
ironic note. So does Callimaco's "Gratia habbi el ciel, poi che ti ci ha
renduto," if we remember Virginia's role as heaven's agent. The theme of
divine direction is most clearly and ironically sounded at the climax when
the Prince, pitying the dejected lady before him, swears "per quello
immortale / Che'n cielo e'n terra ha somma monarchia" that "ogni gratia
da me fatta ti fia / Se ben m'havessi offeso" (sig. E8$^r$). Within this
religious context Virginia expands and contracts the magnitude of her
guilt to suit the changing directions of her theme. The Prince was rightly
offended by what Love compelled her to do, yet he should easily forgive
what was engineered "con pietoso inganno" (sig. F1$^v$). Whether "pietoso"
is here taken as "piteous" or "pious," the "inganno" is defended with the
heroine's customary "ingegno"—139 lines of sweeping rhetoric that cul-
minate in her offering her breast to his blade, provided, of course, that he
later open up her heart to find his name inscribed (sig. F2$^r$).

True to his course throughout the play, however, Accolti is more skeptical as well as more sentimental than Neifile. When her two-line, matter-of-fact comment concerning Beltramo's return to Rossiglione is inflated into Salerno's twenty-four-line agonizing, we almost expect to find the speaker's sincerity—"Ruffo io son disperato, anzi son morto"— eventually qualified by his ignorance—"Se visto havessi el corpo pere-grino" (sig. E1ʳ). The same technique of exaggerating only to undercut is found in the nine impassioned octaves that conclude Act IV. Silvio, created out of nothing more than Neifile's passing reference to Giletta's suitors (I, 419), laments his beloved's imminent death for lack of sufficient "forza, o ingegno" and vows to undertake "ogni impossibil cosa" to find her, first questing among the conventional "selve, & fere impaste" and then through places and times increasingly removed, from a realistic "Danubio veloce" to an exotic "Eufrate che l'arene coce," from "le selve nude" of the ancient Parthians to the never-existing "sette Insule pie" and, just for good measure, "le sette crude." There is a similarly facetious tone behind the expansive geography of Act V as the Seneschal, turning Neifile's brief notice of Beltramo's "gran festa" (I, 430) into fifty-two lines of unrelieved hyperbole, bids the Prince's hunters bring back an eagle, a griffin, a phoenix, and the fishermen, everything from oysters to whales—"Et se possibil fusse una serena" (sig. E6ᵛ).

In Virginia's extravagant summation of her sorrows before the Salernese nobility we find the same uneasy balance between high seriousness and high comedy. While the befuddled hero speaks more and more ironically—directing his Seneschal, for example, "Non lasciar cosa entrar che ci dispiaccia"—the clear-eyed heroine publicly maintains her inno-cence and privately admits her cunning. To Sabina she explains that the "stelle fortuna, & fata humano. / M'hanno arrichita di doppio figliuolo," but she next addresses the babes themselves as precious things "Acquistati da me con tanto ingegno" (sigs. E7ʳ-E7ᵛ). To her husband and his court, however, it is mainly a matter of making "ingegno" look "piatoso." The Prince's "per quello immortale" therefore becomes "Per quel sommo fat-tor, ch'el tutto vede" and is joined to "Per le cener del tuo pio genitore" and "Per mio fervente & infinito amore" (sig. F1ᵛ). Such parallelisms support the "logic" of Virginia's claim: the mercy that family honor or tradition encourages is the mercy that God upholds and her own love deserves. But if such grand theater outdoes Neifile's melodramatic resolution—Accolti turns the weeping heroine into the weeping everyone (sig. F3$^r$)—it also seems to question its credibility, transforming the husband who loves so suddenly and unreservedly into a weary actor feeling out various roles to meet an astonishing turn of events: the good sportsman grudgingly admiring such "inaudito extremo ingegno," the good ruler bending to his subjects' wishes, the proud man trying to become magnanimous, first as Griselda's repentant husband, next as an anguished Ovidian lover, then as Orpheus, praising Apollo's will, and finally as the husband humbled before heaven's will (or comic conventions): "Andiamo poi ch' el ciel qui te compiace / Di quel ch'a me non creder gia che annoglia" (sig. F3$^v$).

The concluding comment on all ending well, however, comes in the Seneschal's three-octave epilogue. For the man who has done so much ordering and arranging during the last two acts there is a natural reluctance to extend the festivities; hence, the play's final joke—each spectator is invited to dine in his own house. But for this loyal servant there is no question of the couple's future happiness or of the play's moral import: the fact that Virginia, "Per suo ingegno, & virtu," has achieved her desires is proof that

> il meritato premio al fin raccoglie
> Ciascun, de l'opra sua, o bona, o fella
> Che cosi da d'Iddio le giuste voglie.
>
> (Sig. F4$^r$)

Like Neifile, the Seneschal is prone to gloss over minor problems: the frequent coupling of "ingegno" and "inganno," a "virtu" that is more efficient than virtuous. Notice, too, that his conviction that all must be well is based not on what has happened but on his notion of what God's just will must grant or allow, a faith in a perfectly ordered, poetically just universe that is both unrealistic and un-Christian. What supports his faith is precisely what supports Neifile's, a clever heroine who dresses God's just will to her own advantage. The playwright whose own performances before princes and popes made him ideally suited to expand upon the meaning of Giletta's ingenious deceits is once more reminding us that Boccaccio's allegedly simple virtue story is fraught with affectations and ironies.

IV

The foregoing consideration of Accolti's high-comic dramaturgy offers some evidence of the *Virginia*'s intrinsic worth and also suggests its value in interpreting Boccaccio. But of what use is this neglected play in glossing the greatest "chapter" of the *All's Well* story? Weighing every part of Accolti's play against every part of Shakespeare's is of course beyond an article's scope, but we can at least conclude by measuring Helena's seeming and being against those of her predecessors. After all, both Boccaccio and Accolti not only give us a common theme to look for in Shakespeare but an assurance that our search for an ironic or cynical treatment of that theme is not necessarily anachronistic.

As we might expect, Shakespeare voices the theme of shaping divinity, as well as his tradition's subordinate motif of sexual desire initiating action, principally through his heroine. Bertram is no sooner off to Paris with his mother's prayers than Helena laments the heavenly order that opposes her love for him, that "bright particular star" so removed from her "sphere." [39] But whereas her first soliloquy concludes that her "idolatrous fancy / Must sanctify [only] his relics," she is soon sanctifying her quest for his person. The first step in translating what heaven opposes to what heaven allows to what heaven actively supports occurs in her second soliloquy: "Our remedies oft in ourselves do lie, / Which we ascribe to heaven" (I.i.212–213). Although her use of "nature" to challenge Fortune's "mightiest space" sounds like the vain self-reliance of Iago or Edmund, her new self-confidence is too guileless to be interpreted as "Now, sex, stand up for wenches!" It is in soliloquy—in Shakespeare, a sure indication of sincerity, however misguided—that she asks, "Who ever strove / To show her merit that did miss her love?" Rather than denying heaven, Helena quite innocently manipulates it, a process that is completed when she finally etherealizes that remedy first forbidden and then allowed:

> There's something in't
> More than my father's skill, which was the great'st
> Of his profession, that his good receipt

39. I.i.84 ff. All citations to Shakespeare are from the Arden edition of *All's Well That Ends Well*, ed. G. K. Hunter (London, 1959).

Shall for my legacy be sanctified
By th'luckiest stars in heaven.

(I.iii.237–241)

It is impossible to determine whether the "something" supporting
Helena's designs relates to Fortune or nature, deity or desire, for during
every one of *All's Well*'s critical moments Shakespeare reflects his tradition's mingling of the sacred and profane. Even as Helena is rationalizing
her way into Bertram's orbit, Lavatch is listing those "holy reasons" (or
raisings) that drive him to Isbel (I.iii.30 ff.) with a mock piety much like
Dioneo's or Ruffo's. A similar sexual-religious interplay is achieved in the
next scene when Lafew approaches his "royal fox" as "Cressid's uncle" to
announce "Doctor She" and her miraculous powers "to araise" (II.i.69 ff.).
The most ironic sounding of the theme of divine direction, however,
occurs as Helena, much in the manner of Virginia's "di mie prove / Tu
stupirai," brings France through a mixture of miracles and bombast to
insist that

most it is presumption in us when
The help of heaven we count the act of men.

(II.i.150–151)

As both the play and its tradition repeatedly make clear, counting in
reverse, no matter how innocently, is no less presumptuous. The path to
Helena's own desires is inevitably paved with religious intentions, even
the *"sainted vow"* of *"Saint Jaques' pilgrim"* to *"sanctify"* Bertram's *"name
with zealous fervour"* (III.iv.4 ff.).

Although suggestions of high-handed France are found in both the
*Decameron* and the *Virginia*, Helena's second agent is far closer to Accolti's
Costanza than Neifile's good and honest woman, who acts without a
thought of being rewarded. Whereas Boccaccio could use Dioneo's story
to qualify Neifile's idealism, Shakespeare, like Accolti, had to raise his
questions more quickly. The Widow's faith in Helena's spiritual credentials is certainly nourished by something akin to Accolti's "oro," "that
which well approves / Y'are great in fortune," the "purse of gold" and
offer to "over-pay, and pay again" (III.vii.13 ff.). Notice, too, that it is
only after Helena offers to "add three thousand crowns" that the Widow is
suddenly able to grasp the bed trick's subtle moral basis, and she now
yields to "this deceit so lawful" (ll. 36 ff.).

The resemblance between such sentiments and Accolti's euphemisms—"Che va a l'util" and "Quando si sappi un si piatoso inganno" (sig. D3ʳ)—may be another coincidence. So also the two dramatists' common technique of underlining the pursuer pursued—within twenty lines (III.vi.102–III.vii.3) Shakespeare shows us one French lord about to collect twigs to lime Parolles, another to stalk Diana with Bertram, and Helena to shore up "the grounds I work upon." Before Act IV is over Ruffo is bragging about "El fin" revealing his "piu senno fido" (sig. E3ᵛ). At the same point in his play Parolles is "hoodwink'd." But so are their masters. Like Salerno, Rossillion implies that all is well with a conventional Petrarchan compliment, "A heaven on earth I have won by wooing thee," but he is gone before Diana, with a glance at the play's title, accommodates its theme: "For which live long to thank both Heaven and me! / You may so in the end" (IV.ii.67–68).

None of these relationships *prove* that Shakespeare borrowed from or even knew of Accolti; it is just as impossible to *prove* that he dramatized Neifile's tale with an eye to her subjects' contributions. If we wish to use our evidence imaginatively, we must be content with probabilities based on assumptions that seem well within reason: that Shakespeare had access to the whole of Boccaccio's Third Day, not just to Painter's translation of the ninth tale; that the *Virginia* enjoyed a surprising (to us) popularity.[40] What these relationships do indicate is a tradition that is usually witty, ironic, skeptical, and sometimes even cynical in its handling of fairy-tale motifs and virtue-story conventions. Where we cannot be sure that one innovator knew another, we can be sure that he would have understood him.

The *Virginia*'s success as one of the modern world's earliest high comedies makes Accolti important irrespective of Shakespeare. Beyond granting him his due, we may regard his clever exploitation of Boccaccio as one of Shakespeare's sources, a full-blown literary model, or as merely an

40. For Shakespeare's indebtedness to Antoine le Maçon's French translation of the *Decameron*, which went through nineteen editions between 1545 and 1616, see Herbert G. Wright, "How Did Shakespeare Come to Know the 'Decameron'?," *MLR*, L (January, 1955), 45–48. Mazzuchelli, I, 67–68, lists six editions of the *Virginia*: 1513, 1515, 1519, 1553, 1565, 1586; to these we should add our text (Venice, 1535), first noticed by Enrico Narducci, *Atti della R. Accademia dei Lincei, XII* (Rome, 1884), XII, 6; an eighth edition (Florence, 1518) not noted by either bibliographer is found in the University of Illinois Library.

obscure analogue, one of *All's Well*'s several sources of inspiration. At the very least Accolti is for Shakespeareans a potentially valuable source of information, telling us what to expect or to look for in a play that certainly requires frequent glossing. Something like the spirit of Dioneo appears to animate Lavatch's puns on grace and grass (IV.v.16–19) and Bertram's ironic complaint about being subdued to Diana's "modern grace" (V.iii.215–216). But it is the ghost of the *secentismo* showman and god of *improvvisatori* that seems to stand behind the needlessly complicated ways in which Helena performs her final wonders, beginning with Lafew's inspired detection of a ring new to the *All's Well* tradition and properly glossed by royalty itself:

> The heavens have thought well on thee, Lafew,
> To bring forth this discov'ry.
>
> (V.iii.149–150)

# Jessica's Turquoise Ring and Abigail's Poisoned Porridge: Shakespeare and Marlowe as Rivals and Imitators

## MAURICE CHARNEY

C HRISTOPHER MARLOWE was baptized at Canterbury on February 26, 1564, and William Shakespeare was baptized at Stratford on April 26, 1564, thus beginning one of the most intriguing rivalries in the annals of English literature. By the time Marlowe was killed in a tavern brawl at Deptford on May 30, 1593, his accomplishments at age 29 were considerably greater than those of Shakespeare at age 29. Had Shakespeare died in the same year, our literary history of Elizabethan drama would need to be radically revised, with Shakespeare among the lesser dramatists like Greene and Peele. Shakespeare not only outperformed his contemporaries, but also outlived most of them. It is not entirely conjectural, therefore, to see Shakespeare in 1593 laboring under the anxiety of influence exerted by Marlowe, his more famous, more energetic, more brilliant, and more personally exciting coeval.

Marlowe is the "Dead shepherd" of Phebe's couplet in *As You Like It*:

A shorter version of this paper was presented to the Drama Division of the Modern Language Association in December 1977.

Dead shepherd, now I find thy saw of might,
"Who ever loved that loved not at first sight?"

(III.v.81–82)[1]

And Marlowe is constantly erupting in allusive and parodic fashion in
Shakespeare's early plays. As Nicholas Brooke puts it: "There are a
number of eruptions in Shakespeare's work of passages which are unmis-
takably Marlovian in tone and attitude, to a degree which would almost
justify a disintegrator in identifying them as Marlowe's work."[2]

Marlowe may perhaps be the Rival Poet of the Sonnets, who keeps
Shakespeare's "ripe thoughts" from coming to fruition by "the proud full
sail of his great verse," and who, by writing "Above a mortal pitch,"
strikes Shakespeare dead. Shakespeare calls up his own truth and strength
of devotion—perhaps only a "worthless boat" after all—against his rival's
great rhetorical pinnace "of tall building, and of goodly pride." Whether
or not he is literally invoking Marlowe, Marlowe was, as F. P. Wilson
claims, "the only man of Shakespeare's age who could have been a rival
poet."[3] Shakespeare's nervous verses show a marked sense of diffidence
and inferiority to Marlowe's "mighty line"; it is as if Shakespeare felt that
it was hopeless ever to try to match him.

If we confine our perspective to *The Jew of Malta* and *The Merchant of
Venice*, we can speculate within a narrower range about how Shakespeare
tried not to compete with Marlowe in his own excellences, but to convert
him into a less heroic and more complex mode. *The Jew of Malta*, from
around 1590, became a great hit of the Admiral's Men, the chief rival to
Shakespeare's company, with Edward Alleyn as Barabas. *The Merchant of
Venice*, from about 1596, draws directly on Marlowe's Jew-play for the
action in Venice.[4] Shakespeare undoubtedly studied his rival's play in

1. All quotations from Shakespeare's plays are from the Signet paperback series edited
by Sylvan Barnet and published by New American Library.

2. Nicholas Brooke, "Marlowe as Provocative Agent in Shakespeare's Early Plays,"
*ShS.*, XIV (1961), 34. See also Brooke's lively and original essay, "Marlowe the Drama-
tist," in *Elizabethan Theatre*, ed. John Russell Brown and Bernard Harris, Stratford-upon-
Avon Studies #9 (London, 1966), pp. 87–105.

3. F. P. Wilson, *Marlowe and the Early Shakespeare* (Oxford, 1953), p. 131.

4. See Geoffrey Bullough, *Narrative and Dramatic Sources of Shakespeare*, Vol. 1 (London, 1957), esp. pp. 454–456. Bullough sees *The Jew of Malta* as "one of Shakespeare's
major sources in developing the character of the Jew" (p. 454).

order to prepare to write his own. It is also likely that he saw it performed. The transformation of Marlowe is profound, yet the indebtedness is still deep.

There are other ways of phrasing this relation. Marlowe influenced Shakespeare, but Shakespeare also recoiled from that influence. It is everywhere apparent that Shakespeare thought *The Jew of Malta* an inadequate play, weak and inconsistent in characterization and deprived of those richly ambiguous touches of psychological truth that make *The Merchant of Venice* so compelling. Yet Shakespeare's play, at least in the Shylock action, is surprisingly close in spirit to its source in *The Jew of Malta*. It is as if Shakespeare were trying to conceal the intensity of his own indebtedness to Marlowe, as if he were trying to prove that, although he could not rival Marlowe on his own ground, he could explore areas of dramatic awareness in which Marlowe would never dare to venture.

The title of this paper, "Jessica's Turquoise Ring and Abigail's Poisoned Porridge," is not entirely frivolous, because, even though it is difficult to compare turquoise rings and poisoned porridge, the two daughters have an analogous function. Jessica is clearly modeled on Abigail. Both are motherless daughters, like Ophelia and the daughters of King Lear. The absence of the mother strengthens the bond with the father, and there is a curiously incestuous scene in *The Jew of Malta*, in which Barabas, with the aid of Abigail, has just recovered his treasure from the nunnery in which Abigail has falsely immured herself. The exhilarated Barabas speaks in a style that strongly anticipates the wooing of Romeo and Juliet:

> But stay! what star shines yonder in the east?
> The lodestar of my life, if Abigail.
>
> (II.i.41–42)[5]

Before Abigail exits above, her father closes with her in an exuberantly romantic style very different from the heavy paternalism of Shylock, Polonius, and Lear:

> Farewell, my joy, and by my fingers take
> A kiss from him that sends it from his soul.
>
> (II.i.58–59)

5. *The Jew of Malta* is quoted from the edition by Richard W. Van Fossen in the Regents Renaissance Drama series (Lincoln, Nebr., 1964).

The exclamation of Barabas links his ducats and his daughter in a context that is celebratory: "O girl, O gold, O beauty, O my bliss! *Hugs his bags*" (II.i.54). With Shylock the association is grotesque and melodramatic, as in Solanio's malicious report:

> "My daughter! O my ducats! O my daughter!
> Fled with a Christian! O my Christian ducats!
> Justice! The law! My ducats and my daughter!"
> (II.viii.15–17)

Solanio revels in the sexual implication of "two stones, two rich and precious stones, / Stol'n by my daughter!" (II.viii.20–21), as if Shylock were speaking directly about the "family jewels"—"stones" is a standard Elizabethan word for testicles. Jessica has symbolically emasculated her old father, while Abigail has filled Barabas full of lusty, incestuous vitality. Admittedly, the passages are from different parts of the action, but they still use the same symbolic means to produce opposite effects. This is characteristic of Shakespeare's attempt to thoroughly revamp his old script.

Abigail and Jessica both enact the folk-tale role of the ogre's daughter: "the story of a girl who betrays her own inhuman father, sometimes letting him be killed, always permitting the stealing of his treasure—and all for the sake of a human hero, with whom she afterward tries to flee back to his world." [6] The archetype does not fit the dramatic characters as well as Leslie Fiedler would have us believe, yet we are grateful to him for his subterranean exploration of *The Merchant of Venice*. As fair Christians, Abigail and Jessica redeem the sins of their dark and villainous fathers. They do not, of course, succeed in converting their unrepentant ogre-fathers, but they manage to separate themselves from their own tainted origins. Here the absence of the mother simplifies the dichotomy. The desertion of the daughters isolates the fathers and sets them up as the villain-scapegoats of a corrupt, money-dominated society.

The dynamics of *The Jew of Malta* and *The Merchant of Venice* correspond with surprising closeness. Both Barabas and Shylock react with anguish to their daughters' betrayal. There is never any objection to the daughters' Christianity on theological grounds; the issue is never pursued doctrinally

6. Leslie A. Fiedler, *The Stranger in Shakespeare* (London, 1972), p. 111.

or ideologically. It is simply the revolt of the daughter against a hard but loving father—"How sharper than a serpent's tooth it is / To have a thankless child" (I.iv.295–296), as Lear puts it with more than fatherly exigence. The disloyalty cuts deep and feeds, especially in Shylock, a monomaniacal rage. It is the biological shock of separation.

In *The Jew of Malta*, the ogre's daughter does not immediately reveal her darker purpose, but first delights her father with the ingenious recovery of his treasure. We know, however, that this optimistic mood cannot last. Abigail refuses to be a party to the Machiavellian games of Barabas and Ithamore—and the Turkish slave bought in the market place soon replaces her, both figuratively and literally, as Barabas's adopted son. After the murder of Lodowick and Don Mathias, Abigail abjures her father, "Hard-hearted father, unkind Barabas," in an important soliloquy:

> But I perceive there is no love on earth,
> Pity in Jews, nor piety in Turks.
>
> (III.iii.47–48)

When Abigail becomes a nun again in good earnest, her father casts her off with cruel but logical arguments: "False and unkind! What, hast thou lost thy father?" (III.iv.2). Barabas correctly understands that the Catholic church is his rival and that his daughter has irretrievably abandoned him. In this hostile choice, she may actually be a threat to him for what she knows. Unlike Shylock, Barabas speaks of the loss of his daughter with a matter-of-fact, sardonic lucidity:

> For she that varies from me in belief
> Gives great presumption that she loves me not;
> Or loving, doth dislike of something done.
>
> (III.iv.10–12)

In a revenge tinged with incestuous overtones, Barabas, like old Abraham (the prototype of all "heavy" Jewish fathers), is now ready to slay his child. We have already had some alarming signs of this impending murder. In the smooth colloquy with Lodowick, Barabas says savagely (aside): "ere he shall have her, / I'll sacrifice her on a pile of wood" (II.iii.52–53). This is uncomfortably close to the Abraham and Isaac story. There is also foreboding in Barabas's early declaration that he has only "one sole daughter, whom I hold as dear / As Agamemnon did his Iphigen" (I.i.135–

136). Like the Jeptha's daughter of Polonius (*Hamlet*, II.ii.412–421), this allusion is dire, since Agamemnon sacrificed his daughter Iphigenia to get his fleet moving.

Once Barabas curses his daughter, he proceeds to a witty expedient by which to rid himself not only of her, but also of a whole nunnery of his enemies. The comfortingly domestic pot of rice porridge that stands by the fire is cunningly "spiced" by Barabas and sent secretly as an alms offering to the nunnery on Saint Jacques' Even. Ithamore as villainous straightman makes his witty contribution: "Troth, master, I'm loath such a pot of pottage should be spoil'd" (III.iv. 84–85), which is in the mocking spirit of Barabas's delight in mass murder:

> There is no music to a Christian's knell.
> How sweet the bells ring now the nuns are dead
> That sound at other times like tinkers' pans!
>
> (IV.i.1–3)

This is a good example of the farcical energy celebrated by T. S. Eliot in his essay on Marlowe: "it is the farce of the old English humour, the terribly serious, even savage comic humour, the humour which spent its last breath in the decadent genius of Dickens."[7]

Abigail dies as an all-loving saint:

> Ah, gentle friar,
> Convert my father, that he may be sav'd,
> And witness that I die a Christian.
>
> (III.vi.38–40)

As surrogate for Barabas, Friar Barnardine undercuts the unctuous beatitudes: "Ay, and a virgin, too; that grieves me most" (III.vi.41). Is this "savage comic humour," or is Barnardine merely an evil-minded wise guy in the style of Lucio in *Measure for Measure*? In any case, Abigail's death has a curiously maternal aspect to it as her father offers the speciously comforting rice porridge—a dish often given to the sick. Marlowe seems to miss the implications of Abigail's death, since the rage of Barabas is so limited and so controlled, and the murder of his daughter is so unclimactically merged with a whole anonymous nunnery.

7. T. S. Eliot, "Christopher Marlowe" (1918), in *Selected Essays 1917–1932* (New York, 1932), p. 105.

This is the very point on which Shakespeare puts such overwhelming emphasis. After the stealing away of Jessica—and her own self-indulgent stealing from her father's coffers—Shylock is enraged with an intensity of hate that can never be placated. The teasing, "merry" bond has disappeared, and Shylock is now out for blood. Shylock's passion in Act III, scene i, cannot be appeased, and the loss of his daughter marks the loss of everything that has made life meaningful for him in Venice. I don't mean this as a sentimental justification of the savage Shylock, but only as a way of understanding the new and literal viciousness of Act III, scene i. Shylock is suffering, and, in characteristic fashion, he wants to make sure that all those around him suffer more than he does.

Shylock has sent to seek for his daughter, and in III.i Tubal gives his lacerating report of Jessica and Lorenzo on their frivolous honeymoon in Genoa. "Your daughter spent in Genoa, as I heard, one night fourscore ducats" (III.i.101–102). The exact amounts and their modern equivalents are unimportant. Shylock is cut to the quick by his daughter's mindless extravagance: to him it translates what it means to be a Christian wife. The culminating insult is Tubal's report from a creditor of Antonio: "One of them showed me a ring that he had of your daughter for a monkey" (ll. 111–112). We think of Othello's fulsome "Goats and monkeys" (IV.i.263), both animals associated with lechery. "Were they as prime as goats, as hot as monkeys" (III.iii.400), as Iago has said before, and we remember that in Falstaff's report, Justice Shallow was in his youth "lecherous as a monkey" (2 *Henry IV*, III.ii.324). The monkey is a type image for the derogation of human decency, as in the railing Apemantus's conclusion: "The strain of man's bred out / Into baboon and monkey" (*Timon of Athens*, I.i.255–256). Jessica's monkey affronts her father's serious, puritanic values—we are reminded that Jews and Puritans were closely associated in the minds of Shakespeare's audience as pharisaical believers in the literal word of the Old Testament.

From Jessica's monkey we move back to Shylock's ring, which represents the final, excruciating turn of the screw:

Out upon her! Thou torturest me, Tubal. It was my turquoise; I had it of Leah when I was a bachelor. I would not have given it for a wilderness of monkeys.
(III.i.113–116)

For a moment, Jessica is no longer a motherless daughter. The mention of Leah, Shylock's deceased wife, evokes a human landscape that has long since disappeared. That Shylock could have been a bachelor and a wooer and the receiver of a turquoise ring as a love token from his girl-friend Leah—all these humanizing details seem incredible at this moment.

Turquoise is the semi-precious stone from Turkey—Ithamore's country—usually spelled and pronounced "turkis" (or "turkie"). Its special property was to mirror the state of health and the mood of its wearer. Thus Donne, in his "First Anniversary," describes the stone "As a compassionate Turcoyse which doth tell / By looking pale, the wearer is not well" (ll. 343–344).[8] In Jonson's *Sejanus*, it is "true as turquoise in the dear lord's ring, / Look well or ill with him" (I.i.37–38).[9] The lapidary meaning gives the turquoise special significance as a reflector of the reciprocal feelings of lovers. The point of Shylock's intense and almost hysterical grief is that Jessica has desecrated her mother's ring (and therefore her mother's memory).[10] The hyperbolic and commercial conclusion about the wilderness of monkeys is both grotesque and poignant. Shylock does not have at hand any easy terms by which to express his emotions.

It is curious that Barabas has quantities of precious and semi-precious stones—

> Bags of fiery opals, sapphires, amethysts,
> Jacinths, hard topaz, grass-green emeralds,
> Beauteous rubies, sparkling diamonds—
>
> (I.ii.25–27)

but no turquoise. It seems obvious that if all these splendid stones are heaped together in one grand hyperbole in Marlowe's play, then they are no longer available to Shakespeare, who has to turn to the humbler and more anthropomorphic turquoise. If this detail carries any conviction, then Shakespeare was also obliged to avoid many of the poetic felicities of *The Jew of Malta*. Barabas has a vaunting, heroic style, not unlike Tambur-

8. Quoted from *John Donne: The Anniversaries*, ed. Frank Manley (Baltimore, Md., 1963), p. 77 and note on p. 157.

9. Quoted from *Sejanus*, in *Ben Jonson*, ed. C. H. Herford and Percy and Evelyn Simpson, 11 vols. (Oxford, 1925–1952).

10. See the animated moral attack on Jessica by Arthur Quiller-Couch in the introduction to the New Cambridge edition of the play (Cambridge, Eng., 1926), pp. xx–xxi. "Jessica is bad and disloyal, unfilial, a thief; frivolous, greedy, without any more conscience than a cat and without even a cat's redeeming love of home" (p. xx).

laine's, that would be completely out of keeping for Shylock. The Jew of Malta holds himself above ordinary, dull-witted mortals:

> No, Barabas is born to better chance,
> And fram'd of finer mold than common men,
> That measure naught but by the present time.
> A reaching thought will search his deepest wits,
> And cast with cunning for the time to come. . . .
>
> (I.ii.218–222)

The illusion is offered, almost from the beginning, that his wealth is the aesthetic product of his soaring imagination.

In his most characteristic utterance, Shylock insists on his common humanity:

Hath not a Jew eyes? Hath not a Jew hands, organs, dimensions, senses, affections, passions?—fed with the same food, hurt with the same weapons, subject to the same diseases, healed by the same means, warmed and cooled by the same winter and summer as a Christian is?

> (III.i.56–61)

It would never occur to Barabas to rationalize his revenge in these humanistic terms; he is never put in a position where he needs to justify what he is doing, even to himself. This is hardly a comic speech, even if Shylock is dressed in the Jewish clown costume inherited from Judas: red wig, hooked putty nose, and long, loose-fitting gown or smock—his "Jewish gaberdine." Barabas has a much wider range, but Shylock is more intense. His crudeness of speech and manner—halting, inconsequential, wheedling, insistent, insinuating, menacing, irrelevant—is meant to characterize him as a Jew very different from the elegant, eloquent, and worldly Barabas. We are never allowed to feel that Barabas is desperate, wild, and frenzied as Shylock is, with his back to the wall and at bay in a totally hostile setting. By a nice paradox, although Barabas moves in a tragic action, he is thoroughly insulated from the tragic emotions that Shylock arouses in a play that is unquestionably a comedy.

If Marlowe was indeed Shakespeare's rival poet, then the limits he set had a salutary effect on Shakespeare's development. There was no chance that the boy from Stratford, not even university trained, could match the boy from Canterbury's soaring and classically derived rhetoric. In an early

play like *Titus Andronicus*, for example, Shakespeare may have tried to
out-Marlowe Marlowe. The splendid speeches, heavily indebted as they
are to Ovid, resemble *Tamburlaine* and *The Jew of Malta*, too. There is no
lack of persons with aspiring minds in *Titus*, and the insouciant Mach-
iavellism of Aaron the Moor must be directly indebted to Ithamore and
Barabas both. But Shakespeare moved away from grand rhetoric to a more
difficult exploration of the details of character and consciousness. There is
a certain flatness in Barabas that Shakespeare must have found disturbing.
When Ithamore, for example, asks him: "Do you not sorrow for your
daughter's death?" (IV.i.16), Barabas answers with energetic vitupera-
tion, but his speech is disappointing because it lacks any psychological
dimension:

> No, but I grieve because she liv'd so long.
> An Hebrew born, and would become a Christian!
> *Cazzo! diabolo!*
>
> (IV.i.17–19)

"*Cazzo! diabolo!*" is very un-Shakespearean and just on the edge of high-
class, Italianate rant.

Shylock's deviousness is an improvement on the plain-spoken villainy of
Barabas. When the Duke importunes Shylock to explain his murderous
passion against Antonio, he sardonically refuses any answer:

> What if my house be troubled with a rat,
> And I be pleased to give ten thousand ducats
> To have it baned? What, are you answered yet?
> Some men there are love not a gaping pig,
> Some that are mad if they behold a cat,
> And others, when the bagpipe sings i' th' nose,
> Cannot contain their urine. . . .
>
> (IV.i.44–50)

But there is a savage answer concealed in these insinuations that Bassiano
presses out of Shylock:

> BASSANIO
> Do all men kill the things they do not love?
>
> SHYLOCK
> Hates any man the thing he would not kill?
>
> (IV.i.65–66)

This has a hateful energy and resonance very different from the smoothly articulated speeches of Barabas, yet without Marlowe's *Jew of Malta* it is hard to see how Shakespeare could have created *The Merchant of Venice*. The one play overlays the other.

The relations between these two great dramatic poets, almost exact contemporaries, have not yet been fully understood. Among the many critics who have written on this difficult subject—most to needlessly reiterate Shakespeare's superiority to Marlowe [11]—Nicholas Brooke best grapples with the complexity of the relationship. His conclusion is that "Marlowe seems to have been for Shakespeare not only a great poet, as his tributes imply, but the inescapable imaginative creator of something initially alien which he could only assimilate with difficulty, through a process of imitative re-creation merging into critical parody." [12] We tend to forget that, even though Marlowe died in 1593, a significant part of his theatrical career overlapped Shakespeare's, and the reverse question of Shakespeare's influence on Marlowe is even more teasing than the one we have been considering. In *Edward II*, for example, Marlowe is moving in a distinctly Shakespearean direction, with Shakespeare's earliest history plays serving as models. It is also true that Shakespeare is increasingly able to shake off Marlowe's influence, which virtually disappears in the progress from *Titus Andronicus* to *King Lear*.

How to account for these shifting dependencies and autonomies? It looks as if Shakespeare was finally able to exorcise his fascination with the demonic Marlowe, but Marlowe at the end of his career suddenly glimpses a new Shakespearean way of writing tragedy. In the absence of any relevant biographical data, we need to reconstruct the artistic relations of Shakespeare and Marlowe from the tentative, anxious, and perhaps even grudging influences of the plays. It seems apparent that Shakespeare, at

11. I strongly disagree with the point of view of Irving Ribner in "Marlowe and Shakespeare," *SQ*, XV (1964), 41–53. Ribner thinks the influence of *The Jew of Malta* on *The Merchant of Venice* has been overestimated and that the influence of Marlowe on Shakespeare is generally very small. See also the more moderate position of Wolfgang Clemen in "Shakespeare and Marlowe," pp. 123–132, of *Shakespeare 1971: Proceedings of the World Shakespeare Congress, Vancouver, August 1971*, ed. Clifford Leech and J.M.R. Margeson (Toronto, 1972). In making the comparison between Marlowe and Shakespeare, it all depends on what criteria are invoked. Dramaturgic criteria are likely to yield more positive results than those drawn from an ideational, thematic, or strictly verbal approach.

12. Brooke, "Marlowe as Provocative Agent," *ShS*, XIV (1961), 44.

least in his earlier career, was not only actively imitating, but also trying to outdo his formidable rival playwrights and poets—Marlowe as well as Kyd, Greene, Peele, Lyly, and others. *The Merchant of Venice* is so radically different from *The Jew of Malta* because Shakespeare was so intensely aware of his powerful rival. Without directly imitating Marlowe, he is attempting to surpass him in writing a tragic-comic play about an overweening Jew. Shakespeare tempers Marlowe's splendid rhetoric with a wide variety of unheroic, wheedling, and malicious touches that make Shylock less grand than Barabas but more dramatically compelling. On his side, Marlowe was trying to discover in Shakespeare a more theatrical, more character-oriented, and less rhetorical way of writing plays. This mutual give and take obviously influenced both playwrights to strive for dramatic effects they could not possibly have accomplished alone.

# Shakespeare and Jonson Again: The Comic Forms

## NANCY S. LEONARD

T HE DISTINCTION BETWEEN Shakespearean romantic comedy and
Jonsonian satiric comedy is now canonical. For a long time, it was a
liberating idea which put an end to the habit of taking one playwright by
the other's measure. More recently, though, a sense of the difference
between the two kinds of comedy has tended to obscure the perception of
their relationship to each other. The use of the terms "romantic" and
"satiric" to distinguish Shakespeare's comedies from Jonson's implies a
mutual exclusiveness which there is good reason to mistrust. Recent
criticism has shown a certain uneasiness in this matter, particularly in its
recognition of Jonson's exploitation of romantic sympathy in the audience.[1] Most readings, however, still assume the privileged authority of

---

1. M. A. Shaaber has observed that in Shakespeare's romantic comedy "the stress is on
the noun rather than the adjective"; "The Comic View of Life in Shakespeare's Comedies,"
in *The Drama of the Renaissance: Essays for Leicester Bradner*, ed. Elmer M. Blistein (Providence, R.I., 1970), p. 172. For the recognition of elements in Jonson which elicit
romantic sympathy, see Jonas A. Barish, review of *Jonson's Moral Comedy* by Alan C.
Dessen, *MP*, LXXI (1973), 80–84, and Robert Ornstein, "Shakespearian and Jonsonian
Comedy," *ShS*, XXII (1969), 43–46. Milton Crane has argued for a definition of
Elizabethan comedy broad enough to include romantic and satiric modes in a single kind,
in *"Twelfth Night* and Shakespearean Comedy," *SQ*, VI (1955), 1–8.

the distinction between the comic kinds. My aim in this essay is to modify that authority by arguing that the two forms of comedy are essentially and inextricably involved with each other, even dependent on each other, in four representative comedies, *As You Like It, Twelfth Night, Volpone*, and *The Alchemist*.

To be specific, the two great comic forms, Shakespearean romantic comedy and Jonsonian satiric comedy, are mirror images of each other. Each kind of comedy develops in active opposition to the other; and in order for either form to realize itself, it must first get rid of the other form. To enact and then to defeat the antagonist form are essential for arrival at persuasive closure, and problematic endings reflect the occasional (and interesting) draw. In making my own point about their structural interrelation, I intend no surprising definitions of what romantic and satiric comedy are. We might agree on the following features as defining ones. First, of course, romantic comedy is usually a love comedy, satiric comedy most often an intrigue. Second, a romantic comedy constructs its implicit values in the process of the play, which it closes by a hierarchically ordered whole that displays those values symbolically. Satiric comedy, conversely, deconstructs delusive values in its temporal process, and closes with a symbolic scene which marks the absence of false values to signify the presence or possibility of true ones. Third, romantic comedy affirms an essential congruence between character and role, while satiric comedy often shows up a disparity between them. It follows that romantic comedy tends to confirm the beliefs of its characters, while satiric comedy tends to disconfirm them. Finally, and perhaps most importantly, the characters in a romantic comedy almost always appear to the audience (though not to each other) as what they really are, and the play evolves in a way that endorses audience attitudes toward them. In satiric comedy, certain central characters are presented duplicitously, and appear to the audience in an ambiguous light. In particular, the rogues of Jonsonian comedy elicit in the audience a form of sympathetic admiration that William Empson has called "rogue-sentiment," a sentiment that the comedy ultimately tries to expunge by its exposure of the rogues.[2]

2. Empson's term comes from his *Hudson Review* essays on *Volpone*, XXI (1968), 651–666, and on *The Alchemist*, XXII (1969), 595–608. To Empson, rogue-sentiment makes the audience "half-sympathize" with the tricksters; I borrow the term but use it to refer only to the romantic elements of sympathy and admiration. The ironic elements, which

On the surface, it would seem that contrasts like these leave romantic and satiric comedy hopelessly far apart. But neither Shakespeare nor Jonson is content merely to let a play be romantic or satiric by virtue of certain generic features. A play's generic markings are likely to be clear from the outset, but also volatile, easily threatened by attitudes bound up with the opposite form. Consequently, a play must become an instance of its own mode by making the features of the mode more secure, and it is the necessity of becoming that creates the mirror relationship which is my subject here. Naturally, there is no one way for a play to enact and defeat its mirror image, but Shakespeare and Jonson do return to the ways that suit them, and draw on common resources in the process. Shakespeare's romantic comedies characteristically absorb their satiric elements by subordinating them in a large synthesis of disparate attitudes. Jonson, by contrast, prefers to ridicule or expel the romantic aspects of his comedies; he offers an analytical logic of parts rather than Shakespeare's logic of the whole. In both men's work, primary elements of form are recruited to articulate the basic opposition: dramatic relations between characters, between scenes, between different aspects of a single character's psychology, between crisis and resolution. The particular stress on the generic characteristics of the endings of these plays is deliberate, for they mirror the goals of the comic process.

*As You Like It* is commonly acknowledged to dramatize a war between romantic and satiric views in the roles of Touchstone, Jaques, and Rosalind, but this by no means exhausts the subject.[3] In fact, the Renaissance pastoralism represented by *As You Like It* would lead us to expect a much more thorough mingling of generic and moral points of view.[4]

---

compete with admiration to create half-sympathy, are identified separately in my paper for convenience in making contradistinctions. See also Barish's expanded discussion of Empson's terms in his review of Dessen's *Jonson's Moral Comedy*, cited above.

3. For the classic position that Rosalind's wit, the functions of Touchstone and Jaques, and the parallels among the play's lovers are the ways by which the play mingles satiric and romantic attitudes, see Helen Gardner's essays and Jay L. Halio's introduction to his *Twentieth Century Interpretations of As You Like It* (Englewood Cliffs, N.J., 1968), pp. 1–8.

4. See Rosalie L. Colie, *Shakespeare's Living Art* (Princeton, N.J., 1974), pp. 243–283: She makes the important point that "With these literary or generic and social mixes, comes also moral mixture, a mixture of ways of life set in actual or implied contradistinction or even contradiction" (p. 253).

What needs to be recognized is the extent to which the play builds the opposition between romantic and satiric elements into the main love plot, as essential to each of its couplings. *As You Like It* intends to vindicate perhaps the most extravagant of romantic impulses, love at first sight. Other comedies assume the more modest aim of vindicating what one might call love on second thought. Orsino, Benedick, and Demetrius, for instance, are all lovers who realize only belatedly (and almost too late) their true love's identity. Despite its sophisticated tone, *As You Like It* is more reckless, even supplying itself with the famous Marlovian motto, "Who ever loved that loved not at first sight?" From a satirical point of view, love at first sight is ridiculous because it almost guarantees a misalliance, a prospect *As You Like It* takes very seriously. For the couples of the play, the experience of courtship tends to fuse with the rhetoric of misalliance. This gives way, however, to a repetition of the love-at-first-sight impulse: an act of surrender to romance even after misalliance has become a part of its texture. The play recognizes the essential mysteriousness of this surrender by its use of a supernatural figure and formalized stage emblems to bring the lovers together.

The play's treatment of romantic and satiric elements is epitomized in the extreme case of Silvius and Phebe. The two are such hypertrophied romantics that they turn into quotation marks for their own speeches, but paradoxically they lose little by it. Silvius and Phebe are not persons betrayed by conventionality; they *are* their conventionality, and therefore they belong together, no less than Rosalind and Orlando do. Their postures are so complementary that Phebe's consent should be enough to pronounce them well-matched. Yet when Rosalind delivers her satiric diatribe against this pair, the balance of conventional union is upset. Rosalind's language collapses Silvius and Phebe from exalted anguish to commonplace nature, with Phebe appearing as "the ordinary / Of Nature's sale-work" and Silvius "Like foggy South puffing with wind and rain." [5] In a straightforwardly satirical setting, this kind of ridicule would imprison its objects in their ridiculousness, but here it leads to an unusual

5. *As You Like It*, III.v.42–43, 50. References to Shakespeare are from the Arden editions: *As You Like It*, ed. Agnes Latham (London, 1975); *Twelfth Night*, ed. J. M. Lothian and T. W. Craik (London, 1975). Latham's discussion of the luring of characters in *As You Like It* into traps and ridicule is suggestive; introduction to the New Arden, pp. lxxxiii–lxxxiv.

reversal. The thrust of Rosalind's remarks is that Phebe needs to take on the burden of self-knowledge, to recognize that she is "not for all markets" and that "a good man's love" is the real aim of her desire. This kind of educative change, a conversion of identity by knowledge, is traditionally associated with the heroines of romantic comedy, characters like Rosalind herself. Here, however, the most lightweight, most stereotypical character conceivable is asked to change at a level of personality she does not, apparently, even have. Meanwhile, Rosalind and Celia, characters more eligible for such an education, don't appear to need one, or at least to get one. Celia, whose credentials for psychological depth are established by the loyalty to Rosalind for which she rejects her father, undergoes the kind of sudden conversion more appropriate to a Phebe; while Rosalind does not so much get a sentimental education as she gives one.

The Ganymede-Silvius-Phebe triangle that mediates Phebe's education is the most extreme development of Phebe's unexpected position. Certain elements of the situation are explicitly educative, and need only be recognized for what they are. The mismatching of Phebe with a woman both mocks the self-love that motivates her cruelty toward Silvius and exposes the illusion that one's lover is or must be the "perfect" man or woman. Likewise, when Phebe suffers from "Ganymede" the same abusive language she has administered to Silvius, she takes on his role of abject wooer and is prepared to appreciate his "faith," as she does in the end. At the same time, though, Phebe's mismatching with "Ganymede" is a severe sexual blunder (compare the nature of Orsino's feelings for "Cesario," which remain hidden to him until "Cesario" becomes a woman). The exercising of Phebe's erotic feelings toward a devastatingly inappropriate object carries undeveloped suggestions of sexual ambivalence, vulnerability, and instability which do not "belong" to a character of Phebe's type. The play explicitly suggests that Phebe can be protected from these things by romantic faith, accepted when the true basis of alliance is acknowledged. For Phebe, a true alliance has seemed to be a misalliance, for reasons of vanity and self-mystification. For her, the experience of actual misalliance turns out to be a cure; her surrender to "Ganymede" is vindicated in her belated surrender to Silvius.

With Celia and Oliver, love and betrothal are both instantaneous, and no one in the play questions either one. Yet the lovers are a surprisingly unlikely couple. For one thing, they respond in opposite ways to the obligations of natural loyalty raised by their relations as brother to Orlando and cousin to Rosalind. The brotherly "discretion" with which Oliver advises Charles to break young Orlando's neck is utterly at odds with the cousinly loyalty with which Celia pleads Rosalind's case before her own father. The reformed Oliver, of course, is on the stage long enough to convince us of his repentance, but not, perhaps, of his capacity for the kind of sustained enactment of obligation that Celia has performed in Rosalind's behalf. Further, if Celia's moral energy, unlike Oliver's, is unquestioned, her belief in romantic love is not. Oddly, Celia's predominant mode of encouraging Rosalind in love is to mock both erotic impulse and romantic faith. What makes this more than merely witty temperament is the frequency of her skeptical remarks. Her parrying of Rosalind's "petitionary vehemence" to discover the identity of the verse writer in III.ii clearly plays with Rosalind's impulsiveness, yet this play takes on a caustic character when she continues to stress her own witty similes, against Rosalind's ardent interruptions. Celia's suspicion of the volatility of eroticism is also clear in her retort to Rosalind's assertion of bottomless love ("as fast as you pour affection in, it runs out" IV.i.199–200), and this may be the basis for her questioning of Orlando's truth (III.iv.19, 25) and of the oaths of all lovers (III.iv.27–30). However playful the skepticism, it is still genuine.

Celia's ironic attitude toward love meets its match when she meets hers and suddenly turns into the type of romantic extravagance. The love between her and Oliver is simultaneously a problem and a solution, an ironic joke and a romantic statement. Celia's skepticism does not become problematical until Celia herself becomes a lover, and the solution to the problem lies in the vow, an act of romantic faith, which surrenders her skeptical self to Oliver. On his side, Oliver is well aware of the "giddiness" of his betrothal, and even enjoys it, thereby suggesting his capacity, and the play's, to absorb ironic perspectives without diminishment. Rosalind and Orlando make the same point more decisively, when they subject Celia and Oliver to a bout of humorous deflation. The language they use is satirical, but its purpose is affectionate and accepting; it actually celebrates love in the guise of denigrating it. Satire, here, becomes the trope by which the affirmation of spontaneous passion is created: Celia and Oliver no sooner met, but they looked; no sooner looked, but they loved; no sooner loved, but they sighed; no sooner sighed, but they asked one another the reason; no sooner knew the reason, but they sought the remedy. And in these degrees have they made a pair of stairs to marriage, which they will climb incontinent, or else be incontinent before marriage. They are in the very wrath of love, and they will together. Clubs cannot part them.

(V.ii.31–40)

The affirmative impulse of this language goes beyond just Celia and Oliver. Immediately after this speech, Orlando expresses his desire for the "real" Rosalind, and Rosalind decides to end her masquerade. Throughout the play, she and Orlando have used satire as an instrument of courtship; here, a transformed satire incorporates the two of them in an affirmation intended for someone else.

Rosalind and Orlando become true lovers after acting out a mock wooing which is more than the misalliance of comic masquerade—two "boys" playing at courtship—although much comedy comes from that. It is not "Ganymede," but Rosalind, who makes this playing risky, for "Ganymede's" satirical remarks about the vows and illusions of love are projections of a Rosalind quite uncertain about what she is able to believe and is capable of saying.[6] To Orlando's wish to make "Ganymede" believe in his love for Rosalind, "Ganymede" replies:

Me believe it! You may as soon make her that you love believe it, which I warrant she is apter to do than to confess she does.

(III.ii.377–79)

What "Ganymede" admits is Rosalind's difficulty in committing herself to her love by expressing it to her lover. Orlando, for his part, needs to surrender his conventional romantic oaths; otherwise, his language of love will be a "tedious homily" which will not overcome Rosalind's anxiety. The "Ganymede"-Orlando dialogues expose real strains in a future match between Orlando and Rosalind; the scenes are thus not only generally satiric, by mocking romantic illusion, but specifically ironic, by sustaining for characters and audience the prospect that Orlando and Rosalind

6. For good recent discussion of the ambiguities of the courtship play, see D. J. Palmer, "*As You Like It* and the Idea of Play," *CritQ*, XIII (1971), 234–245; and "Art and Nature in *As You Like It*," *PQ*, XLIX (1970), 30–40, esp. 37 ff.

may be fundamentally mismatched. The strains in the relation occur because Rosalind is unsure how to interpret a language so unlike her own, and is uncertain how to respond to it, as we see here:

ROSALIND

But are you so much in love as your rhymes speak?

ORLANDO

Neither rhyme nor reason can express how much.

ROSALIND

Love is merely a madness, and I tell you, deserves as well a dark house and a whip as madmen do.

(III.ii.386–389)

What is unsaid is as interesting as what is said. "Ganymede" risks a direct question, from the twin impulses of passionate curiosity and frustration with Orlando's conventional way of putting things. Orlando, pressed for sincerity, continues to affirm it in a doggedly predictable idiom. Rosalind replies by withdrawing from her impulse to direct statement; "Ganymede" energetically returns Orlando's conventional volley. Perhaps exasperation makes Rosalind do this, perhaps fear of her impulse to believe him. Or perhaps she takes refuge in the comfortable scoffing of her role as "Ganymede." In any case, we are made aware that Rosalind and Orlando speak in colliding languages, and no one is sure what to make of it.

This potential misalliance is not averted by a surrender of conflicting idioms during the play. Orlando, though he does show effective wit, as in his defeat of Jaques, never loses the steady, if sometimes stylized, language native to him. Rosalind, though she shows repeatedly her capacity for seriousness, does not show it directly to him until the final scene. She never stops being witty; even Hymen must silence the "confusion" of her wit to solemnize the marriages (V.iv.124–125). Having enacted an ironic perspective on the compatability of the play's most attractively romantic lovers, by showing that Orlando talks too much like Silvius and Rosalind feels too much like "Ganymede," the play leaves us, remarkably, with lovers who no one doubts are true ones.

The form by which this is accomplished is the same symbolic surrender to the idea of true marriage that marks the other characters, in this case symbolized by "Ganymede's" claim that Rosalind will be united to Orlando by magic (V.ii.51–75). Magic is a potent idea in the play, though a relatively understated one. Its role is to resolve irresolvables, as in the conversions, and here what is resolved is the inner tension in Rosalind's and Orlando's relationship. Nothing that either character has actually done can be shown to sanction the lovers' impulses and harmonize their disparate qualities; the common assumption that their role playing does so is based on the reasonable premise that something must. Yet the play insists that that something be Hymen, direct from heaven; that the gesture of unity, in other words, share equally in the nature of fiat and grace. The play dramatizes, and endorses, the "magical" origin of its romantic faith by the elaborate, celebratory formality of its ending, with its stage images of lovers. In fact, it works a careful transformation, replacing the chorus of unsatisfied lovers chanting in response to Silvius (V.ii.82–125) with the emblematic array of matched couples that Hymen blesses (V.iv.130–139, 185–195). This amounts to displacing a stage figure that represents the difficulty of subordinating passion and anxiety to genuine relationship by a figure that enacts that subordination—and is confirmed in its validity by being given twice. But it is important to emphasize that this resolution does not seem "arbitrary," even where it includes such fabulously misallied characters as Touchstone and Audrey. Rather, the resolution is extravagant, in a play where everything that is most attractive springs from extravagance—Rosalind's wit, Orlando's decision to "play along" with it, Oliver's conversion, and so on. True, extravagance has also appeared in ironic and satiric ways, but it is meanness that the play finally condemns: the meanness of Duke Frederick, of Oliver before Arden, and of Jaques, whose only power (before his grudging blessing) is to take the joy out of life. His blessing, importantly, allows that joy its day. But the Duke senior has the last word on this subject, and the right one: that one must *trust* that things will end in "true delights" (V.iv.197).

Most readings of *Volpone* severely limit its romantic elements to the play's enlistment of partial sympathy for the rogues, and their Marlovian aspiration, in three powerfully eloquent scenes: Volpone's apostrophes to gold and to Celia, and Mosca's soliloquy. Nonetheless, despite the eloquence, readers usually find their sympathy only partial, given the implicit irony that plays about the rogues. Jonson is seen to reject the rogues' appeal in the end, and it is clear that the play judges them adversely

enough to make the survival of that appeal an interpreter's burden. Yet
the ending of *Volpone*, with the unusual severity of its punishments, has
troubled many readers,[7] and I would argue that this is so because the
romantic appeal of Jonson's rogues is by no means confined to the particular scenes that give it expression, or strongly qualified there. Characters
like Volpone have an imaginative energy that overwhelms the moral
energy opposed to it and compels an audience to the kind of instinctive
sympathy usually reserved for the protagonists of romantic comedy. The
romantic presence is a rooted one, in conflict with the play's satirical
movement at many levels of structure; and Jonson's ending is as harsh as it
is because the romantic presence is too strong to be merely rejected. It
must be expunged, purged, from the play. One may well feel that the
purgation is incomplete, and my discussion, which will point to the
various planes of conflict between the two presences, may help to explain
why.

Volpone's opening apostrophe to gold is usually read as the key to the
play's irony about visionary ambition. But the rhetorical design of the
scene, and Mosca's pivotal role in it, lend Volpone's aspirations a surprising authority. Paradoxically, this is achieved by a heightening of satire.
When Mosca flatters Volpone, making the cosmological visionary into a
parasite's dupe, Jonson creates for the scene an explicit satiric presence
that goes beyond the irony implicit in Volpone's speech. The satire
triumphs when Volpone pays Mosca off, but only momentarily. Volpone
immediately sends Mosca on an errand, then reasserts with undiminished
pleasure the authority of his romantic delight:

> What should I doe
> But cocker up my *genius*, and live free
> To all delights, my fortune calls me to?[8]

Mosca is displaced, his view of Volpone banished, and in its stead an
appealing tribute to freedom is offered, one which continues for a full

7. On this point, see Jonas Barish, "Feasting and Judging in Jonsonian Comedy,"
*RenD*, N.S. V (1972), 20–21; Alan C. Dessen, *Jonson's Moral Comedy* (Evanston, Ill.,
1971), p. 104; Una Ellis-Fermor, *The Jacobean Drama* (1936; rpt. New York, 1964), pp.
113–114.

8. I.i.70–72. References to Jonson are from *Ben Jonson*, ed. C. H. Herford and Percy
and Evelyn Simpson, 11 vols. (Oxford, 1925–1952).

twenty lines until the close of the scene. The handling of the scene almost suggests a technique of romantic comedy: an enactment, then expurgation, of satiric presence. Of course the implicit verbal ironies remain, but the romantic authority of Volpone in this scene is a good deal stronger than it might have been.

Something similar happens with Mosca's soliloquy in Act III. Not even Volpone, whose concern with the transforming freedoms of the human imagination is larger than Mosca's, is allowed to articulate his vision with no one else on stage for an entire scene. Mosca's tribute to himself as a "fine, elegant rascal" emphasizes the metamorphic fluidity of the actor, a freedom from place and fixed identity which is, to Mosca, proof and privilege of the parasite's "most excellent nature." Though his conclusion, in its consummate egoism, cannot fail to be ironic, what he says about his acting talent is not. The speech underlines what we have already seen, the genius by which Mosca has managed the plunder of son by father and of wife by husband. If the soliloquy anticipates the conclusion by celebrating the very self-love which will help bring Mosca down, it more directly affirms the romantic aspirations symbolized by the rogues' acting. In effect, the scene furthers our rogue-sentiment by supporting our confidence in Mosca, just before the growing complexity of the action will even more emphatically require his special talents.

Volpone's seduction of Celia is a scene that so triumphantly combines lyricism with farce that it is easy to overlook the importance of its structure. The tug-of-war over Celia's body, with Celia pulling toward heaven and Corvino pulling toward Volpone's couch, is so grotesque that we only begin to understand the complex meanings and effects of the seduction when the stage is cleared for Volpone and Celia. Volpone's apostrophe to Celia, with her replies, takes up half of a long scene, which suddenly closes with the entrance of Bonario. This collapses the seduction attempt, rescues Celia, and shames Volpone to a Bonarian expostulation: "I am un-mask'd, unspirited, un-done" (III.vii.278). Thus the intense romanticism of Volpone's seduction of Celia is framed by an intensely satirical opening action, and by a similar closure. But during the seduction itself there is no one to answer the magnificent rhetoric of Volpone but the ineffectual Celia.

Celia and Bonario are conventionalized romance characters, but unlike Silvius and Phebe they have no hidden dimensions. They are so deliber-

ately wooden that their presence in this scene enhances Volpone's appeal
by the contrast of insipid virtue and magnificent vice.[9] The virtuous pair
are naïvely innocent and linguistically impoverished; their powers are
summed up by Bonario's entry line: "Forbeare, foule ravisher! libidinous
swine!" (III.vii.267). In particular, Celia's reductive way of embodying
chastity makes Volpone's lust harder for the audience to condemn. Her
stock delicacy ("Whether, whether, / Is shame fled humane breasts?"
(III.vii.133–134) is ludicrously inadequate as a response to what Volpone
says and is. Only Bonario is more absurdly virtuous. Volpone's song to
Celia, and his mimicry of Ovidian fable, on the other hand, consciously
will to exhaust all forms of the imagination in the search for the capacities
of human desire. Volpone's romantic tribute to sensuality and imagination can be faulted—when it is—only for the scope of its aspiration;
Celia's decency is no answer to it.

The attractiveness of the rogues, to which their rich rhetoric so notably
contributes, is not diminished by a sustained dramatic contrast with
richer or wiser characters. The community of the foolish offered by the
play is lacking in characters of Volpone's and Mosca's size and success;
even Peregrine, who acts as a rogue in his exposure of Sir Pol, is merely a
mimic of their dramatic authority. Though Sir Pol's exposure does antici-
pate the ending, Sir Pol is an easy gull for a rogue to dupe, and the farcical
stage turtle is no match for the subtle contrivances of Volpone and Mosca.
Peregrine may act in a good cause, but his common sense is not the
quality we admire in a rogue.

One thing that helps to make Volpone and Mosca more "normative"
(though not more normal) than Peregrine is the combination of aspiration
and fallability reflected by their own self-images. Remarkably, the rogues
not only supply a vision and a virtuosity lacking in the other characters,
but they also show that ironic awareness of self-limitation without which
we could not admire them. When Mosca, for example, bleeding from
Bonario's sword, acknowledges his own role in the mishap, he mocks
himself and Bonario in a neat fusion of idioms: "Where shall I runne,
most wretched shame of men, / To beate out my un-luckie braines?"
(III.viii.1–2). And there are instances in Volpone, too, of the self-directed

9. Cf. John J. Enck, *Jonson and the Comic Truth* (Madison, Wis., 1957), p. 129.
Leonard F. Dean points out that Celia "does not really hear" Volpone, in "Three Notes on
Comic Morality: Celia, Bobadill, and Falstaff," *SEL*, XVI (1976), 264.

outrage that absorbs the brunt of folly by admitting to it: "To make a snare, for mine owne necke! and run / My head into it, wilfully! with laughter!" (V.xi. 1–2). Rogues so aware of overreaching are not free from satire, but without such recognition there could be little identification with their aspirations or their collusions.

The relationship between Volpone and Mosca is the most persuasive one in the play. Unquestionably, it is a profoundly deceived and self-limiting one, and its symbolic degradation by the use of disguise does articulate an ironic logic central to the play.[10] Nevertheless, the betrayal that ends the play comes as a shock, and part of its satiric power comes from the strange authenticity in the bond it breaks. Volpone and Mosca work as perfect complements, and their delight in their powers and successes is a ground, at least on Volpone's part, for extravagant affection. And though Mosca often withholds from Volpone the affection Volpone showers on him, thus anticipating his ultimate duplicity, there are moments when he, too, affirms the bond in emotionally charged terms:

VOLPONE
Deare Mosca, shall I hope?

MOSCA
Sir, more than deare,
I will not bid you to despaire of ought
Within a humane compasse.

(II.iv.18–20)

In short, Volpone and Mosca offer a roguish version of the romance ideal of male friendship. Whatever its ambiguities, their relationship sustains its intrinsic appeal, and does so all the more because the play does not offer a single case of genuine, intense affection outside of the two rogues.

Ultimately, perhaps, the bond between these two is assimilated to the tenuousness that marks the frail ties among the gulls. Yet the revelation of this weakness is postponed for a strikingly long time; it does not become clear until late in Act IV. Instead, throughout most of the play the facts of plot continually reaffirm the rogues' successful mutuality; the accumulating successes so thoroughly demonstrate their genius that their outbursts of self-praise and mutual appreciation receive continual dramatic support. This is not to deny that the evidence of betrayal is implicit from Mosca's

10. Alvin Kernan, introduction to *Volpone* (New Haven, Conn., 1962), pp. 20 ff.

first scene, or that the affectionate tribute to the partner is mostly Volpone's, or that their misalliance so identifies need with greed that even affection is suspect. But it is to assert Volpone's right to be angry, and to uncase himself, in the final scene.

At the end of the play, Jonson tries to expunge romantic presence from the play by the irony of the rogues' collusion in their own downfall, and even more by the severity of their punishments, punishments much fiercer than those assigned to the duplicitous gulls. These punishments are made to fit the crimes of Volpone and Mosca with a kind of savage literalness. Mosca, whose only relationship to others has been to use them, will now be chained to others, and made use of. Worse yet, Volpone, fettered and ill-treated, will be made to be the thing he pretended to be, "sick and lame": that is, the self that exalted its power by playing a role will be destroyed by absorption or identification with the role he created. Spirit is reduced to matter: "cramped in irons." These punishments seem to suggest an essential resentment on the part of the social order toward the extravagant self-assertion of those who defy it; and the court's preference for small selves over large ones is clear in the ways it mitigates the punishments of its own, the gulls. Beyond that, the severe punishments meted out to the rogues, understood as meted out by the play, not the court, are Jonson's way of dramatizing the necessity not merely to subdue but to explode the presence of the rogues' egotism and the "rogue-sentiment" of the audience. If the gesture is extravagant, it has to be; the rogues are too compelling to be dismissed lightly. The problem of the ending is that the rogues' continued resistance to satiric reduction may well make it unacceptable to condemn them so severely.

The boundaries of the satiric presence in *Twelfth Night* are usually confined to the subplot, especially to its Jonsonian ridicule of Malvolio, but the structure of the main love plot turns out to be a more important antagonist to romantic vision.[11] Though it is common to perceive the lovers struggling toward a unity or fullness of self,[12] we need to perceive

11. David Bevington discusses the subplot of *Twelfth Night* as a deliberate experiment with Jonsonian satire: "Shakespeare vs. Jonson on Satire," *Shakespeare 1971: Proceedings of the World Shakespeare Congress, Vancouver, August, 1971*, ed. Clifford Leech and J. M. Margeon (Toronto, 1972), pp. 107–122.

12. See the influential readings of John Hollander, "*Twelfth Night* and the Morality of

more clearly that the means to this goal is a course of experience in which ridicule and humiliation are inevitably risked by love. The outcome of the lovers' struggle, moreover, is uncertain, as much so as Viola's confidence in the eventual reappearance of Sebastian. Until the end, love means vulnerability as well as faith, and the self is as likely to remain partial as to achieve wholeness. Unlike *As You Like It*, in which erotic humiliation is mainly ritualized, as in Rosalind's and Orlando's playing, *Twelfth Night* makes it dangerously real. In fact, self-abasement is fused with erotic feeling from the beginning:

> O spirit of love, how quick and fresh art thou,
> That notwithstanding thy capacity
> Receiveth as the sea, nought enters there
> Of what validity and pitch soe'er,
> But falls into abatement and low price,
> Even in a minute!
>
> (I.i.9–14)

"Abatement" and "low price" are the humiliating costs of the "quick and fresh" impulses of romantic passion, and the first act, as prologue to the rest of the play, contrasts "abatement" and "pitch" as symbolic prospects for the self.

The predicaments of Viola, Orsino, and Olivia all reflect states of fragmentation.[13] The state of being fragmented, with its openness to folly and failure, is in itself an invitation to satiric presence, an invitation that Malvolio for one accepts. But the characters are not all fragmented in the same way. Viola offers an image of fragmentation which is intrinsically romantic. Her disguise suggests a partiality which emerges from wholeness and seeks it again. She is self-divided, as one-half of a pair of twins, but her longing for Sebastian suggests a fundamental condition of natural alliance, and her assumption of disguise is an act of alliance with Orsino. Though her confusions are invested in her duality as "boy and girl," the

Indulgence," *SR*, LXVII (1959), 220–238, and of Joseph H. Summers, "The Masks of *Twelfth Night*," *UR*, XXII (1955), 25–32. For a recent development of the theme in terms of the psychology of adolescence, see J. Dennis Huston, "'When I came to Man's Estate': *Twelfth Night* and Problems of Identity," *MLQ*, XXXIII (1972), 274–288.

13. Alexander Leggatt thinks of fragmentation in *Twelfth Night* in Jonsonian terms: "this sense of sharply distinguished individuals adrift in a fragmented world, each with his own obsession," *Shakespeare's Comedy of Love* (London, 1974), p. 223.

essential unity in duality that she symbolizes is confirmed by her identity as twin. Olivia and Orsino, at the play's opening, are fragmented selves of a different order. Each is assimilated to the satiric posture of a Sir Andrew, if not a Malvolio, by the essential folly of self-absorption, and each neatly impersonates the stance of romantic lover by a love committed to ally itself only with the impossible, and thus with no one. Olivia and Orsino are images of partial selves which cannot be wholes. They are the play's "only children," the metaphorical antithesis to twins.

What the play does with these contrastive prospects for the ultimate integration of the self is to bear them out, by so identifying the course of love with the experience of humiliation that every romantic lover is vulnerable to it. Humiliation threatens the potential wholeness of the self by inviting obsessiveness, by inviting, that is, preoccupation with what shames one. Olivia is obsessed by "Cesario," Viola by the "Cesario" in herself, and Orsino by that "Olivia" which is a covert self-image. Hand in hand with the growth toward love is a dramatic enactment of obsession and an exploration of potential recovery from it.

Olivia's experience in the play is the most fully dramatized case of the vulnerability of the play's romantic characters to humiliation and ridicule. Her first meeting with "Cesario" suggests both an ironic exposure of her self-imposed isolation and a romantic prospect that she may go beyond it. "Cesario," with a keen wit that transcends Orisino's "suit," clarifies Olivia's position by combining a critique of her self-absorption with a reduction of it:

VIOLA

Are you the lady of the house?

OLIVIA

If I do not usurp myself, I am.

VIOLA

Most certain, if you are she, you do usurp yourself: for what is yours to bestow is not yours to reserve.

(I.v.185–190)

By falling in love with the "peevish" messenger, Olivia enters a transitional phase in her progress from self-absorption to romantic faith. If there is something of herself in "Cesario's" femininity, which ironically suggests an analogy to Phebe's pursuit of "Ganymede," Olivia is also no Phebe, and "Cesario," by virtue of her twinship, is "other" enough to call forth erotic feeling for a masculine partner who will ultimately be Sebastian. That erotic feeling, however, is consistently intertwined with shame, and a shame not only associated with the audience's pleasures in mistakes of gender.

The sense of humiliation Olivia feels in her pursuit of "Cesario" is more central: our cue to the starts and stops in her movement outward. There is self-recognition and acknowledgment of otherness in Olivia's apology to "Cesario" for pursuing him with her ring ("So did I abuse / Myself, my servant, and, I fear me, you" III.i.115–116). Here, she shows a readiness to risk humiliation in love's behalf which compares favorably with her earlier self-protective grief; yet her occasional tendency to embrace her shame can also make her ludicrous: "O what a deal of scorn looks beautiful / In the contempt and anger of his lip!" (III.i.147–148). This response to erotic passion cherishes the self-abasement that so terrifies Rosalind, and it has an immediate answer in "Cesario's" reply to her. Also a shamed self, all too conscious of being wooed by a woman, "Cesario" replies by a romantic reassertion of self-integration: "I have one heart, one bosom, and one truth . . . never none / Shall be mistress of it, save I alone" (III.i.160–163). This subtly answers Olivia, for what "Cesario" wants to acknowledge is the unity of self which preserves vulnerability from shame.

Shame, however, is still necessary to Olivia. Though she has had to perceive her love for "Cesario" as "shameful cunning" (III.i.118), she must continue to do so until "Cesario" is transformed into Sebastian. Her endurance of shame creates for her a kind of undoing of it. Olivia has seemed ridiculous in the sudden dropping of her mourning vow, and has felt herself so in her pursuit of "Cesario," but she is not ridiculous in her sudden marriage. The reason for this is not only Sebastian's acceptability. At her marriage she recognizes that her haste might seem vulnerable to ridicule (IV.iii.22), but she accepts this as an inevitable element of both romantic faith and her own self-understanding:

> Plight me the full assurance of your faith,
> That my most jealous and too doubtful soul
> May live at peace.
>
> (IV.iii.26–28)

Her love accepts the "doubtful" without attempting to eliminate it. Thus Olivia's growth toward self-integration is not assumed by the play but earned during it, and her recovery from humiliation finally attests to her unsuitability for the gulls who have sought to marry her.

Viola's experience of humiliation is more modest in scope but as painful in character. She must undergo the consequences of the mask she has chosen,[14] and while we know that to be "Cesario" is right in its winning of Orsino's favor (I.iv.1–4), Viola knows "Cesario" too well not to be shamed by "his" falseness. Her soliloquy bears this out:

> My master loves her dearly,
> And I, poor monster, fond as much on him,
> And she, mistaken, seems to dote on me:
> What will become of this?
>
> (II.ii.32–35)

Since she calls Orsino "my master," the pronoun "I" clearly refers to "Cesario," not Viola, and if "Cesario" is "fond" of Orsino, selfhood does become a monstrosity. Viola finds no problem in loving Orsino, but "Cesario" must, and both the reticence and the frustration of "Cesario's" colloquy with Orsino in II.iv reflect the self-division imposed by her disguise. Being "Cesario," and not Viola, she is subject to the wit others sometimes make of her appearance, as Malvolio does (I.v.158–164) and as Feste does (III.i.45). These remarks can bounce off lightly, since they merely make her look ridiculous, but when the primary consequences of her disguise as "Cesario" are to woo Olivia for Orsino, be loved by Olivia, and answer Andrew's challenge to a duel, she feels her "abatement" more strenuously.

These situations are, of course, funny, but they also subject "Cesario" to real ridicule. For example, "Cesario" seriously works to persuade Sir Andrew not to fight with her, but her lack of success aligns her with Andrew, since they are both victims of Toby's joke; the play confirms her own awareness that the duel shames her (III.iv.306). She is saved only for another humiliation, her inability to answer to Antonio's charges of Sebastian's ingratitude; her generalizations about hatred of ingratitude (III.iv.361 ff.) can hardly fail to be comically inappropriate. Once again, Viola is shamed by the self-falsification that being "Cesario" entails.

14. Viola's assumption of disguise must reflect, for one thing, the conflict between human will and comic providence. See Joan Hartwig, "Feste's 'Whirligig' and the Comic Providence of *Twelfth Night*," *ELH*, XL (1973), 501.

Indeed, the play does not disentangle Viola's love from "Cesario's" humiliation until the arrival of Sebastian; and while we have come to admire the Viola within "Cesario," we are as glad to be rid of him as she is to be free from embarrassment.

Unlike the other characters, Orsino is not actually humiliated until the last scene. His blindness and infatuation may make him ridiculous to the audience, but the audience cannot bring him down. Only Orsino himself can do that, and he does it in a climactic scene which threatens to drag the entire play into satire, something which is avoided only in the most hairbreadth way with the arrival of Sebastian. What humiliates Orsino is, of course, his sense of "Cesario's" treachery, and his response to being humiliated, with its extravagantly silly rant about "perverseness," tyranny, and savage sacrifice, presents a combination of desire and absurdity all too close to that of a Jonsonian gull. His vehemence and self-delusion are the most extreme in the play at this point, and for many readers they cloud over his subsequent recognition of his love for Viola, which represents his self-knowledge and transcendence of fragmentation. What's more, Orsino is not only debased here, but is the cause of debasement in others. Viola, faced with his ravings, abuses herself with a cheerful fatuity that makes her look like a female Silvius (in male clothing): "To do you rest, a thousand deaths [I] would die" (V.i.131). Olivia, faced in turn with this treachery, also goes under, sounding a little like Jonson's Celia: "Ay me detested! how am I beguil'd!" (V.i.137). If we are to believe Viola's earlier remark, this knot of circumstance is to be untied by time; but time needs some help from the man at the center of the melee, whose love on the one hand and attractiveness on the other have caused it all: Orsino.

The prospect of restored harmony lies hidden in Orsino's mind; his self-debasement and self-recovery are paradigmatic for the play as a whole. Significantly, it is Orsino who first perceives the truth of the situation, as if his love for Viola were speaking for him: "One face, one voice, one habit, and two persons! / A natural perspective, that is, and is not!" (V.i.214–215). What must follow is an interpretation of this perspective which comprehends the mysteries of unity and duality symbolized by the twinship of Sebastian and Viola. Orsino's response to the natural perspective is a combination of the shock of a factual truth which negates his self-absorption, and the shock of an emotional truth which frees him from it and makes him eligible, like the others, to be unified in a pairing:

> Be not amaz'd, right noble is his blood.
> If this be so, as yet the glass seems true,
> I shall have share in this most happy wreck.
>
> (V.i.262–264)

He recovers from his amazement by accepting faith in the paradox, seeing it as "true," and understanding, in consequence, the tie of self to other selves that issues from an awareness of what wholeness means. The play ends, then, in a logic of wholes, by multiplying sibling relationships as it creates new marriages, by offering "solemn combination" to every part. Olivia offers Malvolio both justice (V.i.354–355) and sympathy (V.i.368); by his rejection of them, Malvolio is self-excluded from the whole. Surely this is appropriate to the only character in the play incapable of recovering from humiliation.

Jonson's *The Alchemist* is different enough from *Volpone* to suggest the complexity by which romantic and satiric comic forms can reveal their active antagonism. For one thing, the romantic elements that elicit rogue-sentiment in *Volpone*, imaginative scope and cleverness strong enough to survive deflation and moral exposure, are distributed to characters who attenuate them by competing with each other. Cleverness, of course, is given to Subtle, Face, and Doll and later to Lovewit, while imaginative scope is assigned to a gargantuan gull, Sir Epicure Mammon.[15] Problems appear in this distribution, which I will discuss, but what needs comment here is the sheer multiplicity of rogues. Subtle, Face, Doll, and Lovewit are in anyone's court, and one should also count Surly, who acts as a rogue of an inferior stripe during a good part of the play. This multiplicity is a reflection of the complexity of intrigue, and of the play's defiant cynicism about human nature. Yet despite the striking number of rogues, their formation into two main groups—the "venter tripartite" which controls the action until late in Act IV, and Lovewit-Jeremy, an alliance which takes over from there—helps to shape not only the action but the specific values of the play.

Subtle, Face, and Doll are presented by the opening scenes as an alliance of rogues which bears little relation to its counterpart in *Volpone*;

---

15. On Mammon's scope, cf. Barish, review of Dessen, p. 82; cf. Ornstein, p. 43. Both point to the appeal of Mammon, though not quite as strongly, or in quite these terms.

they form an exclusively commercial venture. Egotism, temper, and aptitude for betrayal doom them from the start, and the presence of Doll's sexuality is not an encouraging sign. The structure of the opening quarrel is a cue to the problem of the audience. First Face rants about Subtle's dependence on him, and creation by him; then Subtle presents a contradictory story making the same points; then Doll contradicts them both in a hilarious satiric deflation. The progress of the quarrel obscures the rogues' essential differentiation as characters, and obscures too the answer to the question of primacy among them. What it does clarify is the extraordinary frailty of their alliance, despite their virtuosity.

The members of the "venter tripartite" in *The Alchemist* are superior to the gulls only in cleverness, and the rhetorical design of the play, by its contrast with *Volpone*, makes this clear. While Volpone and Mosca remain on the stage throughout the play, the "venter" breaks up at the end of Act IV, to be replaced by a new one.[16] Where *Volpone* offers an alternation of gulling scenes and scenes of the rogues' plots and self-celebrations, which assists rogue-sympathy and imparts a sense of their superiority to the gulls, *The Alchemist* offers a different pattern. At least before Lovewit's arrival, the presence or absence of the gulls makes little difference to the emphatically satiric presentation of the rogues. Since Subtle, Face, and Doll are too busy, or too ill-tempered, to engage in huddles that plot strategy, our appreciation of their craft is not based on a capacity to identify with the rogues' own appraisal of tactics. Our sympathies are further limited by the fact that the rogues rarely share a sense of triumph, although there is a little jollity over the gulling of Mammom (II.iv). The rhythm of the scenes, then, has an unambiguously satiric effect; we are rarely fooled into admiration.[17]

The texture of the scenes, with its predominance of insults, supports this. Insults are sometimes gulling strategy, as when Face calls Subtle "Doctor dogs-meate" in front of Dapper in order to call forth Dapper's belief in Face (I.ii.45). Elsewhere, insults are uncontrolled reflections of

16. Dessen sees the ending of *The Alchemist* as creating a new "venter tripartite" composed of Lovewit, Face, and the audience. *Jonson's Moral Comedy*, pp. 133–134.

17. Perhaps this structural rhythm reflects what Lester Beaurline has described as a change in Jonson's methods of composition after *Volpone*, toward a method of "gradation within strict limits." "Ben Jonson and the Illusion of Completeness," *PMLA*, LXXXIV (1969), 56.

egotism and greed—when Face, for example, greets Drugger's exit by hurling an insult at Subtle: "you smoky persecuter of nature" (I.iii.100), the point of which is to prove his own superiority. Because the motives and effects of the insults in the two kinds of scenes are indistinguishable, the rogues are reduced to the level of the gulls, and this is true in the play as a whole. The consequence of this dramatic texture and structure is that rogue-sentiment is stripped of identification with specific characters, a pattern that persists until the entrance of Lovewit. What rogue-sentiment becomes instead, during a large part of *The Alchemist*, is sheer pleasure in ironic artifice; Subtle, Face, and Doll are voices for the play's virtuosity and energy, its center of force rather than its major persons.

*The Alchemist's* rogues are creatures of talent, not genius, and their ironic idiom never rises to that romantic hyperbole which renders Volpone so magnificent a visionary of deluded aspiration. Though the play offers a splendid display of the range of desires that bring the gulls to the alchemist, and keep the rogues together, the romantic spokesman, the Marlovian of this play, is not a rogue but a gull: Sir Epicure Mammon. Mammon's cheerfully obscene formulation of his desire to "firke nature up, in her owne center" (II.i.28) reflects a longing to transform the rhythms of human destiny which is quite unlike the other characters' desires to get a leg up by gold or wit. Mammon, like Volpone, is a cosmological visionary, and his presence disrupts an otherwise straightforward duping of foolishly aspiring gulls by clever but not visionary rogues. Though Mammon is only one of several gulls, he dominates most of the second act, and two scenes of the fourth. Subtle's alchemical imagery implies that the duping of Mammon is the rogues' centerpiece,[18] and its importance is also suggested by the size and complexity of their strategy against him, their delight at succeeding, and the noise that brings down the house at Mammon's defeat. The reason for this centrality, I think, is the form it provides for the enactment and expungement of the romantic idea of the world transformed by human desire.

When Subtle steps forward to introduce Mammon, his characteristi-

---

18. On the implications of Subtle's alchemical imagery in assigning centrality to the duping of Mammon, see Kernan's note to II.iii.96 ff. in the Yale Ben Jonson (New Haven, Conn., 1974). By analogy, Subtle's tribute to Nature's progression from imperfect to perfect (II.iii.158–159) also applies to the duping of Mammon.

cally ironic idiom passes gradually but emphatically into romantic vision, particularly in conclusion (I.iv.25–29); Subtle's speech is an unconscious anticipation of the arrival of Sir Epicure, though his own focus on deformity is only a partial element of Mammon's inclusive concerns. Mammon's conception of the "Novo Orbe" in Act II is a gigantic expansion of Volpone's evocation of metamorphosis in the seduction scene. Mammon's desire is to reinvent all experience, not just eros, as a paradise of transformation and transvaluation. Self will be multiplied: Mammon cuts mirrors in subtle angles to "multiply the figures, as I walke" (II.ii.47); and sensuality will be at once refined and intensified: "My shirts / I'll have of taffata-sarsnet, soft, and light / As cobwebs" (II.ii.88–90).

In all this, human desire takes on a gargantuan scope and inclusiveness, and if Mammon is scarcely a disinterested shaper of magnificence, he is genuinely magnanimous. The basis of his vision is not only egoism but also the generous intent to "confer honour, love, respect, long life . . . safety, valure: yea, and victorie" (II.ii.50–51) at large. Of course, Mammon's generosity is absurdly indiscriminate. He will have for poets those "that writ so subtly of the *fart*" (II.ii.63), while his flatterers "shall be the pure, and gravest of Divines" that money can buy (II.i.60–61). Yet the ludicrous and preposterous character of these desires can deflate their wild imaginative vitality without finally eliminating it. It is to the point that Mammon's visions are continually deflated by Surly's irony, and as continually spring back unflattened, in new forms. It is also true that Mammon absorbs some of Surly's satiric thrust by praise of his "excellent wit" and by the even more important acknowledgment of the satiric view of human folly in his own speeches. He absorbs, in these first two scenes of Act II, anything Face and Surly can say.

What defeats Mammon is a process of a satiric size equal to his romantic weight. First, he is gradually reduced for us by his own obsessive absorption in the literal instruments of his effort at transvaluation: the process of alchemy and the body of Dol Common. He is as trapped in the *matter* of his idea as a Shakespearean heroine in her disguise—but he can't throw it off at the end. Mammon's reduction begins in II.iii.; his willing surrender of his goods, and later the extravagance of his desire for one talk with the "madwoman," make him ridiculous to us. Yet his speeches when closeted with Doll reassert, in a diminished form, the romantic scope of his desires. Mammon is expunged not so much by the carefully coordinated strategy of all three rogues, though there is that, nor even by his own enormous tendency to folly, distraction, and self-betrayal. What is most effective, I think, to the audience's comprehension of Mammon's defeat is Doll's undoing of his romantic vision in her "ravings" in the "tongue of Eber and Javan" (IV.v). Aptly enough, his apocalyptic vision is undone by an imitation that burlesques it; her "kingdom of God" is so "Brimstony, blew and fiery" (IV.v.29) that Mammon's new world goes up in smoke. The "great crack and noise within" (s.d.IV.v.55) that follows Mammon's defeat is a sign of the importance of the conflict between Mammon and the play's fundamental vision, as well as the end of it.

Romantic presence is not expunged from the play by the defeat of Mammon. It reappears at the beginning of Act V, with the entrance of Lovewit. The stage of folly is thoroughly purged at the close of Act IV, except for Face, who strips to Jeremy, shaves, and so begins a new role for a new comedy. The alliance between Jeremy-Face and Lovewit is much less simple than Lovewit implies when explaining why authority would join up with a rogue: "I love a teeming wit, as I love my nourishment" (V.i.16). His love of wit is surely natural, but it is as natural as appetitite: a motive all too easily implicit in the rewards he reaps. Lovewit's disguise as a Spaniard, by which he marries Dame Pliant, not only demonstrates his witty success in a role that had defeated the other wearers of the disguise, but also emblematizes the difficulties of his role in the play's conclusion. The role of the Spaniard was first Surly's mask to win Pliant and expose Subtle and Face to justice; on his failure, the disguise passed to the rogues, as part of their efforts to win Pliant and control the gulls. As "the Spaniard," Lovewit is thoroughly ambiguous: an exposer of rogues and a cohort of them, a type of the failed satirist, and the last and truest form of the play's rogues. Lovewit's cleverness, his success at surmounting all antagonists and winning all spoils, is united with generosity toward Jeremy-Face, good humor, and the capability of fusing in the bond between himself and Jeremy the normative value of good sense. By these means he earns all the rogue-sentiment that has been held in reserve for him during the rest of the play. But the qualities that make him succeed are the romantic elements of a rogue in Jonsonian satiric comedy. Indeed, he acts like a roguish parody of a romantic protagonist—wooing and winning the lady by the use of disguise, relying on and supporting the ideal of male friendship, reaping, as the reward of virtue, wealth, woman, and sympathy.

Yet he also must function as the figure of satiric authority, the representative of justice by virtue of his distribution of penalties. In this capacity, he functions in a severely limited way, expunging all the egotism and greed, except his own and Jeremy's. But the rest of the play lives on in Jeremy, who is not even roguishly romantic, and this makes Lovewit's acknowledgment of Jeremy's importance troublesome: "I will be rul'd by thee in anything, Jeremy" (V.v.143). He is so, in how he acts, and that is the problem. The ending of *The Alchemist* is a tribute to theatrical genius, and it is also evidence of Jonson's willingness to indulge romantic rogue-sentiment, even at the cost of strict satiric justice, in order to insure the triumph of wit.[19]

To conclude, we have for too long taken the essential competition between Shakespeare's vision and Jonson's to mean that their forms of comedy are mutually exclusive. We have acknowledged the mingling of romantic comedy with satiric comedy only in minor and occasional ways, and so have too often read the presence of a satiric element in Shakespeare, or a romantic one in Jonson, as evidence of failure, inspiration, or a new turn in the dramatist's understanding of his genre. But *As You Like It, Volpone, Twelfth Night*, and *The Alchemist* demonstrate that the mutual engagement of romantic and satiric comedy is much more central than we usually think. This is consistent with the value placed on *genera mixta* by the theory and practice of genres in the Renaissance.[20] To interpret these comedies, therefore, should be to ask how a given play responds to the antagonism of modes, what methods Shakespeare and Jonson use to mingle them, and what this might mean for our definitions of Renaissance comedy. In taking this approach, we acknowledge that the sophistication of each dramatist is realized rather than undermined by his adaptation of methods associated with the other.

19. For different views of the problems of the ending, see Gabriele Bernhard Jackson, *Vision and Judgment in Ben Jonson's Drama* (New Haven, Conn., 1968), pp. 67–69, 90–92; Barish, "Feasting and Judging," pp. 25–28; Judd Arnold, "Lovewit's Triumph and Jonsonian Morality: A Reading of *The Alchemist*," *Criticism*, XI (1969), 151–166; and A. Richard Dutton, "*Volpone* and *The Alchemist*: A Comparison in Satiric Techniques," *RMS*, XVIII (1974), 36–62.

20. Rosalie L. Colie, *The Resources of Kind: Genre-Theory in the Renaissance* (Berkeley, Calif., 1973), esp. pp. 103 ff.

# "Tragedy, Laugh On": Comic Violence in Titus Andronicus

## RICHARD T. BRUCHER

D ESPITE THOMAS HEYWOOD'S CONTENTION that tragedy depicts "the fatal and abortive ends of such as commit notorious murders, . . . aggravated and acted with all the art that may be, to terrify men from the like abhorred practices," [1] the effect of Elizabethan stage violence may not be moral at all. Nahum Tate did not think so, because he was determined to "improve" *King Lear*. By concluding his adaptation (1681) "in a success to the innocent distressed persons," Tate made the ending more "just" and avoided encumbering "the stage with dead bodies, which conduct makes many tragedies conclude with unseasonable jests." [2] The problem of the catastrophe causing laughter rather than pity, fear, or moral gratification is more acute in *Titus Andronicus* (1593?), in which the hero Titus, the "Patron of virtue, Rome's best champion" (I.i.65), [3] be-

---

1. Quoted (and modernized) from *An Apology for Actors* (1612), ed. Richard H. Perkinson (New York, 1941), Sig. F3ᵛ.

2. Nahum Tate, Dedicatory Epistle, *The History of King Lear*, ed. James Black (Lincoln, Nebr., 1975), p. 2.

3. *Titus Andronicus* is quoted from the Arden edition, ed. J. C. Maxwell (London: 1953).

comes *"a cook, placing the dishes"* (V.iii.26 s.d.). Dressed as a chef, Titus
feeds Tamora her two sons, whom he has baked in a pie, kills his daughter
Lavinia, and murders Tamora, before being killed by Saturninus. The
effect of the atrocities, which are conducted onstage with a savage wit, is
baffling. With some justification, John Dover Wilson compares *Titus* to a
"cart, laden with bleeding corpses from an Elizabethan scaffold, and
driven by an executioner from Bedlam dressed in cap and bells."[4]

The comic effect of violence was a problem for the Elizabethans, too. In
the Induction to *A Warning for Fair Women* (1599), the figure of Tragedy,
brandishing *"in her one hand a whip, in the other hand a knife"* (l. 1 s.d.),[5]
insists that her purpose is to stir the spectators:

> To rack a thought, and strain it to his form,
> Until I rap the senses from their course.
> This is my office.

> (ll. 40–42)

But to Comedy and History, who vie with her for control of the stage,
Tragedy is "a common executioner" (l. 6), and the stuff of tragedy is not
exalted passion and moral instruction, but rant, bloodshed, and grotesquerie. Comedy sardonically suggests that the conqueror plays popular
in the 1580s and '90s merely show "How some damn'd tyrant to obtain a
crown / Stabs, hangs, impoisons, smothers, cutteth throats" (ll. 43–44).
The revenge tragedies go after more hysterical and fantastic effects:

> a filthy whining ghost,
> Lapt in some foul sheet, or a leather pilch,
> Comes screaming like a pig half stick'd,
> And cries, *Vindicta!*—Revenge, Revenge!
> With that a little rosin flasheth forth,
> Like smoke out of a tobacco pipe, or a boy's squib.
> Then comes in two or three [more] like to drovers,
> With tailors' bodkins, stabbing one another—
> Is not this trim?

> (ll. 47–55)

4. John Dover Wilson, Introd., *Titus Andronicus* (1948; rpt. Cambridge, Eng., 1968),
p. xii.

5. *A Warning for Fair Women* is quoted from Richard Simpson, ed., *The School of
Shakespeare*, Vol. II (London, 1878).

Comedy points to an unpredictable, darkly comic effect that must be reckoned with. Some staged atrocities are so outlandish that they seem funny. I contend that the playwrights deliberately made some violence comic in order to thwart conventional moral expectations. I have in mind a form of violence which is shocking in its expression of power and evil, and yet so outrageous in its conception and presentation that it causes laughter as it disrupts our sense of order in the world. *Titus Andronicus* is an extreme play, but Shakespeare draws on a common interest in sardonic depictions of violent actions. In its crudest form, in a play like *The Tragical Reign of Selimus, Emperor of the Turks* (1594?), the comic savagery celebrates barbaric power. In its more witty and complex form, as in Marlowe's *The Jew of Malta* (1590?), the comic savagery reflects an ingenious malevolence which defines its own order in a world of doubtful values. This more sophisticated form of aesthetic, or artfully plotted, violence is at once more appealing and subversive, because it derives from a highly developed, if perverse, human intelligence.[6] The aesthetic conception of violence creates a histrionic context which involves the audience more directly in the fun. Understanding both the crude and the subtle expressions of witty depravity helps us to grapple with the perplexing effect of the violence in *Titus Andronicus*. Shakespeare combines the two forms of comic savagery and directs the onslaught against sympathetic victims. Consequently, the audience becomes engaged in an experience of moral chaos which painfully tests assumptions about human values and behavior, but which cannot comfortably be called tragic.

*Selimus* is not a very good play, but it is interesting as a derivative work which exploits the Elizabethans' love of violence and their delight in the extension of human power. The play brings directly onstage the atrocities casually committed by aspiring tyrants, unmitigated by the inspired poetry and vision of a Tamburlaine. Selimus would simply "set barrels of blood abroach, / And seek with sword whole kingdoms to displace" (ll.

---

6. Erich Segal explores the long literary tradition of comic malevolence and the delight at someone else's misfortune in "Marlowe's *Schadenfreude*: Barabas as Comic Hero," in *Veins of Humor*, ed. Harry Levin (Cambridge, Mass., 1972), pp. 69–91. Segal ascribes to Barabas the comic aggression of Homer's Odysseus and the wiliness of Aristophanes' comic heroes. What is important, as Segal argues, is not the psychological explanation *for* the protagonist's behavior, but the psychological appeal *of* his behavior (p. 76).

240–241).[7] Selimus kills his father, brothers, and sister to secure the
Turkish crown, but he never rivals his brother Acomat in viciousness.
Selimus's crimes are perfunctory, utilitarian, and slightly paranoic. He
delights in the power of violence. Acomat delights in cruelty, as his
treatment of Aga, a peace ambassador from Bajazet, demonstrates. Aga
says he hopes he never lives to see the day when Acomat kills his father, to
which Acomat replies:

> Yes thou shalt live, but never see that day,
> Wanting the tapers that should give thee light.
> > *[Pulls out his eyes]*
> > (ll. 1413–1415)

Acomat anticipates Cornwall's wit in *King Lear*, when the Duke denies
Gloucester the justice of seeing vengeance on unnatural children,[8] but
Aga becomes the straightman in Acomat's grisly routine rather than
simply a terribly violated old man. Convinced of Acomat's cruelty by the
blinding, but still believing in justice, Aga presumptuously claims to
have "my hands left on to murder thee" (l. 1429). This inspires Acomat to
more sardonic cruelty:

> 'Twas well remembered: Regan cut them off.
> > *[They cut off his hands and give them Acomat]*
> Now in that sort go tell thy Emperor
> That if himself had but been in thy place,
> I would have used him crueller than thee:
> Here take thy hands: I know thou lov'st them well.
> > *[Opens his bosom, and puts them in]*
> Which hand is this? right? left? canst thou tell?
> > (ll. 1430–1437)

7. *The Tragical Reign of Selimus* is quoted (and modernized) from the Malone Society
Reprint (London, 1908).

8. The Arden *King Lear*, ed. Kenneth Muir (London, 1952):

> GLOUCESTER
> > . . . but I shall see
> The winged vengeance overtake such children.

> CORNWALL
> See't shalt thou never. Fellows, hold the chair.
> Upon these eyes of thine I'll set my foot.
> > (III.vii.64–67)

With vicious jocularity Acomat transforms Aga into "The woefullest, and sadd'st ambassador / That ever was dispatch'd to any king" (ll. 1453–1454).

Aga's blinding, amputations, and thoracotomy probably form the most gratuitously disgusting sequence in Elizabethan drama. The scene is less terrifying than simply repulsive, but the onstage presentation makes the horror palpable. Yet the scene is uncomfortably funny, too. Acomat performs with malevolent glee, and his insolence prompts our laughter as it adds to Aga's humiliating anguish. The scene is designed to arouse laughter, but it is the kind of laughter, as Nicholas Brooke suggests, through which "we become aware of the total collapse of any reliable forms of behaviour."[9] In part, we laugh at the inhumanity. The brutish wit and the terrible violence define Acomat's freedom from the constraints of decency and protocol, and invite us to marvel at his sense of power and invulnerability. The crimes in *Selimus* are repulsive, but the audience can laugh at the tyrants, who can be viewed as subhumans outside civilized order.[10] The laughter is painful, because the depraved action makes naïveté the object of vicious contempt. But Aga, a minor character to begin with, never gains our full sympathy, and, for want of a more certain response, we can laugh at his incredible durability. He survives his mutilation to be poisoned by an agent of Selimus.

It is clear that the author intends to titillate his audience with spectacular barbarisms, because the "Conclusion" promises a second part, "If this first part gentles, do like you well," which "shall greater murders tell" (ll. 6–7). The play safely indulges a taste for vicarious thrills by playing to Elizabethan prejudices. All the characters, killers and victims alike, would be barbarians to the Elizabethans. As offensive as the violence is, when Turks annihilate one another it is no real threat to Elizabethan values. Shakespeare uses sardonically brutal violence in *Titus*—Chiron and Demetrius could pass for Selimus's brothers—but the effect of the violence

---

9. Nicholas Brooke, "Marlowe the Dramatist," in *Elizabethan Theatre*, ed. John Russell Brown and Russell Harris (New York, 1967), p. 95. Brooke is discussing Preston's *Cambises* (1569?) and its relation to *The Jew of Malta*.

10. See Daniel Gerould, "Tyranny and Comedy," in *New York Literary Forum*, I (Spring, 1978), 3–30. Gerould amasses an impressive array of data from modern drama to demonstrate that "the arbitrary exercise of absolute power by a deranged tyrant can be a source of comic pleasure to an audience" (p. 4).

is more complicated. The victims are more sympathetic and the evil deeds are more wittily conceived. The distancing effect achieved by the stereotypes is less secure in *Titus*, because Shakespeare undermines the stereotypes and directs the barbaric evil against "noble" Romans. The effect of the evil is more compromising, because Aaron, the "Chief architect and plotter" (V.iii.122) of the woes, engages in artful villainy. By establishing its own crafted, amoral disorder to replace the moral order it subverts, aesthetic villainy makes a more persuasive statement about evil. It is more compromising, because the duping of victims can be richly comic, and thus a source of pleasure for the audience. This is the kind of villainy Marlowe vigorously develops in *The Jew of Malta*.

Maurice Charney reminds us that "in Elizabethan drama one may distinguish between clumsy skulduggery and the fine artistic stroke of a graduate Machiavel."[11] The distinction is aesthetic, not moral, and it helps us to appreciate the dramatic energies of *The Jew of Malta*. Marlowe endows his hero Barabas with a brilliant sense of improvisational artistry and an untiring wit, traits which put him closer to Jonson's Volpone and Subtle than to the morality vice figure or a barbaric cutthroat. The histrionic energy of Barabas and his slave Ithamore creates a context which is aesthetically rich but morally neutral, and this context governs our response to the play's violence. The violence, though it is not illusory, is an extension of the histrionics. One of Barabas's most entertaining roles is that of a French musician, and in that guise—"Must tuna my lute for sound, twang, twang, first" (IV.iv.30)[12]—he kills three extortionists with a bouquet of poisoned flowers.

There is an insistence in *The Jew of Malta* that murder "be cunningly performed" (II.iii.369). Appropriate details focus our attention on the murderers' expertise and the lively interest they take in their work. Ithamore immediately realizes Barabas's intention to use Abigail to unwittingly incite Lodowick and Mathias to jealousy and violence. Given a letter to take to Mathias, Ithamore responds like an eager student in Italianate villainy: "'Tis poisoned, is it not?" (II.iii.374). "No, no," the master explains, "and yet it might be done that way. / It is a challenge

---

11. Maurice Charney, "The Persuasiveness of Violence in Elizabethan Plays," *Ren D*, N.S. II (1969), 67.

12. *The Jew of Malta* is quoted from the Revels Plays, ed. N. W. Bawcutt (Manchester, Eng., 1978).

feigned from Lodowick" (ll. 377–378). Barabas's reply to Ithamore's query is of a piece with his other casually erudite remarks on Mediterranean trade routes, Catholic ritual, and Malta's drainage system.

This pervasive sense of performance, professionalism, and seeming omnipotence undermines conventional moral attitudes toward villainy and establishes the comic detachment with which we watch the violence. The violence of the duel between Lodowick and Mathias is real enough, but the rivals simultaneously stab one another as if on Barabas's cue. Their deaths attest more to Barabas's skill than to the horror of two deceived friends killing each other. Abigail's discovery of her father's responsibility for her lover's death complicates our reaction by reminding us of the real pain caused by Barabas's villainy, but her sentiments are part of what the play denies. Her solemnity follows Ithamore's delight. The success of Barabas's device transports the Turk:

> Why, was there ever seen such villainy,
> So neatly plotted, and so well performed:
> Both held in hand, and flatly both beguiled?
>
> (III.iii. 1–3)

Ithamore functions as an intermediary between the reality of the stage action and our perception of it. His gleeful interest in the fine art of murder reduces seemingly tragic events to farce and directs us to appreciate Barabas's artistry. The comic presentation makes the vision of evil tolerable, but more than that it makes us laugh at violence which yields fatalities. The comedy is the most obvious part of a process by which values are being redefined. Our laughter reveals our delight in witty mayhem.

The murders in *The Jew of Malta* form a sequence of tightly connected set pieces. Barabas plots the first killings very carefully. To avoid detection and prosecution he has to commit more murders, but there is no sense, as events close in, of encroaching, inevitable justice, and Barabas is no suffering Macbeth. The precipitating events unleash great comic energy, as each successive threat of detection presents a new test of the murderers' wits. As soon as Barabas discovers Abigail's defection to the nuns he sends Ithamore for "the pot of rice / That for our supper stands upon the fire" (III.iv.49–50) and pulls out his Ancona poison to spice it. Seizing on the "Saint Jaques' even" (l. 76) tradition of anonymously sending alms for the nuns' sustenance, he poisons the entire convent to silence Abigail. No sooner are the nuns dead than Barabas dissembles repentance to buy enough time to work out a scheme for murdering two importuning friars. Barabas's feats are hugely villainous, but he displays the flexibility and witty opportunism of the classic comic hero.[13] His appeal makes the subversion of values more subtle and complete than in a play like *Selimus*, in which the protagonist relies on brute force for his survival.

Having overreached himself as a double agent, Barabas dies when he falls into the steaming cauldron he built to entrap Calymath, the Turkish general. The fiery cauldron is a type image of hell, and, as Brooke suggests, this seems a "very moral conclusion," except that it is "as funny as it is startling."[14] The ambivalence derives from the clash between our moral expectations and our natural admiration for comic inventiveness. Just before the catastrophe, we see Barabas *"Enter with a hammer, very busy"* (V.v.1 s.d.), putting the finishing touches on his machine and shouting orders to his carpenters. With Hieronimo, Barabas believes that "it is for the author's credit / To look that all things may go well."[15] Ferneze, the Maltese governor, thinks the device "excellent" (l. 42), and it works perfectly. But as Barabas invites Calymath "To ascend our homely stairs" (l. 58), Ferneze cuts the restraining rope: *"A charge, the cable cut, a cauldron discovered [into which Barabas falls]"* (l. 65 s.d.). Ferneze takes Calymath prisoner and ends the play by giving praise "Neither to fate nor fortune, but to heaven" (l. 123), though it is clear that he might better thank Barabas or himself. The governor's factitious comment is the final reminder of how tenuous the moral order is in this play, where Jews are treated "like infidels" (I.ii.62) and "It's no sin to deceive a Christian" (II.iii.311) or a Turk.

The essential amorality of *The Jew of Malta* justifies Robert Knoll's suggestion that "Barabas and Ithamore use Marx Brothers tricks in a mad world of violence and politics," and that the Jew and the Turk, like

13. In addition to the traits of the morality vice and the Elizabethan Machiavel, Barabas displays the qualities of the comic hero described by Susanne K. Langer in *Feeling and Form* (London, 1953), pp. 326–350. Barabas's ability to adapt in order to survive is particularly impressive. See also "Marlowe's Schadenfreude: Barabas as Comic Hero."

14. Brooke, pp. 92–93.

15. Thomas Kyd, *The Spanish Tragedy*, ed. Philip Edwards (London, 1959), IV.iii.3–4.

Groucho, Harpo, and Chico, hold their audience despite their sadism.[16] Except for Abigail, who is a minority voice, the victims are not sympathetic. We can laugh at Ferneze, because he is outraged by Barabas's villainy but practices no viable morality himself. *The Jew of Malta* is more comic than tragic, but not because it begins in chaos and ends in order. Rather, like a Marx Brothers' farce, Marlowe's play engages us in an anarchic release from moral order. Richard Boston's description of the dreamlike world of the old film comedies as one in which "the normal laws of the universe" are "suspended" and "everything that is repressed in the waking world is let to run riot,"[17] applies well to the experience of *The Jew of Malta*. The violent nature of the comedy makes it clear that Marlowe intends to do more than satirize Christian hypocrisy or make a sardonic statement about the prevalence of evil in the world. He also intends more than simply to provide vicarious pleasure at the expense of conventional moral and political institutions. By causing us to enjoy and admire an ingenious villain like Barabas, Marlowe vindicates the subversive truth of the ubiquitous Machiavel who speaks the Prologue: "Admired I am of those who hate me most" (l. 9). The comic presentation of the violence prevents us from taking too seriously the issues at stake in the play, but it causes us to redefine, or at least to reconsider, our assumptions about our own moral attitudes.

Comic violence vividly depicts the dissolution of commonly held values because it implies that there is no sane order in the world to make the violence seem legitimate. Our laughter signals our participation in the disorder. In both *Selimus* and *The Jew of Malta*, however, there are distancing devices which prevent the disorder from becoming too painful. In *Selimus* the stereotyping of the barbarians keeps the extreme violence from being an immediate threat to civilization. *The Jew of Malta* subverts values more completely because the witty villainy becomes a more persuasive expression of reality than Christian virtue, but the histrionic gusto with which the violence is presented makes the reality seem like a fantasy. *Titus Andronicus* is a more troublesome play because engaging histrionics and raw brutality coalesce. The comically savage depiction of violence arouses the same kinds of reactions as in *Selimus* and *The Jew of Malta*, but it brings

16. Robert Knoll, *Christopher Marlowe* (New York, 1969), p. 99.

17. Richard Boston, "The Rise and Fall of the Custard Pie," *TLS*, 18 June 1971, p. 713.

them into conflict with a more fundamental recognition that violence which causes real pain ought not to be amusing. Consequently, the violence in *Titus Andronicus* is much more cruel than any encountered so far, and it evokes a more disturbing vision of the world.

Late in *Titus Andronicus*, Aaron the Moor reveals to his captor Lucius, Titus's son, the crimes for which he has been responsible:

> murthers, rapes, and massacres,
> Acts of black night, abominable deeds,
> Complots of mischief, treason, villainies,
> Ruthful to hear, yet piteously performed. . . .
>
> (V.i.63–66)

Lucius expects Aaron to show remorse, but the villain rejoices in not having spent many days "Wherein I did not some notorious ill" (l. 127). His zealous confession recalls the mock-heroic interview in *The Jew of Malta*, in which Barabas boasts of killing sick people and poisoning wells, and Ithamore claims to have spent his time "In setting Christian villages on fire, / Chaining of eunuchs, binding galley-slaves" (II.iii.207–208). Like Barabas, Aaron delights in clever villainy, and the comic indulgence partially distances us from the pain he inflicts. But Aaron is not the protagonist of his play, and his victims are sympathetic, even heroic, in their suffering. More disconcerting, the noble Titus must adopt Aaron's witty malice before he can exact his revenge and clear the way for the restoration of order. The atrocities, "piteously performed" by villain and hero alike, engage us in a bizarre world of outrageous violence and suffering. The comic savagery mocks the apparently sane Roman values of Lucius and Marcus, depriving us of conventional moral or tragic responses.[18]

*Titus Andronicus* is more impressive than *The Jew of Malta* because it

---

18. For a different view of the effect of the violence in *Titus*, see Eugene M. Waith's important essay, "The Metamorphosis of Violence in *Titus Andronicus*," *Sh S*, X (1957), 39–49. Tracing the play's style to Ovid's treatment in *The Metamorphoses* of the transforming power of intense emotion, Waith sees the violence in *Titus* as "both agent and emblem of a metamorphosis of character which takes place before our eyes" (p. 46). Waith concludes that *Titus* is Shakespeare's "contribution to a special tragic mode," one that emphasizes "admiration," in the sense of "wonder" or "astonishment," rather than moral edification (p. 48).

moves us over a wider range of feelings. As Brooke argues, our responses necessarily change when fantasies of violence get translated into action: "it is one thing to laugh at the idea of mass-murder, another to see it done [on the stage]. We laugh still; but differently."[19] Even in its most disturbing moments, as when Barabas murders his daughter, *The Jew of Malta* remains comedy. Marlowe does not test our squeamishness too directly, because he keeps the poisoning of the nuns offstage. We see only Abigail die. Her confession briefly establishes the reality of death, but the pathos quickly turns to farce:[20]

> ABIGAIL
>
> Death seizeth on my heart, ah gentle friar
> Convert my father that he may be saved,
> And witness that I die a Christian.     [*Dies.*]

> 2 FRIAR
>
> Ay, and a virgin too, that grieves me most. . . .
>                           (III.vi.38–41)

The atrocities in *Titus* are seen as sardonic jokes by the perpetrators, but they are presented with horrifying realism before the audience. The disjunction between the lurid reality of the murders and mutilations and the way the characters talk about them is one of the play's most troublesome features, and a chief source of laughter. After the discovery of Bassianus's murder, Lavinia makes her startling entrance, *"her hands cut off, and her tongue cut out, and ravish'd"* (II.iv. 1 s.d.). Aaron, who plotted Lavinia's savage defilement, later calls it a "trimming":

> Why, she was wash'd, and cut, and trimm'd, and 'twas
> Trim sport for them which had the doing of it.
>                           (V.i.95–96)

Aaron's sneering jocularity appalls Lucius, as it is supposed to, but Lucius's reactions to the enormity of Aaron's crimes are comic, because they are so inadequate:

> O detestable villain! Call'st thou that trimming?
>                           (l. 94)

19. Brooke, p. 97.
20. *Ibid.*, p. 97.

Lucius is too self-righteously conventional, too middle-class, to understand Aaron's wittily depraved sense of rape and mutilation. And yet Lucius has a real fondness for violence. In a rhyme as grotesque as the intended action, he threatens to hang Aaron's baby, so that Aaron "may see it sprawl— / A sight to vex the father's soul withal" (V.i.51–52). Lucius also speaks the last words in the play, condemning Aaron and Tamora to terrible ends: Aaron to be set "breast-deep in earth" (V.iii.179) until he starves, and Tamora's body to be thrown "forth to beasts and birds to prey" (l. 198). Early in the play, Lucius zealously participates in the sacrifice of Tamora's son. He can hardly contain his satisfaction when he reports the execution:

> See, lord and father, how we have perform'd
> Our Roman rites: Alarbus' limbs are lopp'd,
> And entrails feed the sacrificing fire,
> Whose smoke like incense doth perfume the sky.
>
> (I.i.142–145)

This sacrifice precipitates the rest of the violence in the play, but Lucius talks of hewing and lopping limbs as if it should offend no one. It is not love of violence that distinguishes Aaron from the Romans, but the witty conception of it.

Aaron's rendition of Lavinia's rape and mutilation is no more offensive than her uncle's. Marcus responds uncomprehendingly to his niece's silent, bleeding form:

> Why dost not speak to me?
> Alas, a crimson river of warm blood,
> Like to a bubbling fountain stirr'd with wind,
> Doth rise and fall between thy rosed lips,
> Coming and going with thy honey breath.
>
> (II.iv.21–25)

Shakespeare means to shock us with incongruity in this scene. As Albert Tricomi argues, "the play deliberately 'exposes' the euphemisms of metaphor by measuring their falseness against the irrefutable realities of dramatized events."[21] The bizarre effect of the discrepancy between the

---

21. Albert Tricomi, "The Aesthetics of Mutilation in *Titus Adronicus*," *Sh S*, XXVII (1974), 13.

appalling reality of Lavinia's condition and Marcus's perception of it is part of the dramatic action. By talking so peculiarly about his ravished niece, Marcus contributes to the absurdity of his world, and we laugh at the absurdity.

Marcus's euphemisms are in character, because he refuses to confront a harsh, anarchic world. He would like to know what "beast" defiled Lavinia so "That I might rail at him to ease my mind!" (II.iv.34–35). Wilson suggests that "a woodman, discovering an injury to one of his trees, would have shown more indignation." [22] There is no talk of seeking justice or taking revenge, only of railing. Marcus even claims that the "craftier Tereus" (l. 41) who raped Lavinia would not have "cut those pretty fingers off" (l. 42) had he seen them at work:

> O, had the monster seen those lily hands
> Tremble like aspen-leaves upon a lute,
> And make the silken strings delight to kiss them,
> He would not then have touch'd them for his life.
>
> (ll. 44–47)

The lines are beautifully ludicrous not simply because they are overly sentimental, but because they are absurdly out of relation to what has happened. Marcus has no way of knowing what took place, but the scene is fresh in our minds when he speaks. Lavinia's ravishers have no interest in her musical skills, only in her body. If she carries her chastity to her grave, Chiron says, "I would I were an eunuch" (II.iii.128). Just before Marcus descants on Lavinia's injury, Chiron and Demetrius lead her in, trading crude witticisms:

CHIRON
Go home, call for sweet water, wash thy hands.

DEMETRIUS
She hath no tongue to call, nor hands to wash;
And so let's leave her to her silent walks.

CHIRON
And 'twere my cause, I should go hang myself.

DEMETRIUS
If thou hadst hands to help thee knit the cord.

(II.iv.6–10)

22. Wilson, p. li.

This depraved exchange establishes the context for Marcus's speech, and the disjunction is intentionally wrenching. The vulgar humor of Chiron and Demetrius is as extreme as Marcus's honey-sweet Ovidian poetry, and it, too, is in character. Their wit is crude because they are stupid, mindless villains. They can properly be called "beasts." They even needed Aaron to give them the idea for the joint assault on Lavinia.

The crimes in *Titus* powerfully suggest the collapse of moral order and "the complete absence of 'justice' from Rome," but to argue that Aaron becomes "the symbol of nightmare disintegration and revolting barbarism" is an oversimplification.[23] Until Titus embarks on his revenge, we can distinguish the good from the bad, but the distinction only partially explains the experience of the play. Shakespeare does not provide stable perspectives on the action. We can understand Lucius's outrage at Aaron's enormous villainy, but we cannot share his love of "legitimate" violence, which does not seem to work against Aaron anyway. Marcus argues for reason and decorum, but he does not seem to realize what is happening. The forces of law and order are painfully, laughably inadequate.

Moreover, there are degrees of craft and intelligence in the villainy. Chiron and Demetrius are dangerous buffoons, but their stupidity makes them easy prey for Titus. This is made clear when Titus sends them *"a bundle of weapons, and verses writ upon them"* (IV.ii.1 s.d.). The implications of the verse from Horace, suggesting that the upright man need not fear the Moor's javelins and bow, pass by Chiron, but they instill in Aaron a new respect for Titus:

> Here's no sound jest! the old man hath found their guilt,
> And sends them weapons wrapp'd about with lines,
> That wound, beyond their feeling, to the quick;
> But were our witty empress well afoot,
> She would applaud Andronicus' conceit. . . .
>
> (IV.ii.26–30)

Aaron's contempt for Chiron and Demetrius and his delight in Titus's "conceit" indicate that there is more to villainy than barbarity. There is an aesthetic dimension as well, which represents an even more radical subver-

---

23. Alan Sommers, "'Wilderness of Tigers': Structure and Symbolism in *Titus Andronicus*," *EIC*, X (1960), 282–283.

sion of values. Order now resides in aesthetics, not ethics, and survival becomes a grotesque battle of wits. It is hard for an audience to know how to react: our sensibilities are split by the intellectual appeal of the game and the emotional onslaught of the horrors which give the competition form.               .

The play's action reveals how vulnerable traditional values are to assault, but out of the chaos emerges a hierarchy of awareness. If the malevolent ingenuity represents a symptom of degeneration, it also provides a way to deal with the chaos, once the terrible reality is accepted on its own terms. The awareness, as Titus's experience shows, comes only with great pain, and it is akin to madness. Titus gets his full initiation into this wittily depraved world in Act III, when Aaron makes his proposition. If Titus, Lucius, or Marcus cuts off his hand and sends it to Saturninus, Mutius and Quintus, who are falsely charged with murdering Bassianus, will be freed. Titus has seen his reputation as Rome's exalted defender dissipate in a moment: his daughter has been raped and mutilated, his son-in-law has been murdered, two of his sons accused, and Lucius banished. Yet with comically pathetic naïveté, Titus welcomes Aaron's proposal:

> O, gracious emperor! O gentle Aaron!
> Did ever raven sing so like a lark
> That gives sweet tidings of the sun's uprise?
> With all my heart I'll send the emperor my hand.
> Good Aaron, wilt thou help to chop it off?
>
> (III.i.157–161)

The grisly humor works here as it does in *Selimus*. Perhaps in self-defense, we laugh at the enormity of Aaron's villainy and at the gullibility of the Andronici, who, despite their experience, clamor to mutilate themselves. Titus pretends to relent, but while Lucius and Marcus go off looking for an ax, thinking one of them will make the sacrifice, he exhorts Aaron to perform the necessary surgery:

> Come hither, Aaron; I'll deceive them both:
> Lend me thy hand, and I will give thee mine.
>
> (III.i.186–187)

In an aside Aaron remarks that "If that be call'd deceit, I will be honest" (l. 188), and then *"He cuts off Titus' hand"* (l. 191 s.d.). Titus thinks he has purchased his sons' lives "at an easy price: / And yet dear too, because I bought mine own" (ll. 198–199), but he cannot indulge his joy or sorrow for long, because a messenger enters *"with two heads and a hand"* (l. 234 s.d.). Aaron, fat on his villainy, has made Titus the butt of a cruel joke for which, he later explains to Lucius, Tamora gives him "twenty kisses" (V.i.120). With this combination of maliciously shrewd exploitation of innocence and shocking violence, the scene makes one of the play's most disconcerting attacks on our sense of decency. Just as Aaron's jest mocks Titus's paternalism and his extreme gesture of friendship ("Lend me thy hand, . . ."), the brutality of the scene mocks the heroic ideal the Andronici mean to uphold. The scene demolishes the notion that traditional forms of heroism and nobility have any meaning in Aaron's world, and bitter laughter is a more appropriate response than pity, fear, or indignation.

Now Titus can only laugh: "Ha, ha, ha!" (III.i.264). The mad laughter, which thoroughly dismays Marcus, signals a turning point in the play, but I think it is a mistake to see it as the beginning of Titus's "metamorphosis from man into beast, his noble nature transformed to a barren detested vale, where he searches for satisfaction" in Revenge's Cave.[24] Titus's subsequent actions are not noble, but they are vigorous, witty, and successful, and thus not barren. Titus's reactions seem mad in terms of the reactions of Marcus and Lucius, but his brother and son cling to a normalcy which no longer exists. Conventional moral order has been replaced by Aaron's aesthetic disorder. The apparent disorder in Titus's mind puts him in touch with Aaron's imagination, and he conducts an appropriately aesthetic revenge. Delivering equivocal messages to Tamora's sons, shooting arrows into court, and sending pigeons to Saturninus seem the actions of a madman, but they properly vex the enemy. When Titus seems most mad, deep in contemplation of direful revenge plots, he sees most lucidly through the illusions raised by his enemies, and he acts cunningly.

Shakespeare goes after extreme effects to engage the audience in the experience of an unpredictable world. Although the action of *Titus* derives from literary sources, it denies the reliability of precedents, particularly bookish ones, for understanding the heinous events. "A craftier Tereus"

24. Nicholas Brooke, *Shakespeare's Early Tragedies* (London, 1968), p. 38.

than the legendary one assaulted Lavinia, because he severed her hands as well as her tongue. Her very real defilement, as Titus recognizes, is worse than what we read about, and it requires a more intense reaction:

> Had I but seen thy picture in this plight
> It would have madded me: what shall I do
> Now I behold thy lively body so?
>
> (III.i.103–105)

Titus contrives a witty, grisly revenge because, as he explains to Chiron and Demetrius before he cuts their throats, grinds their bones, and bakes them in a pie to serve their mother,

> worse than Philomel you us'd my daughter,
> And worse than Progne I will be reveng'd.
>
> (V.ii.195–196)

The revenge has literary precedents in Ovid and Seneca, but Shakespeare dresses Titus in chef's clothing and presents the murders and bloody banquet onstage. There is an insistence in *Titus* that its violence is more outrageous than any described in its sources.[25] This spirited competition with the sources yields some intellectual pleasure for the audience, but the comic distortion intensifies the sense of extremity by pushing the audience into an unfamiliar realm of experience where conventionally serious responses are disallowed. The violence in *Titus* is sometimes wondered at, as if it was part of a nightmare, or "fearful slumber" (III.i.252), but it affirms a vicious reality. Even Marcus, after enough atrocities pile up, begins to suspect that "the gods delight in tragedies" (IV.i.60).

A tension between fiction and reality, the tragic and the ludicrous, prevents the ending from being either pure ritual or mere farce. Ritual would allow us to abstract a symbolic meaning and so exorcize the evil, and farce would allow us to dismiss the grotesque action as a bad joke. The bloody banquet with which Titus consummates his revenge builds on shifting, conflicting sensations which provoke equally disconcerting feelings. After the guests arrive—the emperor and empress with regal train,

---

25. For a more detailed discussion of Shakespeare's heightening of the source material (which leads to different conclusions), see A. C. Hamilton, *The Early Shakespeare* (San Marino, Calif., 1967), pp. 63–89.

to the sound of trumpets—Titus enters *"like a cook, placing the dishes"*
(V.iii.26 s.d.). He dresses like a chef to emphasize his role as gracious
host:

> I would be sure to have all well
> To entertain your highness and your empress.
>
> (ll. 31–32)

Titus's comic posture as cook establishes the extreme, histrionic context of
the slaughter, but his frenzied grief and the revolting nature of the revenge establish the horrible and undeniable reality. Our relationship to
the scene is further complicated by a more subtle tension between horror
and fascination. Being privy to Titus's menu, we can appreciate the irony
of his welcome to his royal guests:

> although the cheer be poor,
> 'Twill fill your stomachs; please you eat of it.
>
> (ll. 28–29)

Horror mixes with apprehension: when will the diners discover that they
are eating human flesh? The anxiety can be called comic, though it is an
intensely debasing comedy, because it is not mitigated by sympathy for
the villainous dupes.

Lavinia unexpectedly falls first, again demonstrating that reality is
more savage than legend. Almost as if he were initiating polite conversation, Titus asks Saturninus to "resolve me this":

> Was it well done of rash Virginius
> To slay his daughter with his own right hand,
> Because she was enforc'd, stain'd, and deflow'r'd?
>
> (V.iii.35–38)

When Saturninus glibly replies that "It was" (l. 39), "Because the girl
should not survive her shame, / And by her presence still renew his
sorrows" (ll. 41–42), Titus tests the idea by pulling a knife and stabbing
Lavinia:

> Die, die, Lavinia, and thy shame with thee;
> And with thy shame thy father's sorrow die!
>                   [*He kills her*]
>
> (ll. 46–47)

Because our attention has been divided—Tamora must be eating while Titus quizzes Saturninus—the killing is especially startling. Titus's grief seems genuine, but we are not allowed to view the killing as a sacrificial purging of sorrow, or even as a lurid expression of insane passion. The potential tragic emotion is immediately undermined because Titus, though he declares his profound suffering, must treat the filicide as a diversion which should not be allowed to interrupt the feast:

> Will't please you eat? will't please your highness feed?
>
> (l. 54)

This line, with its reductive insistence that the banquet go on, returns the scene to grotesque comedy while it reveals Titus's increasing frenzy. At the same time, it focuses our attention on the revolting main course. The dinner guests are shocked and bewildered by their host's unpredictable behavior. We are perplexed too, but we share in Titus's grisly joke. Pressed by Saturninus to produce Lavinia's ravishers, Titus finally exclaims:

> Why, there they are, both baked in this pie;
> Whereof their mother daintily hath fed,
> Eating the flesh that she herself hath bred.
>
> (V.iii.60–62)

The diners' sudden revulsion at this revelation must be at once comic and horrible. The witty couplet contrasting Tamora's table manners with her diet intensifies the comic grotesquerie and reinforces the conflict between decency and lurking depravity that runs throughout the play. Titus insists that "'Tis true, 'tis true" (l. 63); and, as if to punctuate the veracity of the moment, he bids his retching guests to "witness my knife's sharp point" (l. 63), as he plunges it into Tamora. This unleashes a burst of violence. Saturninus immediately stabs Titus "for this accursed deed" (l. 64), and Lucius, wondering "Can the son's eye behold his father bleed?" (l. 65), stabs Saturninus. The sudden reversion of the regal banquet to wild butchery effectively visualizes the violent chaos of the play's world. Curiously, but typically, Lucius's sentimental justification for his participation in violence seems out of relation to the spectacle of the cannibalism and the flurry of stabbings. We laugh in an effort to reach an equilibrium, to put the bizarre action in perspective. But the action provides no clear directions, and we are left in a muddle.

As he does later in *Hamlet*, Shakespeare spends time after the climactic bloodbath restoring order and clarifying, ostensibly for the bewildered onstage witnesses, the hero's part in the carnage. In neither play can a character's summary of events do justice to our experience of the play, but the accounts at the end of *Titus* seem particularly inadequate. Titus is exonerated because he suffered "wrongs unspeakable, past patience, / Or more than any living man could bear" (V.iii.126–127). It is because Titus's experience of sardonic malevolence has been so devastating that his behavior cannot be explained or excused in conventional terms. I do not think that "at the end it is as though some vital principle, long withdrawn, were reincarnated, uniting, as Marcus expresses it, 'These broken limbs again into one body'" (V.iii.72).[26] The action of the play indicates that Titus clears the way for the restoration of order by acting on his mad recognition of the aesthetic principles of disorder. Marcus and Lucius are not reliable spokesmen because they ignore the predominant quality of Aaron's villainy and Titus's spectacular revenge: the inspired, disorienting wit. Yet it is this amoral aestheticism, the violence for art's sake, that governs our experience of the play's assault on traditional human values.

Titus's experience, which includes his terrible suffering and his insanely inspired revenge, moves the audience beyond the vision of normalcy Marcus and Lucius adhere to. Like Barabas, and Hieronimo in *The Spanish Tragedy* (1587?), Titus engages in a revenge which transcends what is merely necessary and which transforms the suffering tragic hero into a grotesquely triumphant comic hero. Titus uses his comically hysterical Thyestean feast to engineer a collision between reality and complacent illusion. Tamora had expected to "find some cunning practice" (V.ii.77) with which to defeat Titus, but with her masquerade of Revenge, Murder, and Rape, she placed too much faith in her art and in Titus's lunacy, just as Titus once put too much faith in Aaron's humanity. She is made to surfeit on her evil. Horrors are brought to life to confront the audience with a world more zany and undeniably violent than what we discover in Ovid and Seneca. Brooke suggests that in *Titus* "it is the shock of death itself that restores a sense of reality to the stylized enactment of unleashed destructiveness."[27] Revengers like Titus, Barabas, and Hieronimo build this shock of recognition into their performances, and they use the dis-

---

26. Sommers, p. 283.
27. Brooke, *Shakespeare's Early Tragedies*, p. 45.

tancing effect of comic art to insure the impact of their meaning. Because of the dislocating effect of pain mixed with laughter, comic savagery is useful for engaging the audience in a sense of the chaos afflicting the characters onstage. The comic heightening of the brutality helps to reveal a world in which the malevolence is too witty, the violence too extreme, and the sense of order too illusory, to sustain the redemptive tragic emotions of pity and fear. Our bitter laughter reflects our painful involvement in the disorder.

It used to be argued that "all this violence and cruelty" in the early plays "inspires neither pessimism nor discouragement. The tragic hero is not weighed down by his failure: he boldly continues all forms of life, undeterred by the mutability of his fortunes."[28] Surely, the violence creates a robustness that is one of the distinguishing features of the plays. The generalization certainly fits plays like *Selimus*, in which the violence celebrates power, and *Lust's Dominion* (1600?), in which the villain-hero Eleazar can simply proclaim, "Murder, be proud; and, tragedy, laugh on, / I'll seek a stage for thee to jet upon."[29] But the violence in *The Jew of Malta*, and especially in *Titus Andronicus*, though still robust, witty, and inspired, reveals painful truths about the world and undermines cherished notions about human values and conduct. Insofar as the comedy is an expression and product of the subversion of moral values by the aesthetic violence, it anticipates the more brittle irony of the plays of Tourneur, Middleton, and Webster, in which Tragedy and Comedy again vie for control of the stage.

28. Henri Fluchère, *Shakespeare and the Elizabethans*, trans. Guy Hamilton (1947; rpt. New York, 1956), p. 30.

29. *Lust's Dominion; or, The Lascivious Queen*, in Robert Dodsley's *A Select Collection of Old English Plays*, ed. William Hazlitt (London, 1875), XLV, 176.

# Ideology and Class Conduct in
# The Merchant of Venice

## FRANK WHIGHAM

O NE OF THE MOST SIGNIFICANT ISSUES in *The Merchant of Venice* is the rhetorical assertion of social status. Shakespeare locates this activity in a context of social mobility and class conflict, where language and other modes of self-projection serve as both enabling and repressive forces. The styles of the Christians and of Shylock are calculated: each aims to manipulate its audience, to secure access to the society's resources of power and privilege. In each case the movements of wooing and assault constitute ideological assertion. Insofar as the play presents an examination of political or class interaction, the normative aristocratic style is not simply the medium of presentation, nor even the harmonious sign of authorial approval; it is itself a subject for scrutiny. To accept these words and actions "in the rainbow hues of romance," as some interpreters suggest,[1] is to accept without question a mode presented for questioning, to surrender to the imperatives of the style itself.

Contemporary records attest to a widespread fascination with the uses of stylized identity as a social tool. Queen Elizabeth and Prince Hal carefully

---

1. A. R. Humphreys, *The Merchant of Venice (Shakespeare)*, Notes on English Literature, No. 50 (Oxford, 1973), pp. 62–63.

constructed public images of magnificence in order to defuse their inheritance from problematic forebears. Othello and Sir Henry Sidney artfully
purchased elite status, the former with exotic tales, the latter with a false
pedigree.[2] Tamburlaine and Coriolanus declaimed their transcendent excellence. Sir Christopher Hatton, eventual lord chancellor, was accused of
dancing his way to office and his queen's heart.[3] Sir Fridericke Frigoso
proposed to define the ideal courtier in order "to disgrace therfore many
untowardly Asseheades, that through malapartnesse thinke to purchase
them the name of a good courtier."[4] The analyst might thus focus on the
individual action, or on its representative status, or on its audience. Praise
and blame for achievement or imposture, fiction or perception, were
distributed according to the ideological stance of the viewer.

*The Merchant of Venice* anatomizes this social rhetoric through parallel
focuses of inclusion and exclusion. As style reveals relation with one's
equals and discrimination from one's inferiors, so the plot enacts these
concepts in linear fashion. The marriage plot chronicles Bassanio's courtship of and assimilation into the elite; the trial plot depicts Shylock's
critical invasion of their preserve of power. These actions are parallel,
because each focuses on the promulgation of instrumental style, culminates in an interpretive trial, and results in the clarification of social
identity.

I

The marriage plot takes place in a context where insecurity is held at
bay by reassuring assertions of class solidity and value. In the choric
dialogue of the first scene Salerio and Solanio respond to Antonio's sadness
with a practiced flattery supportive of his social value, and, by reflection,
their own. References to the magnificence of his tonnage overcome any
sense of anxiety and vulnerability through the force of weighty dignity.
Commercial and social superiority are fused:

2. Roger Howell, *Sir Philip Sidney: The Shepherd Knight* (Boston, 1968), p. 18.
3. Neville Williams, *Elizabeth I, Queen of England* (1967; rpt. London, 1971), pp.
185–186.
4. Baldassare Castiglione, *The Book of the Courtier* (1528), trans. Sir Thomas Hoby
(1561; rpt. New York, 1928), p. 29.

> There [on the sea] where your argosies with portly sail,
> Like signiors and rich burghers on the flood,
> Or as it were the pageants of the sea,
> Do overpeer the petty traffickers
> That cur'sy to them (do them reverence)
> As they fly by them with their woven wings.[5]

The social imagery embodying the values of the life of commerce expresses their ideological status: material and aesthetic distinctions take on almost moral force. This accretion owes something to the Marlovian excess of Barabas's world-girdling trade empire in *The Jew of Malta*. However, the emphasis here is not on a heroic imperialism of the sea, with implications of self-determining social mobility and disrespect for established boundaries, but on the solid value of those who are impregnably dignified within those bounds. These first lines go far to suggest the world of the play, where appearances govern reality, money governs appearances, and class expectations and mystifications govern the use of money.

However, the threats of the sea question the security Salerio has invoked. He describes them in terms of social degradation (to "see my wealthy Andrew dock'd in sand / Vailing her high top lower than her ribs / To kiss her burial" [I.i.27–29]) and apocalyptic misdirection and usurpation of Antonio's luxury imports ("rocks, / Which touching but my gentle vessel's side / Would scatter all her spices on the stream, / Enrobe the roaring waters with my silks" [I.i.31–34]). For Salerio thoughts of pleasurable security inescapably arouse fears for its loss; he thus voices the other of the play's twin subjects—the invasion, usurpation, or loss of security and privilege. The safety of position and wealth is continually embattled, not given but achieved, and always requiring vigilant defense. The complexity of the play's treatment of these issues is latent in the fact that the tools of assault and defense are the same—stylized assertion and its enabling force, money.

When Bassanio makes his request for funds to Antonio, his ornate style belies the humility of its content. The comparison of his "project" of

---

5. *The Merchant of Venice*, ed. J. R. Brown, The Arden Shakespeare (London, 1955), I.i.9–14. All quotations are taken from this edition, and are identified by parenthetical references in the text.

Regarding the social moralization of the sea we may also note Morocco's reference to "the watery kingdom, whose ambitious head/Spets in the face of heaven" (II.vii.44–45).

obtaining Portia's hand to Jason's search for the Golden Fleece makes his
plan a quest, magnificent and dangerous (and more deserving of un-
derwriting). The parallel with Jason has a shady side, however, since Jason
and Medea were both associated with untruth and deception, and since the
Golden Fleece image was frequently used to signify the goal of commercial
enterprise, monetary profit.[6] Bassanio's language also has a specifically
commercial vocabulary: he frequently uses such terms as "rate," "owe,"
"hazard," "richly," "undervalu'd," "worth," "means," and "thrift." The
intermixture of heroic and mercantile language emphasizes their relation
to each other; the tonal disjunction suggests an ironic reading, since in
romantic heroics financial foundations are usually suppressed as tawdry.
Bassanio's request is for the "means to hold a rival place" with the other
suitors; this turns out to consist of "rare new liveries," "gifts of rich
value," and followers with "courteous breath." Bassanio romanticizes in
heroic terms the pragmatic web of technique, effort, and self-interest
which baser men work with more openly.

Antonio makes it clear that Bassanio shall have the money for friendship's sake rather than for the art of his appeal. That he should feel the
need to make the appeal, and insist on delivering it in full despite clear
signs from Antonio that it is superfluous, suggests his insecurity in the
friendship. Such covert alienation informs many relationships in this play.
The purest expression of this occurs in Act III, where Solanio tells Salerio
the rumor of the loss of Antonio's shipping. The brief conversation is
mired in rhetorical cleverness:

I would she [Report] were as lying a gossip in that, as ever knapp'd ginger, or
made her neighbours believe she wept for the death of a third husband: but it is
true, without any slips of prolixity, or crossing the plain highway of talk, that the
good Antonio, the honest Antonio;—O that I had a title good enough to keep his
name company!—

(III.i.8–14)

The disjunction of style and content in the obtrusively witty conveyance of
fearful rumor for their friend and patron suggests the tenuous nature of
attachment and regard in this society, where tragic news is an occasion for
gratuitous self-display.

6. See Elizabeth S. Sklar, "Bassanio's Golden Fleece," *TSLL*, XVIII (1976), 502–503.

In scene ii Shakespeare presents aristocratic life from another angle, the boredom of country-house life, where the only activity of interest for a daughter is speculation regarding marriage. Portia's stylized and petulant world-weariness is put in perspective by Nerissa's observation of its origin in surfeit and idleness. Her rebuke does not really register with Portia, who chafes under the curb of a dead father's will. Nerissa soothingly assigns the government of the suitors to heaven, the casket device being sacramental, the inspiration of a holy man. However, the casket device in fact functions with quite secular effectiveness to select, by stylistic tests, a man of just the right sort of awareness, ultimately reaffirming and supporting a particular class-oriented definition of value. Lawrence Stone provides an equation for the relation between money and status:

Money was the means of acquiring and retaining status, but it was not the essence of it: the acid test was the mode of life, a concept that involved many factors. Living on a private income was one, but more important was spending liberally, dressing elegantly, and entertaining lavishly. Another was having sufficient education to display a reasonable knowledge of public affairs, and to be able to perform gracefully on the dance-floor, and on horseback, in the tennis-court and the fencing-school.[7]

Shakespeare presents such items in emblematic moments and small touches, placing at the center of his plot the crucial element implicit in Stone's catalogue: the ability to judge as well as to manifest style. Castiglione had stressed the import of this in general; Shakespeare creates an emblematic test conceived specifically on stylistic lines.

The emphasis on such criteria is central from the first mention of the casket device. All the suitors who are unwilling to risk their futures on such a test are shown to be, in Portia's eye, defective in style. Her mockery of them allows her to demonstrate her own impeccable credentials. Their weaknesses range from innocence of proper styling to obsessive concern with it. The Neapolitan prince seems to have been persuaded to wish himself a horse. The County Palatine is never merry, and Monsieur le Bon is infirm of image ("every man in no man"). Falconbridge, the English baron, is ill-educated (having neither Latin, French, nor Italian) and ill-clothed, with a hodgepodge of fashions from around the world. The German, out of regard for tradition, is a drunkard. The Scottish lord

7. Lawrence Stone, *The Crisis of the Aristocracy* (Oxford, 1965), p. 50.

fares most poorly of all, being only a mark for Portia to shoot wit-cracks at. Portia's mockeries deal primarily with external manifestations of style; as she judges others, she reveals herself.

Shakespeare's comic observation of Portia deepens into irony at the end of the scene, where the two most important suitors, Morocco and Bassanio, are brought together. Of the latter there is a bare mention, revealing at least a visual impression made on his last visit. (Here, presumably, were given the "speechless messages" which led Bassanio's mind to "presage thrift" [I.i.175] in his venture.) Morocco too is considered (and condemned) in visual terms, as having "the complexion of a devil." Throughout the scenes with Morocco the element of complexion provides a measure of the exclusive implications of courtesy in Portia's society.

The remainder of the casket action is divided into three segments: the failures of Morocco and Arragon and the success of Bassanio. The failures provide criteria by which to examine Bassanio's success. The action of Morocco opens with his statement of defiant insecurity regarding his skin color. He dresses in white, and declares that his blood is as red as that of any blond's, asserting inner virtue over outward defect. He converts his color to a virtue by assimilating it to fierceness: "I tell thee lady this aspect of mine / Hath fear'd the valiant" (II.i.8–9). In this, as in many other ways, he reminds one of Tamburlaine.[8] His imagery of martial exploit and confrontation is in the style of early Elizabethan rant, which is ineffective with this young sophisticate. The world of physical action and martial valor, the natural violence of the she-bear and the lion, are all unwelcome in Belmont, legitimate only as figurative language. Morocco finds that what he sees as his "own good parts" gain scant credit with Portia. Unlike Desdemona, she does not love the Moor for the dangers he has passed, but seems to find him something of a barbarian. (Portia is not a rebel against her culture; she is its judgmental representative.) She alludes to his color when she remarks that he stands "as fair / As any comer [she has] look'd on yet" (II.i.20–21). He seems, in sum, to be handicapped by his race, his lack of sophistication, and his outmoded style. The attribute of his style most relevant here is his lavish claims made for his own desert. In the early days of Elizabethan drama the non-European setting and character, presented with extensive rhetorical ornament, gave the exotic an incanta-

8. See M. C. Bradbrook, *Shakespeare and Elizabethan Poetry* (London, 1951), p. 175.

tory power over Elizabethan audiences. In the courtly context, however, the imperialistic titanism of Tamburlaine is ill-adapted to purposes of wooing. In *The Merchant of Venice* the requirements for success have moved into a lower key, more civilized and guileful. A polished Bassanio may succeed where a Morocco weighted with golden attributes will fail. The conqueror no longer spins Fortune's Wheel with his hand, but plays the odds and wins with a "system."

Shakespeare further exposes these patterns in the scene of Morocco's choice, which sets up a major irony for the casket action. Morocco is governed by two assumptions, of his own worth and of the validity of appearance in displaying value. Like Tamburlaine he insists on correct ranking for himself: "A golden mind stoops not to shows of dross" (II.vii.20). He also assumes, like Tamburlaine, that the world dare not deceive him; shows of dross must contain only dross: "Is't like that lead contains her?—'twere damnation / To think so base a thought, it were too gross / To rib her cerecloth in the obscure grave" (II.vii.49–51). So, of course, he chooses the best exterior, and loses. His judgment is rooted in a simpler world, with a more linear scale of value, less obscure and demanding less of one in the way of training and education. It is a world in which men are still intoxicated with the thrill of power attendant upon might, and less concerned to exercise that power within society's complexities. A more discriminating member of a more differentiated society, Portia rejoices because she is not to be allied to an image so primitive and out of place. The displacement of typical Elizabethan ethnocentrism to Italy, where one of the victims is an Englishman, emphasizes the focus on the exclusive motive itself. Portia requires one of her own sort, with whom she can share assumptions and jokes, and her father's device skillfully excludes the unfit. Virtue without appropriate external appeal has no traction in this world.

Unlike Morocco, Arragon recognizes the possible falsity of externals, yet he ignores lead. Gold he condemns as the choice of the many:

> The fool multitude that choose by show,
> Not learning more than the fond eye doth teach,
> Which pries not to th' interior, but like the martlet
> Builds in the weather on the outward wall,
> Even in the force and road of casualty.
>
> (II.ix.26–30)

Here is the sense that judging by externals is risky, and that the wise man will look inward to avoid hazard. The hazard Arragon fears is to be ranked with the barbarous multitude (a class-oriented objection that never occurs to Morocco). He laments the corrupt derivation of place:

> O that . . .
> clear honor
> Were purchas'd by the merit of the wearer!—
> How many then should cover that stand bare! . . .
> How much low peasantry would then be gleaned
> From the true seed of honor!
>
> (II.ix.42–47)

The primary impact of Arragon's speculations is a stress on the disjunction between surface and inner value, and on the frequent misreadings of externals. This complication of Morocco's interpretive approach serves to heighten our awareness of the stylistic character of Bassanio's entry, which follows at once. His gifts of rich value, his retinue with courteous breath, and his resemblance to costly summer manifestly impress Portia and Nerissa, but we should be aware of the reflection of Arragon's words on this flashy entry.

Bassanio's choice of the leaden casket is the culmination of all the motifs suggested so far: by the demonstration of stylistic class affinities Bassanio wins marital bliss, a splendid fortune, and a solid class grounding. The scene is set with a series of allusions to artistic signs of harmony. They conduct a witty duet, cleverly playing variations on the Petrarchan theme of love torture, creating an effect not dissimilar to the sonnet spoken by Romeo and Juliet. As they test and reveal their verbal affinity, they establish social congruence and foreshadow a decorous love match. Each builds on the other's remarks in a fashion reminiscent of the witty games of repartee depicted in *The Book of the Courtier* or Guazzo's *The Civile Conversation*, with the same effect of mutual reinforcement.

Bassanio's meditation on his choice concerns the deceptiveness of appearance, especially ornamental appearance. He finds it in law, in religion, in assertions of valor and beauty. Of all these elements he says that "ornament is but the guiled shore / To a most dangerous sea: the beauteous scarf / Veiling an Indian beauty (III.ii.97–99).[9] There is no reason to

---

9. The verbal parallel with Salerio's earlier description of the threats to Antonio's luxury trade invites us to note the suggestions of danger and falsehood specifically.

question these familiar perceptions (though the racial stereotype is a revealing term for evil: he casts it as dark and non-European). However, when he concludes sententiously, "Therefore, thou gaudy gold, Hard food for Midas, I will none of thee, / Nor none of thee thou pale and common drudge / 'Tween man and man" (III.ii. 101–104), one may wonder how to take his reflections. For we can hardly forget Bassanio's borrowing from Shylock through Antonio, his rare new liveries and costly gifts, all of which, bred from Shylock's gold (as Sigurd Burckhardt notes),[10] were meant to nurture his chances for success in Belmont. Maybe Bassanio is so unreflective as to be unaware of the irony of his words; even his meditations may be so rhetorically ordered as to preclude self-consciousness. Insofar as he may be imagined to conceive the self as a configuration of public gestures, the perception of irony may be somewhat anachronistic. He may be unconcerned with the tension between the artful form of his meditation and its moral content; aesthetic and moral perspectives often seem askew from one another in this play. Perhaps some such compartmentalization, and the instrumental utility it implies, are part of Shakespeare's point here.

Indeed, in *The Book of the Courtier* troublesome moral matters regarding deception are often suppressed or obscured by the proponents of the aestheticized personality. When Lord Gasper Pallavicino, the book's chief devil's advocate, labels a certain rhetorical stratagem "a very deceite," Sir Fridericke Frigoso replies in defense that it is "rather an ornament . . . than a deceite: and though it be a deceite, yet it is not to be disallowed."[11] One might suggest here that Bassanio speaks against falsehood to disguise his own operations, but this would assume an unlikely degree of intellectual self-consciousness on the courtier's part. Perhaps we can only say that an excessive concern for the rhetorical projection of self somehow works against self-knowledge. The irony in *The Merchant of Venice* seems most explicable if placed in the gray area between deception and self-deception, rhetorical conspiracy and illusion.[12]

The actual choice of the leaden casket results logically from this meditation on the implications of appearance. Bassanio seems to act on the basis

10. Sigurd Burckhardt, "*The Merchant of Venice*: The Gentle Bond," *Shakespearean Meanings* (Princeton, N.J., 1968), p. 215.

11. Castiglione, p. 132 (variations in spelling follow the original).

12. For this distinction see Kenneth Burke, *A Rhetoric of Motives* (1950; rpt. Berkeley, Calif., 1969), p. 114.

of stylistic *sententiae* derived from Castiglione. The interlocutors of *The Book of the Courtier* repeatedly enjoin us to hide art with art, to underplay our attributes in order to generate greater impact when the truth is revealed. When Bassanio decides to trust the least prepossessing casket, he assumes it promises reward by the principle of *ars celare artem*. He imputes this paradigm to the test itself; it is the intuition that constitutes passage, into marriage and membership.

Portia, chosen rightly, proceeds to wish herself, her beauty, and her money arithmetically multiplied, that "only to stand high in [his] account, / [she] might in virtues, beauties, livings, friends / Exceed account" (III.ii.155–157). The elaboration of this quantitative imagery belies the "unlesson'd . . . unschool'd, unpractised" girl, whose modesty is an art of ostentation. Her surrender of self emphasizes her own value and its accompanying material benefits almost as strongly as Bassanio did in seeking her:

> Myself, and what is mine, to you and yours
> Is now converted. But now I was the lord
> Of this fair mansion, master of my servants,
> Queen o'er myself: and even now, but now,
> This house, these servants, and this same myself
> Are yours.
>
> (III.ii.166–171)

At this, Bassanio is bereft of words. He would seem to agree with Francis Osborne, who advised his son that "as the fertilitie of the ensuing year is guessed at the height of the river Nilus, so by the greatness of a wive's portion may much of the future conjugall happiness be calculated."[13] Bassanio becomes solvent, Portia is married to a fit mate, and Antonio is to be repaid, after which all are to live happily ever after.

To many this is an adequate reading of the entire play. The hero meets the test and wins the rich and beautiful lady who is the prize. As often happens in fairy tales, beauty, goodness, and right-feeling intelligence have been assimilated to one another; the achievement of the lady is the achievement of the comedy. However, Shakespeare has written a more complex play than this model suggests. Several matters remain to be integrated with what has gone before; some are quite critical, even subver-

---

13. Quoted in Stone, p. 613.

sive, of the dominant ideology articulated in the marriage plot. But criticisms are tucked safely out of sight, and we are left with what appears to be an entertaining play. (The Elizabethan political climate was hostile to playwrights who meddled with matters beyond their proper sphere. Obtrusive neatness is thus often legalistic camouflage, a sign of prohibited criticism underneath.)

When one reads *The Merchant of Venice* as a study of courteous ideology, a different sort of coherence is revealed: the trial plot, far from simply providing an antagonistic movement, *mirrors* the marriage plot. The collective rituals of language and style reaffirm the dominant ideology not only by the induction of consonant suitors, but also by the expulsion of "malapart asseheades." Both actions rest upon assumptions of the revelation of natural hierarchy.

## II

The narrative structure of the trial plot parallels that of the casket plot in that they are both organized by the social rituals surrounding a bid for power. Bassanio and Shylock both seek power in a social context where the old feudal hierarchy is being reordered by the pressures of capitalism. Bassanio's procedure was perceived as reaffirming the model of sanctified natural hierarchy, and thus the bulwarks between the elite and its inferiors. As we have seen, however, his assertion of the natural distinction of the elite is itself positive, in the sense that it is in fact posited, created by the human powers of imagination and money. He therein implicitly represents one major version of disruptive social mobility.

Shylock represents another. Unlike Bassanio, he does not seek membership in the power-wielding class. (Indeed, his contempt for their ways matches theirs for his; both sides endorse the structure of exclusion and the self-righteous perception of elitism.) Shylock does aim at the achievement and exercise of power, and like Bassanio denies the natural status of class distinction. Shylock's overt version of positivism leads him to a disruption of the courtly ideology apparently quite unlike Bassanio's affirmations of it, but the implicit positivist threat to social rigidity is the same. Shylock is also subjected to trial, and is finally punished for his heterodox self-assertion. And just as Bassanio's reward (marriage and enrichment) is fitting to his courtly mode, Shylock's punishment and reduction to insignificance grow out of his legal and commercial mode of self-definition. This portion of the play then reveals the alternative to Bassanio's successful quest: the exclusion and baffling of the unsuccessful impostor or poacher.

The mode of Shylock's bid for power is first registered stylistically. In dealing with Bassanio and Antonio, he strives to demystify their power and prestige, to strip to essences what is romantically obscured. He takes the incantatory terms with which Solanio and Salerio sang Antonio's reputation and stands them on their feet.

. . . His means are in supposition: he hath an argosy bound to Tripolis, another to the Indies, I understand moreover on the Rialto, he hath a third at Mexico, a fourth for England, and other ventures he hath squand'red abroad,—but ships are but boards, sailors but men, there be land-rats and water-rats, water-thieves and land-thieves, (I mean pirates), and then there is the peril of waters, winds, and rocks.

(I.iii.15–23)

Shylock's epistemology threatens their heroic self-concept (and the supremacy it implies), revealing adventure as risk, dangerously akin to weakness. The Christians prefer to control the frame of their public image, needing to be witnessed rather than inspected. Their right to power and privilege will not bear Shylock's demystifying examination.

Similarly, they are unwilling or unable to use Shylock's observations to reexamine themselves from a new perspective. This is revealed as Antonio, with the force of public morality behind him, humiliates Shylock in the marketplace for his "Jewish" business practices: "he rails / . . . On me, my bargains, and my well-won thrift / Which he calls interest" (I.iii.43– 46). The divergent vocabularies suggest a gap in communication, combining in Antonio's case an inability to perceive the object with a readiness to judge it. Shakespeare reveals the social impact of this communication gap in the reception of Shylock's tale of the "scientific" manipulation of Laban's sheep.

Shylock tells the tale to justify his taking of interest. The precedent is obscure, and Antonio's overready interpretation emphasizes the rigidity of his conceptual vocabulary, under which Shylock stands condemned. Before he can even complete the tale of Jacob, Antonio demands to know "And what of him? did he take interest?" (I.iii.70), moving instantly to interpret in the terms of his predetermined code. Shylock responds that his example works in other terms: "No, not take interest, not as you would say / Directly int'rest,—mark what Jacob did" (I.iii.71–72). Antonio's reductive stock response to the obscure story makes clear that he perceives only in his own derivative vocabulary:

> This was a venture sir that Jacob serv'd for,
> A thing not in his power to bring to pass,
> But sway'd and fashion'd by the hand of heaven.
> Was this inserted to make interest good?
> Or is your gold and silver ewes and rams?

Shylock's response, "I cannot tell, I make it breed as fast" (I.iii.86–91), attempts to cut across the arbitrary terms of Christian philosophy to a pragmatic standard that reveals Antonio's response as predetermined and conventional. The latter is unwilling or unable to make the venture of thought required by Shylock's irony; he blatantly ignores Shylock's "But note me signior," turning to Bassanio with a series of complacent *sententiae*:

> Mark you this Bassanio,
> The devil can cite Scripture for his purpose,—
> An evil soul producing holy witness
> Is like a villain with a smiling cheek,
> A goodly apple rotten at the heart.
> O what a goodly outside falsehood hath!
>
> (I.iii.92–97)

These lines demonstrate Antonio's dismissive prejudgment of Shylock's Mosaic tale, which Antonio sees as an attempt to use a Christian argument. Shylock's explanation in biblical terms is seen as *prima facie* proof of falsehood, an illegitimate assumption of (Christian) image: the book is their book, and can only legitimately reveal their truths. His attempt to enlist their language in order to be taken seriously is doomed to confusion.

It is significant that Shylock is condemned in terms of having a false outside: a double attitude toward assumed surfaces is revealed here. The creation of an attractive image can be regarded as a deception when one dislikes the perpetrator, while the same sort of performance by an ally is regarded either as laudable decoration or revelation of consonance of inner and outer value. The flexibility of this attitude allows for any convenient labeling of artificial surface, from moral falsehood to aesthetic accomplishment.

The rest of the third scene, and indeed of the entire bond story, revolves around the assumption that those excluded from the elite circle of community strength are powerless to change their state or affect those within. Shylock speaks bitterly of the contradiction between their normal debasement of him and their suit to him for money, with its implicit trivialization of any resentment he might feel. When he complains of a previous humiliation, Antonio says, "I am as like to call thee [dog] again, / To spet on thee again, to spurn thee too" (I.iii.125–126), inviting all the ruin he believes Shylock can offer. Shylock, more responsively aware of the ambiguity of language and experience than Antonio, conceives a revenge that is primarily a gesture that will evidence his existence as a figure of significance to those who feel safe inside the circle. The plan for revenge is couched in language whose threat is unreal to Antonio. It is more apparent to Bassanio, whose experience on the periphery has perhaps taught him more of life's unfunny jokes. Shylock's "merry sport," like Morocco's she-bear, is so violently and barbarically alien to Antonio's world that he regards it as absurd, and therefore trivial. Shylock has clearly counted on this, and to silence Bassanio, he shows how profitless the pound of flesh is from a mercantile point of view.

> If he should break his day what should I gain
> By the exaction of the forfeiture?
> A pound of man's flesh taken from a man,
> Is not so estimable, profitable neither
> As flesh of muttons, beefs, or goats,—I say
> To buy his favour, I extend this friendship.
>
> (I.iii.159–64)

By trivializing the bond in commercial terms and casting himself in the role of suitor, of "petty trafficker," Shylock suggests his comparative insignificance and the accuracy of the flattering social model earlier proposed for Antonio. Remaining orderly and insignificant in Antonio's eyes will enable Shylock to reduce him to the status of powerless and trivial tool, to be the definer instead of the defined.

In using the law for his own purposes of dominance and self-expression, Shylock performs an act of invasion formally parallel to Bassanio's—both attempt to engineer a change in status through the use of an ideologically weighted language. Bassanio's goal is participation in the group conferring identity, and in the attendant social and financial privileges. He compels desert by the manipulation of the systems of courtesy. Shylock desires not community with but dominance over his social superiors. He wants to invert the hierarchy, using the powers of authentication himself to spite the principles of reciprocity falsely asserted by the aristocratic ideology. This he aims to accomplish by precipitating out another ideologically affiliated system—the law—from its particular social and historical context, and positing it to be objective and available for use by all. In other words, he insists, in his literalist fashion, on taking the law at its face value. He insists on accepting as authentic and natural the law's claim to universality. He sees that his hope of power and parity rests on the separation of the law from single factional affiliation. He fails in the end precisely because the law is itself an ideological expression of the imperatives of the elite. In a most literal way, the ruling ideas here are the ideas of the ruling class; the law remains finally in the sole employ of its owners. The duke (a partial judge) has striven to recall Shylock to subordination through his own positive powers, "generously" attributing to him the "Christian" qualities of mercy and gentleness, contrasting him with "stubborn Turks, and Tartars never train'd / To offices of tender courtesy" (IV.i.32–33).[14] Shylock refuses these proffered signs of social inclusion because they would return him to hierarchical submission.

14. The function of the duke's intervention may be unfolded by reference to an analytic statement by Max Weber regarding the residual presence of such behavior in the legal context in the nineteenth century, when Shylock's perception of the law (though not his use of it in *The Merchant of Venice*) had become normative.

The modern capitalist concern is based inwardly above all on *Calculation*. It requires for its survival a system of justice and an administration whose workings can be *rationally calculated*, at least in principle, according to fixed general laws, just as the probable performance of a *machine* can be calculated. It is as little able to tolerate the dispensing of justice according to the judge's sense of fair play *in individual cases* or any other irrational means of principles of administering the law . . . as it is able to endure a patriarchal administration that obeys the dictates of its own caprice, or sense of mercy and, for the rest, proceeds in accordance with an inviolable and sacrosanct, but irrational tradition. . . . What is specific to modern capitalism as distinct from the age-old capitalist forms of acquisition is that the strictly rational *organisation of work* on the basis of *rational technology* did not come into being *anywhere* within such irrationally constituted political systems nor could it have done so. For these modern businesses with their fixed capital and their exact calculations are much too sensitive to legal and administrative irrationalities. They could only come into being in the bureau-

His power rests on his assertion of the law's absoluteness; admission of the possibility of interpretation or compromise would return him to the realm of the contingent, and place his status in the determination of others. He insists on staying beyond their reach, refusing to justify his acts in their terms. He replies instead in language which to them is irrational, beyond the pale of intelligibility, a language of other inexplicable acts, of cats and pigs and hatred which, long denied entrance to the system of civilization, now refuses to be domesticated. Shylock is no longer bound to communicate at all, for he now sees himself as not bound to the hierarchical social body, but to the law. He is therefore not bound to confer upon them the commensurate status that conversation implies.

Shylock has engineered a figure-and-ground reversal by forcing the elite to accept the sort of diminution of identity and social stature which grows directly from their own systematic oppression. In this way he universalizes his own plight as dehumanized tool and disposable slave of order.

> You have among you many a purchas'd slave,
> Which (like your asses, and your dogs and mules)
> You use in abject and in slavish parts,
> Because you bought them,—shall I say to you,
> Let them be free, marry them to your heirs?
> Why sweat they under burthens? let their beds
> Be made as soft as yours, and let their palates
> Be season'd with such viands? you will answer
> "The slaves are ours,"—so do I answer you:
> The pound of flesh which I demand of him
> Is dearly bought, 'tis mine and I will have it:
> If you deny me, fie upon your law!
> There is no force in the decrees of Venice:
> I stand for judgment,—answer, shall I have it?
>
> (IV.i.90–103)

At the moment of his greatest power, Shylock presses his audience to recognize the implications of the ideology of universal harmony by redi-

---

cratic state with its rational laws where . . . the judge is more or less an automatic statute-dispensing machine in which you insert the files together with the necessary costs and dues at the top, whereupon he will eject the judgment together with the more or less cogent reasons for it at the bottom: that is to say, where the judge's behaviour is on the whole *predictable*.

(Quoted in Georg Lukacs, "Reification and the Consciousness of the Proletariat," in *History and Class Consciousness*, trans. Rodney Livingstone [Cambridge, Mass., 1971], p. 96).

recting its oppressive faculties onto one of their own, thereby forcing them
to confront an example they cannot ignore. In demonstrating its oppression of one, he reveals its oppression of many, demystifies the universal
harmony of the dominant ideology, and stops the dance. It is an arresting
moment in Elizabethan literature.

It is also very brief, for the play shifts its tone from tragicomic insight
to saturnine *deus ex machina*: ironically named Portia, the voice of
inequity[15] enters to restore the imbalance after Shylock's profound demystification. Her famous "quality of mercy" speech is specifically presented as a *compulsion* ("on what compulsion must I be mercifull," he has
asked); mercy itself is presented as an attribute of power. Portia also offers
Shylock apparent membership in the class establishment in return for his
assent to a vocabulary that would wash away the foundation of his power.
She argues that they are governed by a Christian rule of mercy, and that
Shylock is one of them:

> Though justice be thy plea, consider this,
> That in the course of justice, none of us
> Should see salvation: we do pray for mercy,
> And that same prayer, doth teach us all to render
> The deeds of mercy.
>
> (IV.i.194–198)

Therefore, she reasons, "must the Jew be merciful." Shylock scoffs at her
concern for his salvation ("my deeds upon my head!") and insists on the
solidity of his claim at written law, rather than trust in the law his
opponents call divine. He knows they are not bound by this law, and he
cannot bind them with it either. His power is contingent upon the escape
from the positive into the putatively natural.

Bassanio sees this, and seeks to have the duke take this weapon from
Shylock by setting aside the law. But this, of course, would involve
setting aside its claim to be natural rather than positive. Shylock, as
Burckhardt notes, would be forcing them to espouse publicly the mode of

---

15. Regarding the discussion of equity in relation to *The Merchant of Venice*, see Mark
Edwin Andrews, *Law versus Equity in 'The Merchant of Venice'* (Boulder, Colo., 1965); W.
Moelwyn Merchant's introduction to his New Penguin edition of the play (Har-
mondsworth, 1967); W. Nicholas Knight, "Equity, *The Merchant of Venice*, and William
Lambarde," *ShS*, XXVII (1974), 93–104.

positivism which he shares with them, but which they deny.[16] To admit
the law's flexibility would call the fictive ground of their power into
question; they dare not do so, and Shylock knows it.

Portia has, of course, a prepared solution to the problem, and the way
she implements it shows, as A. D. Moody observes, that her goal is not
just saving Antonio, but "putting Shylock at the mercy of his enemies."[17]
By repeated ironic demonstration of the irreducible nature of the stated
law she leads Shylock to be utterly confident in it, and to reveal his
murderous urge to destruction and revenge; in so doing she creates an
emotional setting ideal for his destruction.

This she accomplishes with great economy by means of two graceful
strokes of positive power. First, she reveals that the objective certainty of
the law, by means of which Shylock thought to bind its makers, is still
subject, despite all his efforts, to creative interpretation. When she finds
no mention of a jot of blood, she reveals the language of the law as
infinitely interpretable, as the ongoing creation of its native speakers, who
maintain their power precisely by "ad libbing" with it. Portia discovers
the necessary escape clause in the white spaces between the lines, where no
strict construction is possible.

Though the reading regarding the blood is sufficient for Shylock's
destruction (loss of lands and goods and—according to line 328—life),
Portia adduces a second legal weapon (Shakespeare's own creation, not in
the sources) which not only renders Shylock's defeat irrevocable, but
places it in an explicitly ideological perspective. It seems that any *alien*
who plots against the life of a citizen loses his goods and places his life at
the mercy of the duke. As W. H. Auden observes, the effect of this is to
show that factional bias is built in even in law, that Shylock was excluded
by definition as alien to begin with.[18]

The ideology is redeemed, and the aristocratic identity reaffirmed,
through Shylock's destruction. Portia's speech on mercy functions precisely as an ideological weapon. The final driving-home of this irony is
Shylock's forced conversion. Blatantly a mockery and punishment (here an

16. Burckhardt, pp. 229–230.

17. A. D. Moody, *Shakespeare: The Merchant of Venice*, Studies in English Literature,
No. 21 (London, 1964), p. 43.

18. W. H. Auden, "Brothers and Others," in *The Dyer's Hand* (1963; rpt. New York,
1968), p. 229.

alternative only to death), compulsory conversion is associated historically with confiscation of goods by the state.[19] Shylock is denied his wealth, his original means to power, which excludes him thoroughly from creative activity in the world of significance.[20] In this light the brilliance of the solution to the Shylock problem is evident even now: it still has such power to bend the perception of observers to its will as to lead some readers to say, with Nevill Coghill, that "Shylock [has] at least been given the chance of eternal joy"![21] This issue of generosity is a phantom, however; Shylock has simply been rendered totally powerless in the secular world of the play (the only world there presented—real Christian transcendent options are completely absent). He equates his impoverishment with death: "you take my life / When you do take the means whereby I live" (IV.i.372–373). Spiritual generosity to Shylock is in fact a guise for material generosity to Antonio, the state, and Lorenzo and Jessica. The dissonance of this ironic windfall of goods with the traditional schematic access of joy and riches in comic resolution suggests that Shakespeare began earlier than is usually thought to test the implications of genre (and the awareness of his audiences) as he later did in the "problem comedies." The resolution fits in letter but not in spirit, as is appropriate for its legalistic content.

Shylock's defeat concludes with one last reminder of positive power. If Shylock refuses to submit to the proposed conversion, the duke says he will withdraw the pardon just offered. The immutably natural law of Venice is shown again to be open to interpretation and revision whenever it is advantageous to its own. The trial finally crushes Shylock between the law's immutability and its fluid capacity to redefine itself at will. Shylock cannot maintain his heterodox identity; he is stamped into the mold designed for him.

---

19. See Wilbur Sanders, "Appendix A: Barabas and the Historical Jew of Europe," in *The Dramatist and the Received Idea* (Cambridge, Eng., 1968), p. 349.

20. It is interesting to note a sexual parallel here with the unsuccessful suitors for Portia's hand, who are forbidden to wive, to build a family. Shylock, whose loss of his bags and stones has already been mocked in implicitly sexual terms, and whose "gentle" daughter has (been) stolen away, is here financially castrated, rendered impotent. In yet another way Bassanio and Shylock ventured for similar rewards, and ran similar risks.

21. Nevill Coghill, "The Basis of Shakespearean Comedy," *Essays and Studies*, N.S. III (1950), quoted in Moody, p. 18.

## III

The deflation of Shylock is the enabling event for the fifth act's generically typical articulation of harmony. The denseness of Shakespeare's resolution of the play's issues goes beyond the concerns of this essay, but certain of his uses of traditional symbols for harmony infold and bring to summation the problem of class invasion and the ideological hedges which render it so difficult. The obtrusive references to art and the folk motif of the ring are the two chief such tools.

Lorenzo and Jessica effect a counterpoint to the actions of Bassanio and Portia which provides a context for the allusions to artful harmony. In each case an outsider enters the privileged group by means of manipulated appearance. Jessica's entry recasts Bassanio's in such a way as to reveal much more openly the strategic nature of the venture and the rewards at its end.

> She hath directed [says Lorenzo]
> How I shall take her from her father's house,
> What gold and jewels she is furnish'd with,
> What page's suit she hath in readiness.
>
> (II.iv.29–32)

Jessica has prepared to direct and act in her own drama, the fictional status of which is appropriately offensive to her father on various grounds. His mode of dealing with Christian assertions of status has been shown to be that of demystification. He objects repeatedly to the public legitimation of licensed display and disguise ("varnish'd faces") embodied in Lorenzo's masque; the creative and interpretive mode which governs the wooing plot is contemptible to him. He condemns this prominence of style as merely superficial, as "shallow fopp'ry," under which hide the same selfish motivations belied by the elite's abstract claims to law and honor. These motivations are made quite clear during the actual "theft" of Jessica: "Here catch this casket, it is worth the pains," she says; "I will make fast the doors and gild myself / With some moe ducats, and be with you straight"; "Now, by my hood, a gentle, and no Jew," Gratiano observes; Lorenzo judges that "true she is, as she hath prov'd herself" (II.vi.33,49–51,55). Jessica proves her truth by falsehood to her father, and she is finally a more faithless Jew than he. She is true, however, to the canons of truth of the class she has joined, both in her acquisition of her financial inheritance and in her celebration with Lorenzo in Genoa, where they display their credentials by lavish spending and revelry, trading Leah's ring for a monkey. True love, exploitation, and the demonstration of identity here coalesce.

They continue this demonstration in Belmont, trading classical allusions and reflexively apostrophizing the music of the spheres, praising its reduction to order of the "wild and wanton herd." "The man that hath no music in himself," Lorenzo says, "nor is not moved with concord of sweet sounds, / Is fit for treasons, stratagems, and spoils" (V.i.83–85). Given the ideological connotations of art already established in earlier acts, Lorenzo's assimilation of himself and Jessica to the celestial harmony is suggestive. While his lines do assert Shylock's unmusical discontinuity with the romantic world of Belmont, as has often been noted, their underlying reference here is to the "treasons, stratagems, and spoils" of the elopement of Lorenzo and his bride. The familiar redemptive force of the harmonious consciousness is questioned here. The imagination is turned to competitive uses, the "concord of sweet sounds" is chiefly a stratagem, and the spoils accrue to those who artfully elevate private urges to the status of universal harmony. The comic decorum of Act V is achieved with many of the same tools of poetic assertion which make the endings of happier plays glow with warmth and love, but their earlier use for gain, and to maim Shylock, render their full credibility suspect in this play. The mythic glow of the final circle's inclusiveness is founded upon the suppressed factional benefit of its exclusions.

The ring motif with which the play ends makes this concrete. In the first place, it presents the resolution of the trial (in the destruction of Shylock) as a comic matter for the Christians, in the risible as well as beneficent sense. Portia had always found it so, laughing from the start in Act III about the fun she and Nerissa should have at their play-acting. During the trial there are repeated comic asides and ironies, and after Shylock is expelled Portia institutes the practical joke of taking the rings as payment. Auden has noted in his analysis of Iago, another Venetian, how the practical joke depends on the contemptuous objectification of its victim.[22] This principle underlies Iago's destruction of Othello, and Portia's defeat of Shylock in this play. Her game with the ring echoes the trial

22. "The Joker in the Pack," in *The Dyer's Hand* (1963; rpt. New York, 1968), pp. 246–272.

in a comic key, judging Bassanio's transgression to be insignificant and including the victim in the final mutuality. The risk of the loss of community emphasizes its value: the social fabric is intentionally torn and then reestablished by the revelation of the threat's ludic status. The strategy is similar to the use made of Shylock: the threat is made ludicrous (as Gratiano's graceless laughter shows), and the shared joke again confirms the group's identity.

The play closes on a final note of joking anxiety combining the major themes of sharing and exclusion: "Well, while I live, I'll fear no other thing / So sore, as keeping safe Nerissa's ring" (V.i.306–307). The comedy ends not with the departure for a wedding, since that has already taken place, but with an anticipation of future anxiety. The obsessive Elizabethan cuckoldry joke was founded on both fear of and delight in the burglar. Here its application to the play's themes of inclusion and exclusion, invitation and invasion, wooing and assault, allows Shakespeare to synthesize the erotic and class-oriented aspects of his purposes in one image. The fascination with cuckoldry seems to have arisen from the conjunction not primarily of sexes, but of classes: the typical cuckold is bourgeois, his burglar a socially elevated or pretentious rake. If in this play the lover enters through the front door, and gains rank and status as well as sex, he still partakes of the scheming trickster. He must still pick Portia's locks with the keys of courtesy, while Lorenzo, his masked alter ego, steals daughter, stones, and ducats alike. Both circumvent the safeguards of possessive old men. Gratiano, Bassanio's most figural alternate, is most given to blunt signals; his itch and his fear, on the way to the marriage bed, close the play with a carefully infolded emblem of these major themes of class interaction. For, as Kenneth Burke suggests, "the relations between classes are like the ways of courtship, rape, seduction, jilting, prostitution, promiscuity, with variants of sadistic torture or masochistic invitation to mistreatment."[23] If the audience delights in the cuckoldry joke, if the climber, the social second-story man, cannot think of enjoying his bride without crossing himself with the talismanic invocation of the housebound husband, *The Merchant of Venice* must simply be seen to end with, and arouse in its audience, the contradictions of the socially mobile culture it reflects.

23. Burke, p. 115.

## IV

Lawrence Stone provides a convenient summary of the nature and function of the dominant ideological patterns of late-sixteenth-century England. They

> present a picture of a fully integrated society in which stratification by title,
> power, wealth, talent, and culture are all in absolute harmony, and in which
> social mobility is consequently both undesirable and unthinkable. Reality, how-
> ever, is always somewhat different.
>     This ideological pattern and . . . measures designed to freeze the social struc-
> ture and emphasize the cleavages between one class and another were introduced
> or reinforced at a time when in fact families were moving up and down in the
> social and economic scale at a faster rate than at any time before the nineteenth
> and twentieth centuries. Indeed it was just this mobility which stimulated such
> intensive propaganda efforts.[24]

Carefully restricted social and sexual intercourse played major roles in this
ideology of harmony, which presented itself as a natural model of reciprocal interaction while exploiting the less artful. Despite his investment in
the discriminations of hierarchy, Castiglione provided "conventions of
enrichment and fantasy"[25] both to those who would freeze the class
structure and to those who would invade its upper reaches from below. At
the same time Elizabethan jurists were energetically elaborating a legal
system which came increasingly to be used as a major weapon in the war
between those who sought and those who denied. The outcry against
law-mongering from all sides reveals its universal employment. These
pursuits of power through stylistic nuance and verbal complexity had by
the century's end generated profound disorder among the supposedly
mutual and well-beseeming ranks of the Elizabethan polity. Yet the pursuit of status and privilege was always coated with the necessary legitimat-
ing colors—for which the justification of another charming Shakespearean
thief may stand: "Why, Hal, 'tis my vocation, Hal, 'tis no sin for a man to
labour in his vocation."[26]

24. Stone, p. 36.
25. See note 1 above.
26. *The First Part of King Henry IV*, The Arden Shakespeare (London, 1960), I.ii.101–
102.

# Renaissance Magic and the Return of the Golden Age: Utopianism and Religious Enthusiasm in The Alchemist

## JOHN S. MEBANE

T HE OCCULT SCIENCES had a symbolic significance for Ben Jonson and his contemporaries which modern scholarship is just now beginning to appreciate. Heavily influenced by ancient Gnosticism, intellectual Renaissance magic embodied a view of man as a divine creature who can learn to control the creative forces of nature. It carried to its logical extreme the optimistic strain of Renaisance thought which emphasized man's ability to purify both his own soul and his social and natural environment, and in some instances it was a significant force behind movements for political and religious reform in the period.

In the following pages I propose to show that Ben Jonson was acutely aware of these philosophical, political, and religious implications of Renaissance magic when he wrote his masterful satire on occultism, *The Alchemist*. He had correctly observed that occultism often went hand in hand with utopianism and millenarianism, and he saw that it was dependent upon an unorthodox theory of private divine inspiration, or "enthusiasm." He sets out in *The Alchemist* to satirize the entire concept of human nature which magic had come to symbolize. In the most general terms, Jonson mocks the idea that man is a demigod who can perfect his

own nature, control time and change, or perfect through his art—whether
literary, magical, or political—the fallen world. More specifically, Jonson
ridicules the notion that the soul of the magus—or of a Puritan, or of
anyone else—can enter into a special relationship with God and become a
vehicle of His creative power. No one man or sect is God's unique representative on earth, Jonson tells us, and the claim to private religious
revelation made by magicians or by Puritan dissenters is merely a
rationalization of their delusions of grandeur and their concealed, self-
centered ambitions.

The foundations of philosophical occultism in the Renaissance were
established by Marsilio Ficino and Pico della Mirandola. The movement
was popularized by Paracelsus, Cornelius Agrippa, and others, and became prominent in Jonson's England through John Dee, Giordano Bruno,
and a host of English Paracelsians.[1] In this tradition, which draws heavily
upon the ancient Gnostic *Hermetica*, the pseudo-Hermetic writings, and
the Jewish Cabala, we hear consistently that the magus who can perform
such miracles as the alchemical transformation of *species* is a contemplative
soul who has developed a special relationship with God. The soul which
performs magic is, in Ficino's terms, "that which commands the fantasy
to lie silent, and burning with desire for the supernal divinity, relies not
on the common discourse of natural reason, but lives in the mind alone,

1. One of the seminal works on the occult tradition is Frances Yates's *Giordano Bruno
and the Hermetic Tradition* (1964; rpt. New York, 1969), a book to which I am deeply
indebted. Additional relevant works by Yates are *Theatre of the World* (Chicago, 1969); *The
Art of Memory* (Chicago, 1966); *The Rosicrucian Enlightenment* (London, 1972); and *Shakespeare's Last Plays: A New Approach* (London, 1975). Daniel P. Walker provides basic
information on magical theory in the Renaissance in *Spiritual and Demonic Magic from Ficino
to Campanella* (1958; rpt. Nendeln, 1969) and in *The Ancient Theology* (Ithaca, N.Y.,
1972). On the influence of occultism in England and on connections between magic and
both politics and art see the following: Walter Pagel, *Paracelsus: An Introduction to
Philosophical Medicine in the Era of the Renaissance* (New York and Basel, 1958); Allen G.
Debus, *The English Paracelsians* (New York, 1965); Keith Thomas, *Religion and the Decline
of Magic* (New York, 1971); Peter French, *John Dee: The World of an Elizabethan Magus*
(London, 1972); R.J.W. Evans, *Rudolf II and His World: A Study in Intellectual History,
1576–1612* (Oxford, 1973); and S. K. Heninger, Jr., *Touches of Sweet Harmony: Pythagorean
Cosmology and Renaissance Poetics* (San Marino, Calif., 1974).

My own initial research on magic was generously guided and encouraged by Professor
Frank Manley of Emory University. Portions of my subsequent research were aided by a
grant from the Troy State University Research Fund.

becomes an angel, and receives God entirely within his breast."[2] Pico, like Ficino, describes specific stages of a process of "purgation, illumination, and perfection," and he refers to this process of self-purification, as did the alchemists, as a series of "transformations" or "metamorphoses" through which the individual psyche proceeds upward on the Chain of Being toward union with the divine. The final stage of the soul's ascent is the direct illumination of the *Mens*, the highest human faculty, through the descent of the Holy Spirit.[3] It is in this final, suprarational stage of enlightenment that man receives the power to perform the highest forms of magic. He comes to understand all of the occult correspondences between earthly things and the celestial and supercelestial powers which govern them, and his knowledge brings with it the ability to control, through the manipulation of names and numerological symbols, the creative forces of nature. "Magic," Pico proclaims, "is the practical part of natural science."[4] Once the magus has completed the contemplative ascent he perceives the relationships between the divine Ideas and the imperfect reflections of those Ideas in fallen nature. His aim in transitive magic is to regenerate earthly creatures by bringing them into more perfect conformity with their archetypes.

This desire to reform both man and nature became the central motif of philosophical alchemy in the Renaissance. Paracelsus, in particular, makes clear that the role of the alchemist is to perfect and purify what nature leaves imperfect.[5] As an alchemical physician, he claimed to be able to

2. *Theologia Platonica*, ed. Raymond Marcel (Paris, 1964), II, 237. Translations are my own unless I note otherwise.

3. Pico describes the stages in the soul's ascent in his famous *Oration*, trans. Charles Glenn Wallis as *On the Dignity of Man* in *Pico della Mirandola: On the Dignity of Man, On Being and the One, Heptaplus* (Indianapolis, Ind., 1965), and in his magical and Cabalist *Conclusions, Opera Omnia* (1557; rpt. Hildesheim, 1964), I, 104–109, and passim. Many of the most important implications of Pico's *Conclusions* are drawn out and made much more explicit in Cornelius Agrippa's *De Occulta Philosophia Libri Tres* ([Mechlin?], 1533), especially in passages in which Agrippa incorporates statements he has obviously copied from Pico into his own text and then expounds them. Agrippa's interpretations of Pico, Ficino, and others are especially significant because of the direct influence of his work upon Jonson's contemporaries, particularly John Dee. In addition to the original edition of Agrippa an English translation exists in *Three Books of Occult Philosophy*, trans. J. F. (London, 1651).

4. Magical Conclusion Number Three, *Opera Omnia*, I, 104.

5. See, for example, "Alchemy: The Third Column of Medicine," trans. A. E. Waite in *The Hermetic and Alchemical Writings of Paracelsus* (London, 1894), II, 148.

extract from natural substances certain elixirs, tinctures, and quintes-
sences which could renovate the human body, restore youth and strength,
and drive out disease and impurity. He asserted that he had received
special revelations which made him the leader of a new era of enlightenment in which the common man—if he would follow Paracelsus's teach-
ings and the promptings of the Holy Spirit—could possess an occult
wisdom which was denied to established religious, intellectual, and political authorities.[6] Philosophical alchemy in the sixteenth and seventeenth
centuries, then, was not simply an attempt to transform base metals into
gold; it was an extension of the process of redemption to the entire
terrestrial realm. The adept first purifies his own personality, then proceeds to carry out God's plan for the perfection of the cosmos.

The idea that the magus can act as God's agent on earth became a
significant force behind some of the messianic millenary movements of the
Renaissance. With increasing frequency as the sixteenth century
progressed the magicians' dream of bringing heaven to earth came to
include not only the perfection of man and nature, but a universal religious and political reform, as well. Many of the reformers, such as Paracelsus and Guillaume Postel, relied primarily upon a program of universal
enlightenment; others, however, engaged in various kinds of overt political activities. Tommaso Campanella, whose utopian *City of the Sun* is
modeled after the magical city founded by Hermes Trismegistus in the
Arabic *Picatrix*, led a revolt in Calabria in 1598–1599; he later came to
center his hopes for the creation of a universal Christian empire around
Louis XIII of France and, subsequently, Pope Urban VIII, for whom he
performed magical ceremonies.[7] The researches of Frances Yates, R.J.W.
Evans, Peter French, and others are also bringing to light the enormous
importance of occultism in stimulating the creation of cults of mystical
imperialism around such monarchs as Rudolf II of the Holy Roman Empire and Elizabeth I in England. Among the central figures behind imperialistic projects are Giordano Bruno and John Dee, both of whom were

6. A good summary of Paracelsus's claims may be found in "The Book Concerning the
Tincture of the Philosophers," in *ibid.*, I, 19–30.

7. Basic information on magic and millenarianism in Postel may be found in William
J. Bouwsma's *Concordia Mundi: The Career and Thought of Guillaume Postel* (Cambridge,
Mass., 1957). On Campanella see Yates, *Giordano Bruno*, pp. 360–397, and Walker's
chapter on Campanella in *Spiritual and Demonic Magic*.

active in London in the late sixteenth century and helped, through their own notoriety, to initiate the debate over magic which began in the literature of those years. It is well known that Dr. Dee was one of the most influential spokesmen for Elizabethan imperialism, and in his recent study of the English magus Professor French has shown that Dee's plans for British expansion sprang directly from his occult studies and his "mystical vision of Britain as the leader in reuniting Christian Europe and re-establishing the new golden age of civilization."[8] In fact Dee actually proposed to use practical magic in the service of the British army and navy. In 1581 he had begun to use the Cabalistic mathesis of Agrippa's *Occult Philosophy* in an attempt to summon angels from the supercelestial world and learn from them the secrets of the universe. He was aided by Edward Kelley, who acted as his medium and who probably duped him. Dee always approached these experiments in the pious spirit of a man who hoped to be granted a closer relationship with God, but he also planned to use the knowledge he gained from the angels for practical purposes. He believed it was his sacred duty to harness the occult forces of the universe (which he thought of in mathematical terms) in order to ameliorate man's earthly condition. This amelioration involved the extension to all men of the benefits of the just rule of Queen Elizabeth and the true religion of English Protestantism (tempered with Dee's Hermeticism), and he therefore placed his knowledge at the service of Elizabeth's armed forces.

In *The Alchemist* Jonson alludes prominently to Dee in Act II, scene 6, and at IV.i.89–91 he mentions Edward Kelley's association with Rudolf II of Bohemia.[9] It seems likely, in view of these and other topical allusions in the play, that Jonson is reminding us that the magicians' theories about imminent reform in Christendom apparently had had some influence upon English foreign policy, particularly Queen Elizabeth's formation of political alliances in the mid-1580s. Dee, Kelley, Bruno, and other occultists seem to have been involved in numerous secret political negotiations which were connected with their hopes of reform. As *The Alchemist*

8. *John Dee*, p. 56. In my account of Dee I have relied largely on French, though I have also referred to Evans, *Rudolf II*, esp. pp. 218–228; Yates, *Giordano Bruno*, pp. 148–150, 206–210, and passim, and *The Rosicrucian Enlightenment*. On Bruno's activities in England, see Yates, *Giordano Bruno*, pp. 205–256.

9. References to *The Alchemist* are from *Ben Jonson*, ed. C. H. Herford and Percy and Evelyn Simpson, 11 vols. (Oxford, 1925–1952).

suggests, they were an important influence not only upon the cult of Elizabeth in England, but also on the apocalyptic mood of Europe in general in the late 1500s.

Students of English literature are probably most familiar with the millenary hopes of the 1580s and 1590s through *The Faerie Queene*, a work which Jonson is very likely satirizing in his treatment of Dapper's comical quest for Dol Common as "Queen of Faery." Spenser often hints in *The Faerie Queene* that the marriage of Arthur and Glorianna will initiate a new *Pax Anglica*. His epic is the most prominent of the fairly numerous literary works which prophesy, directly or indirectly and with varying degrees of seriousness, that Elizabeth will initiate a new Golden Age. Even poets who were not as deeply absorbed in occultism as I believe Spenser was, found in the terminology of Hermetic alchemy the perfect metaphor for the queen's power to transform the present Age of Iron into an era of peace and justice. A striking example is the following poem written by Sir John Davies, in which we find the symbol of alchemy combined with the conventional equation of Elizabeth with the mythical virgin Astraea, the goddess of Justice who had fled to the heavens at the close of the reign of Saturn but who promised to return to earth when the lost Golden Era was restored:

E   arly before the day doth spring
L   et us awake my Muse, and sing;
I   t is no time to slumber,
S   o many ioyes this time doth bring,
A   s Time will faile to number.

B   ut whereto shall we bend our layes?
E   ven up to Heaven, againe to raise
T   he Mayd, which thence descended;
H   ath brought againe the golden dayes,
A   nd all the world amended.

R   udenesse it selfe she doth refine,
E   ven like an Alchymist divine;
G   rosse times of yron turning
I   nto the purest forme of gold;
N   ot to corrupt, till heaven waxe old,
A   nd be refined with burning.[10]

10. Davies, *Complete Poems*, ed. A. B. Grosart (London, 1876), I, 129, as quoted by Yates in "Queen Elizabeth as Astraea," *JWCI*, X (1947), 63. "Queen Elizabeth as Astraea"

This poem epitomizes the ethos which Jonson is satirizing in his portrait of Epicure Mammon. At the time *The Alchemist* was written there had been attempts to revive the millenary enthusiasm of the late 1500s, and Jonson is intent upon exposing both the foolishness and the dangers of the belief that all of man's troubles in this life can magically disappear. In fact he quite deliberately links the magicians with the one other group which passionately asserted the possibility of radical reform in the seventeenth century—the extreme Puritans. The Protestant reformers and the occultists obviously have their differences, but in *The Alchemist* Jonson emphasizes their very real similarities. Most importantly, he links them together because both are "enthusiasts" who regard their own subjective inspiration as superior to any institutional authorities. It is this enthusiasm, or "possession," to use Jonson's own term, which gives rise to the spirited but unintelligible languages of the play, such as the enigmatic jargon of alchemy and the apocalyptic prophecies from Broughton which Dol spews forth in Act III. It is also what deludes some of Jonson's gulls into thinking they can establish a new political, social, and religious order.

Jonson mentions several groups of Puritan enthusiasts in *The Alchemist*, but one of the most important sects is the one to which Tribulation and Ananias belong, the Anabaptists. It is natural that he would single out this group for attack, since it was one of the most radical of all dissenting denominations. Their absolute faith in the direct revelations they received from God led them to set themselves above the established laws of church and state. The great majority of the Anabaptists were pacifists, but in several well-known instances the leaders of various splinter movements became violent revolutionary millenialists. They planned to initiate an earthly Kingdom of God characterized by egalitarianism, community of goods, and, in some instances, free love. By far the most infamous of the revolutionary Anabaptists were the two with whom Jonson has Subtle explicitly link Ananias and Tribulation: Jan Bockelson, better known as John of Leyden, and Bernt Knipperdollinck.[11]

---

and Yates's more recent *Astraea: The Imperial Theme in the Sixteenth Century* (London, 1974), in which the earlier essay is reprinted, contain a wealth of information on the cult of Elizabeth in general.

11. Allusions to Leyden and Knipperdollinck occur at II.v.13 and III.iii.24. For a detailed account of these and other revolutionary Anabaptists see Norman Cohn's *The Pursuit of the Millennium*, both the original version (New York, 1957) and the revised edition (New York, 1970).

Jonson could not have chosen better examples to illustrate his belief that the rhetoric of individualism and reform can become the tool of a vicious megalomania. After establishing themselves as messianic lords of Münster in the 1530s, Leyden and Knipperdollinck instituted a reign of terror which lasted for nearly a year. Claiming that God had ordered him to transform Münster into the New Jerusalem, Leyden had himself crowned as King of the World. He then appropriated for himself and his "court" of close followers practically all of the worldly goods of Münster's citizens. He also instituted polygamy and collected for himself a harem of fifteen wives. Emissaries from Münster were sent out to Anabaptist communities in neighboring provinces, and a wave of sympathetic rebellions shook northwestern Germany and the Netherlands. After a six-month blockade Münster was recaptured, but not before the population had been decimated by starvation and by Leyden's fanatical executions. The notorious uprising in Münster was often discussed in Jonson's day (in Nashe's *Unfortunate Traveller*, for example), and there was good reason for the authorities to be on guard against a similar outbreak in England. In 1591, for instance, a pseudo-messiah named William Hacket was executed for proclaiming in public that Elizabeth no longer ruled and that the English government must be reformed. The Anabaptist prophet John Wightman was burned as a heretic in 1612, the year of *The Alchemist*'s publication, for calling himself "Elias" or Elijah, the prophet whose return would presage the Second Coming. There is a long tradition of underground radical activity of this sort which surfaced only occasionally until the Puritan Revolution, when a series of utopian schemes and millenarian prophecies broke forth with such fury that even Oliver Cromwell at times found it difficult to control his own supporters. Frequently the radical reformers among the various sects, especially the Family of Love and the Anabaptists, were deeply absorbed in Hermetic alchemy. The occultists' theories of illumination and spiritual perfection coincided with those of the sectarians, and the radicals frequently claimed Paracelsus as a prophet whose predictions of reform were coming true in seventeenth-century England. When the sects felt increasingly free to express their ideas during the interregnum, an unprecedented flood of Hermetic and alchemical works was published. Often these treatises have a strong utopian or millenarian emphasis.[12]

12. *The Works of Thomas Nashe*, ed. Ronald B. McKerrow (London, 1910), II, 232–

Jonson uses the allusions to Leyden, Knipperdollinck, Henric Nicholas (an immigrant preacher of Anabaptist background who founded the Family of Love), Dee, Kelley, Paracelsus, Broughton, and others to make clear one of the contexts in which he wants *The Alchemist* understood. At one level, to be sure, the play ridicules ordinary charlatans who may have had little intellectual background and no political or truly religious motivation. But the grandiose utopian dreams of Mammon, Ananias, and Tribulation were not the usual stock-in-trade of the uneducated village wizard or London con artist. They are characteristic of a far more sophisticated and historically significant occult tradition. One of Jonson's major strategies in *The Alchemist* is to reduce the claims of that tradition to the level of ordinary fraud. The most interesting dimension of the play, to me, is its pointed satirical attack upon attempts at radical reform and upon the new individualism which Jonson saw penetrating into much of Renaissance political, economic, and religious life. Many of the characters' enthusiasms and pretensions are variations upon what Jonson perceives as a new self-centeredness which threatens to overthrow all stable social order. He was quite aware that the new individualism had received metaphysical justification in the occult tradition, and that is one of the reasons why he chose alchemy as the central, unifying symbol of the play. The quest for gold, which can symbolize either the soul's prelapsarian purity or fallen man's cupidity, was uniquely appropriate.

As we enter the opening scene of the play we should keep in mind a distinction between Jonson's concept of self-knowledge and that of the magicians. For the occultists self-knowledge is awareness of one's own divine origins, the consciousness of man's inherent divinity which may drive him, according to Ficino, to seek immediate union with God and to resist all restraints. This awareness of "the immeasurable magnificence of our soul" can even lead to the desire for universal conquest: "Man wishes no superior and no equal," Ficino had said, "and he will not suffer anything to be excluded from his command" (*Theologia*, II, 260). For Jonson, however, this drive for ascendancy is simply the consequence of the Fall. Self-knowledge is knowledge of one's limits, a more traditional

241; K. Thomas, *Religion and the Decline of Magic*, pp. 124–146 and 371–378; P. M. Rattansi, "Paracelsus and the Puritan Revolution," *Ambix*, XI (1963), 24–32; Christopher Hill, *The World Turned Upside Down: Radical Ideas During the English Revolution* (New York, 1972).

view and one which is quite opposed to that of the occultists. Self-awareness leads not to assertiveness, but to acceptance of one's position within a static hierarchy. It enables a man to assume his place in the human community and to enjoy the benefits of an ordered society. And the retreat from genuine self-knowledge into a realm of self-flattering illusion lay, for Jonson, precisely in the direction which the occultists, like the Puritans, believed led to truth: the withdrawal into the subjective.

The interrelated themes of self-knowledge, individualism, and radical reform are all introduced in the opening lines. We enter in the midst of a heated altercation in which Face and Subtle attack each other's false conceptions of self. When Face demands, *"Who am I, my mungrill? Who am I?"* Subtle retorts, *"I'll tell you, since you know not your selfe,"* and proceeds unmercifully to unmask him:

> SUB.
> Yes. You were once (time's not long past) the good,
> Honest, plaine, liuery-three-pound-thrum; that kept
> Your masters worships house, here, in the *friers*,
> For the vacations—
>
> FAC.
> Will you be so lowd?
>
> SUB.
> Since, by my meanes, translated suburb-Captayne.

(I.i. 15–19)

This is clearly not the description of himself which Face was asking for, and he seems momentarily crestfallen. Soon he retaliates, though, by reminding Subtle that he first found him a mere beggar, yet he took him in, exchanged his ragged clothes for a grand conjurer's costume, and gave him a house in which to practice his con-game artistry. On the last point Face leaves himself vulnerable again, for Subtle reminds him that the house in which they are practicing is not Face's, but his master's. Face is not the great man he has disguised himself to be; he is merely a rascally servant who has managed momentarily to turn his master's home into a bawdy house. Throughout the scene we are reminded that we are watching base characters—a dishonest servant, a cheap con man, and a whore—who have tried to rise above themselves through language and

through mere clothing.[13] By assuming theatrical costumes and adopting
an inflated jargon they have undergone illusory transformations to higher
states of being.

The themes of acting and disguise as forms of false metamorphosis are
connected with the central metaphor of "translation," or alchemical puri-
fication, each of the two con-men claiming to have "made" or "sublimed"
the other, to have raised him above his normal station in life. The cozeners
do not take their role playing literally, but it is, nonetheless (as in some
degree role playing always is), a means of acting out imaginatively a
seemingly infinite potential. It is also, for them, a delightful means of
deception, of turning the base passions of others into gold, and of "cocker-
ing up their genius," as Volpone, another consummate role player, might
put it. Subtle makes the connection between disguise, language, and
alchemical transformation clear when he explains how he has taken Face
"out of dung" and raised him above the status of mere butler:

> Thou vermine, haue I tane thee, out of dung,
> So poore, so wretched, when no liuing thing
> Would keepe thee companie, but a spider, or worse?
> Rais'd thee from broomes, and dust, and watring pots?
> *Sublim'd* thee, and *exalted* thee, and fix'd thee
> I' the *third region*, call'd our *state of grace?*
> Wrought thee to *spirit*, to *quintessence*, with paines
> Would twise have won me the *philosophers worke?*
> Put thee in words, and fashion? made thee fit
> For more then ordinarie fellowships?
> Giu'n thee thy othes, thy quarrelling dimensions?
> Thy rules, to cheat at horse-race, cock-pit, cardes,
> Dice, or what euer gallant tincture, else?
>
>                                             (I.i.64–76)

The speech moves to a climax in the sublime, symbolic language of the
magus, then descends rapidly to bathos. The phrase "Put thee in words,

13. Alvin Kernan has discussed the theme of false metamorphosis in Jonson's work in
*The Cankered Muse* (New Haven, Conn., 1959), in his introduction to *Volpone* (New Haven,
Conn., 1962), and in his recent edition of *The Alchemist* (New Haven, Conn., 1974).
Though I differ from Kernan on several points, I regard his insights as quite basic to our
understanding of Jonson. For additional analysis of the language of the play in relation to
the alchemical process see also Edward Partridge's *The Broken Compass: A Study of the Major
Comedies of Ben Jonson* (New York, 1958), esp. pp. 144 and 156–158.

and fashion" reveals that Face's transformation is no more magical than any other ordinary affectation. This movement from the sublime to the ridiculous is typical of many of the speeches of the play, and it characterizes the plot as well. Through disguises and inflated rhetoric the characters attempt to ascend in the social hierarchy, but because their transformations are superficial they are inevitably deflated again. The major action of the play is built upon the model of alchemical ascent and descent and also on the idea of stripping or deflation. Jonson continually reveals the comically ironic gap between the noble roles the characters have assumed and the base persons they really are.

Jonson's specific satire on London con artists is thus a vehicle for his broader attack upon the idea that man can in any way transcend his limits. Largely because of the influence of occultism in the Renaissance, metamorphosis and alchemical transformation had become widely used metaphors for man's ability to act out his infinite potential, and in *The Alchemist* Jonson manipulates these symbols so as to reduce to an absurdity the belief that man has unlimited powers. He loads the play with echoes of the occultists' optimistic praise of mankind, but by connecting the celebration of "man the great miracle" with charlatans and gulls he renders it mock-heroic. The suggestion that the ridiculous Dapper is the nephew of the Queen of Faeries, for example, is an absurd parody of Hermes Trismegistus's teaching that man is "akin to the race of daemons" as well as a mockery of *The Faerie Queene*. The central point of the play is the identification of *magia*, supposedly the highest of all arts and a symbol of man's divinity, with a deceptive con game. The characters transcend their places in the universal hierarchy only through superficial disguises and their own imagination; the entire operation is a cheat.

The theme of deceptive metamorphosis is also connected to Jonson's satire on Renaissance utopianism and millenarianism. As soon as he establishes the theme of false transformation and role playing he moves into the description of the relationship between the con artists as a republic or a commonwealth. Their "venture tripartite" is a political arrangement in which Face plays the role of "Captain" or "General" and Subtle that of "Sovereign." Dol seems at times to be the commonwealth or "body politic" itself, as when she tries to end Subtle and Face's argument by saying "Haue yet, some care of me, o' your *republique*—" (I.i.110). At other times, as when Subtle refers to her as "Royal Dol" or "Claradiana," she

assumes the role of queen. The important point is that the commonwealth
the three clowns have established is ordered in accordance with the
egalitarian ideals that Renaissance thinkers often associated with the lost
Golden Age. The pagan Golden Era, conventionally equated with the
Christian Eden, was frequently described as a time and place in which
man's selfish appetites—particularly lust and greed—had not yet cor-
rupted his will. Men acted out of spontaneous love and friendship, and the
restraint of external laws was unnecessary. They lived as members of one
great family; all goods were held in common, and there was no social
hierarchy. The ideals implicit in the myth sometimes became the basis of
actual programs of social reform.[14]

Dol clearly alludes to these egalitarian principles when she scolds Face
and Subtle for the self-centered bickering which threatens to tear their
relationship apart. She asks what right either of them has to "claime a
primacie, in the diuisions" and insist upon being "chiefe" when their
agreement or "republique" was from the outset a "worke . . . begun out
of equalitie? / The venter *tripartite*? All things in common? / Without
prioritie?" Resolve your differences, she says, "and cossen kindly, / And
heartily, and louingly, as you should," or she herself will become "facti-
ous" (I.i.131–140). Her appeals to their reason and their sense of justice
fail, however, and she finally imposes order only by seizing Face's sword
and threatening to cut their throats. The problem, then, with the cozeners' commonwealth is that each presumably "equal" partner is always
trying to gain ascendancy over the others. The General attempts to take
over the republic, and the Sovereign tries to keep him in awe. Throughout
the play they call each other "rebels" and "traitors." Eventually Face and
Subtle contribute to their own undoing not only by overreaching, but by
ruthlessly competing with each other for Dol and for Dame Pliant. By
describing the trio's relationship as a political venture and then offering us
a comic display of their violent dissensions, Jonson has us laugh ourselves
into the awareness that fallen creatures simply cannot do without traditional restraints. A society built upon individualism and free from law and
social hierarchy becomes a chaos in which each person strives to bind all
others to his own will. Man cannot regain his prelapsarian innocence, as

14. Harry Levin analyzes numerous accounts of the myth and discusses its political
implications in *The Myth of the Golden Age in the Renaissance* (Bloomington, Ind., 1969).

some of the reformers had claimed, and consequently there must be restraints—restraints which Jonson always associates with traditional political and religious institutions—upon his pride and his lusts.

Once Jonson's satiric themes are established in the opening dialogue they develop rapidly. The alchemical symbol comes to embrace all of the areas of Renaissance life into which Jonson saw the new individualism (or, in his view, self-centeredness) penetrating—capitalism, religious dissent, republicanism, Epicureanism. The gulls appear in quick succession, all hoping to be "sublimed" or "raised" by Subtle's art. Each of them expects magic to enable him to escape his limits or to expand his powers. Dapper wants to become a great gamester and a gallant, Drugger to be transformed from a modest shopkeeper into a great merchant prince, Kastrill to become a fashionable quarreler and to rise above his class by marrying his sister to a knight. The Puritans want to become not merely dissenters, but a "faction, / And party in the realme" and perhaps even "temporall lords" themselves (III.ii.25–26, 52). But all of these fall short of Epicure Mammon, who imagines that he will be lord of a new world, "the envy of princes and the fear of states." His fancy carries him beyond the realm of the possible, convincing him that with the stone he will control time and change altogether. He echoes an actual claim of Paracelsus's when he tells Surly that he will "make an old man, of fourescore, a childe. . . . Restore his yeeres, renew him, like an eagle, / To the fifth age; make him get sonnes, and daughters, / Yong giants" (II.i.53–57), and in Act IV he compares Subtle's art to that of Aesculapius, the mythical physician who restored Hippolytus to life and whom Zeus slew lest men become immortal. Mammon's lusts are not merely of heroic proportions (he says he will make himself "a back / With the *elixir*, that shall be as tough / As Hercules, to encounter fiftie a night" [II.ii.37–39]), they are infinite. When he woos Dol in Act IV his description of his boundless appetites combines with the imagery of disguise and metamorphosis:

> Wee'll therefore goe with all, my girle, and liue
> In a free state; where we will eate our mullets,
> Sous'd in high-countrey wines, sup phesants egges,
> And haue our cockles, boild in siluer shells,
> Our shrimps to swim againe, as when they liu'd,
> In a rare butter, made of dolphins milke,
> Whose creame do's looke like opalls: and, with these

> Delicate meats, set our selues high for pleasure,
> And take vs downe againe, and then renew
> Our youth, and strength, with drinking the *elixir*,
> And so enioy a perpetuitie
> Of life, and lust. And, thou shalt ha' thy wardrobe,
> Richer then *Natures*, still, to change thy selfe,
> And vary oftener, for thy pride, then shee.
>
> (IV.i.155–168)

Mammon is one of many characters in *The Alchemist* whose language carries them beyond the bounds of reality and, as an expression of their own peculiar "humor," isolates them from the rest of humanity. He locks himself into a private world in which he imagines himself as a god. We often think of a Jonsonian "humor" as a mere affectation or idiosyncrasy, but in its broadest meaning it is a willingness to abandon the guidance of reason and give way to one's own selfish inclinations. It is allied with instinct, self-love, and inordinate passion.[15] In Jonson's more formidable characters it can become a dangerous monomania. In *The Alchemist* the idea of a "humor" as an all-consuming passion is linked to the theme of enthusiasm, or excessive religious zeal, to the concept of heroic or poetic *"furor,"* to the idea of being possessed by a spirit, and to the madness caused by inhaling the fumes of an alchemical laboratory. Since madness may be caused by syphilis, it is also associated with lustfulness, disease, and perhaps even with the plague which threatens London.

Tribulation makes some of these associations clear when he tells Ananias that even though Subtle's inhalation of fumes may stimulate excessive passion, "This heate of his may turne into a zeale" (III.i.31) and more firmly ally the alchemist with the Anabaptists. Subtle himself describes Mammon as "possessed" (I.iv.16), and the testimony of Mammon's own speeches bears out the accusation. In his case the peculiar excessive passion or "humor" is luxuriousness, and the language which expresses it is highly imaginative poetry. Like the jargon of alchemy, Kastrill's quarreling tongue, or the Puritans' religious cant, Mammon's poetic raving serves to block communication rather than to promote it. Instead of

15. On the relation between Jonson's theory of humors and his moral purposes see Hiram Haydn, *The Counter-Renaissance* (New York, 1950), pp. 385–387, and James D. Redwine, Jr., "Beyond Psychology: The Moral Basis of Jonson's Theory of Humour Characterization," *ELH*, XXVIII (1961), 316–334.

employing language to reach out to others, Mammon uses it to project the self-enclosed world of his own fantasy, an unreal world in which he can escape mortality and indulge his seemingly boundless lusts.

Jonson's exposure of Mammon's delusions is a part of his general attack upon the claims of occultists, prophetic poets, or any other enthusiasts to have special insights into the nature of reality. He reduces such claims to absurdity partially by destroying the idealistic theories of imagination on which they often rested. The occultists, in particular, had claimed that the magus's imagination could become linked to the *Mens* and that he therefore possessed visionary powers. Since images supplied by the fantasy were connected with archetypal Ideas within the *Mens*, the magus could thus apprehend the symbolic meaning of the forms of created things. The aim of the alchemist—and, in a sense, of the poet-as-magician—is to bring physical things into greater conformity with the Ideas that govern them. To be able to do this one must have passed through various stages of enlightenment and attained at least momentary union with God. The desire to thus purify oneself was described as a "divine" or "heroic" passion, and stages of the soul's ascent were the four *"furores."*

It is largely on the ambivalence of these terms in magical theory that Jonson bases his attack on occultism and, by association, the other forms of enthusiasm. He rejects the claim that the imagination can become linked with the mind's intuitive faculties and asserts the traditional view that it is allied with the senses and with physical desire. He agrees with those conservative Renaissance moral psychologists who believed that excessive emotion could distort the fantasy and cause it to form images which did not correspond to physical reality. If strict rational restraint was not exercised objects of desire might deceptively appear more attractive than they really were. This could in turn stimulate even greater passions, so that the soul became involved in a vicious cycle in which passion and imagination continually heightened each other. This cycle could continue until it produced actual madness, a complete divorce from reality.[16]

Almost all of Jonson's characters in *The Alchemist* suffer to some extent

16. Agrippa explains the occultists' theory of stages of enlightenment and the four *furores* in *De Occulta Philosophia*, esp. Bk. III, chaps. iii and xliv–xlix. For surveys of different attitudes toward imagination in the Renaissance see William Rossky's "Imagination in the English Renaissance: Psychology and Poetic," *SRen*, V (1958), 49–73, and George Williamson's "The Restoration Revolt Against Enthusiasm," *SP*, XXX (1933), 571–603.

from this kind of malady. Their idealized view of themselves and of the objects of their desire is not a true vision of a higher reality or of genuine human potential, but simply an illusion prompted by pride and lust and created by a diseased imagination. The gulls come to Lovewit's house predisposed to certain delusions, and it remains for Face and Subtle only to stimulate their ambition somewhat and allow them to gull themselves. Eventually, of course, even the gullers cozen themselves. Obviously they never take occultism per se at face value; in Face and Subtle Jonson has drawn portraits of the enthusiast-as-charlatan, in the Puritans and in Mammon he shows us the enthusiast-as-deluded-fool. But there is, nonetheless, a sense in which Face and Subtle do have an absurdly exaggerated faith in their own powers. As we saw in the opening dialogue, they use their disguises and trickery to inflate their self-esteem, and in the course of the action they become so elated by their own display of wit (e.g., see the image of ascent at IV.v.96–100) that they imagine they can fool an infinite number of gulls simultaneously. At the height of their success their plots explode, and they, much like the gulls, are forced to reassume the limited roles they normally play in society. The effect of all of this, of course, is to render absurd the notion that one can rise above one's place through a "heroic" or "divine" ambition. The "frenzy" which grips Jonson's characters is not a "heroic passion," but an ordinary madness.

Jonson dramatizes the self-delusions of his characters by showing us that their imagination leads them to "see" things which do not in reality exist. Mammon and Surly make the theme of "sight" explicit in the first scene of Act II:

> MAM.
> But when you see th' effects of the great med'cine!
> Of which one part proiected on a hundred
> Of *Mercurie*, or *Venus*, or the *Moone*,
> Shall turne it, to as many of the *Sunne*;
> Nay, to a thousand, so *ad infinitum*:
> You will beleeue me.
>
> SUR.
> Yes, when I see't, I will.
> But, if my eyes doe cossen me so (and I
> Giuing 'hem no occasion) sure, I'll haue
> A whore, shall pisse 'hem out, next day.
>
> (II.i.37–45)

Most of the characters in the play are unlike Surly in that they are quite willing to "see" things which are not there or to see both themselves and the fallen world as more exalted or divine than they really are. The best examples of this can be found in the scenes in which Mammon and, subsequently, Dapper, see Dol Common as a kind of goddess. When Face tells Dapper, "You are made, beleeue it, / If you can see her" (I.ii.154– 155), what he really means is that if Dapper can delude himself into seeing Dol Common as the Faery Queene he can be made a victim of Subtle's fraud. In Act V when Dapper actually does believe the woman whom the audience recognizes as the ridiculously disguised prostitute to be the mysterious Queen of Faeries, the absurdity of his delusion becomes physically visible. When Mammon courts Dol in Act IV he similarly deceives himself about her appearance. To begin with, he manages to see in her face the features of all the noble houses of Europe, while at the same time Face points out that "Her father was an Irish costermonger." As Mammon continues, he begins to wax poetic and to worship Dol. We may grant, of course, that Dol might well possess a kind of earthy attractive- ness; but the earthiness should be apparent enough to give the lie to Mammon's perception of "a certaine touch, or aire" in her face "That sparkles a diuinitie, beyond/An earthly beautie" (IV.i.64–66). What Mammon, like Dapper, sees in Dol is more a projection of his own desires and an indulgence of his own extravagant fantasy than it is a true percep- tion of the woman that stands before him. Jonson implies, I think, that something similar is true of all enthusiasts—lovers, poets, or magicians—who seriously claim to see in the physical world or in mortal women a reflection of a suprasensual reality. His criticism of the tendency to idealize the world (as was often done in the romances to which he mockingly alludes throughout the play) or to project into poetry a subjec- tive spiritual vision is what makes him, in large part, the father of English neoclassicism. He rejects the visionary and the more highly idealistic tendencies of Renaissance art and tries to get his reader back down to physical fact. His art is a search not for transcendence, but for knowledge of how to get on with the actual business of life in this world.

Subjectivism, as I have suggested, not only encloses the individual in a realm of illusion but also gives him a false sense of self-sufficiency which makes him resist all discipline and restraint. The satire on enthusiasm in *The Alchemist* is thus quite intimately related to its exposure of millenary schemes as merely sophisticated forms of outlawry. Jonson saw the old hierarchical order as a system in which love and law work together as the structure and the motivating force of society, and he alludes to love or charity and to law throughout the play. In the new Golden Age of which the "venture tripartite" is a caricature, however, men do away with laws and obey only the dictates of their own selfish humor. Subtle sums up the libertarian Golden Rule of the new era in a casual remark to Dapper, "Your humor must be law" (I.ii.70). Jonson also establishes the theme of lawlessness by having Face threaten to bring Subtle "within / The *statute* of *sorcerie, tricesimo tertio* / Of Harry the eight" (I.i.111–113), and by frequently reminding us that alchemy is illegal. He develops the idea that the new age will be a time of anarchy and self-interest most fully, of course, in his characterization of Mammon, his greatest satiric portrait of those who proclaimed the Renaissance as a new era of freedom in which the individual's potential could be fully unleashed. The deluded knight describes the Golden Age he will make with the stone as a time in which all restraints normally placed upon man's powers (that is, his lusts) will be done away with. He is a mock savior who preaches as the good news of his new dispensation, *"be rich.* / This day, thou shalt haue ingots; and, to morrow, / Giue lords th' affront" (II.ii.6–8). Epicure Mammon is anarchy personified, yet he masquerades as a prophet of humanitarian reform. Jonson establishes this ambivalence in the speech in which Subtle introduces Mammon to us:

> This is the day, I am to perfect for him
> The *magisterium*, our *great worke*, the *stone*;
> And yeeld it, made, into his hands: of which,
> He has, this month, talk'd, as he were possess'd.
> And, now, hee's dealing peeces on't, away.
> Me thinkes, I see him, entring ordinaries,
> Dispensing for the poxe; and plaguy-houses,
> Reaching his dose; walking *more-fields* for lepers;
> And offring citizens-wiues pomander-bracelets,
> As his preseruatiue, made of the *elixir*;
> Searching the spittle, to make old bawdes yong;
> And the high-waies, for beggars, to make rich:
> I see no end of his labours. He will make
> Nature asham'd, of her long sleepe: when art,
> Who's but a step-dame, shall doe more, then shee,
> In her best loue to man-kind, euer could.
> If his dreame last, hee'll turne the age, to gold.
>
> (I.iv.13–29)

*The Alchemist* as a whole builds up a grandiose, mock-heroic portrait of Mammon as an altruistic reformer whose magical power to remedy the ills of our fallen condition surpasses that of Nature herself. At the same time it continually deflates this illusion by revealing that what Mammon really wants is to destroy the social hierarchy and to serve his own lusts, to "Giue lords th' affront" and make old bawds young again. Aspects of his personality are reflected in several of the less important characters, but the most significant parallels are between Mammon and the Anabaptists.

The Puritans, too, have a dream of reforming society, of remaking the modern world in accordance with biblical Christianity. Tribulation calls their plan a "holy worke" (III.ii.16), identifying it as a type of alchemical *magnum opus* and thus bringing it within the scope of Jonson's central metaphor. They have hopes of "rooting out . . . th' *Antichristian Hierarchie*" (II.v.82–83) of the established church and destroying all traditions which conflict with their private revelations. The themes of enthusiasm or "possession" and of the contempt for law are naturally very highly developed in their case, particularly in Jonson's portrait of Ananias. In fact in Act III when Ananias's excessive zeal apparently threatens to alienate Subtle, Tribulation actually attempts to command the "spirit (of zeale, but trouble)" to silence within him (III.ii.84–85). Ananias is "a man, by reuelation,/That hath a competent knowledge of the truth" (III.ii.113–114), and he depends entirely upon his own conscience, not external authority, in deciding questions of ethics. When Tribulation raises the question of whether coining money is lawful, Ananias vehemently protests that the brethren are not subject to temporal authorities.

Jonson comically reveals, of course, that the Puritans' brand of individualism is, like all others in the play, self-serving, for the Anabaptists' appeal to conscience simply permits them to decide that "casting of dollers" for their own profit is lawful indeed. They claim they will use the stone as "medicine" for society's ills, but in reality they plan to use it to corrupt all forms of order. "*Aurum potabile*" is "The onely med'cine, for the ciuill *Magistrate*, / T'incline him to a feeling of the cause" (III.i.41–43), Tribulation tells Ananias, and Subtle explains at length how the stone can obtain political influence for the brethren. He makes it clear that to grant power to the Puritans would be to promote chaos:

> You cannot
> But raise you friends. Withall, to be of power

> To pay an armie, in the field, to buy
> The king of *France*, out of his realmes; or *Spaine*,
> Out of his *Indies*: What can you not doe,
> Against lords spirituall, or temporall,
> That shall oppone you?
>
> TRI.
>
> Verily, 'tis true.
> We may be temporall lords, our selues, I take it.
>
> SUB.
>
> You may be any thing . . .
>
> (III.ii.45–53)

Jonson deals with serious issues in his consideration of Tribulation, Ananias, and Mammon, and occasionally the comedy of *The Alchemist* verges toward the dark satire of *Volpone*. The play maintains its comic mood, however, by reducing the stature of its characters. Mammon's language, for example, is as powerful as Volpone's, but he himself is not really as formidable a threat to society. We never forget that he is a fool. When Lovewit appears at the end of the play, Mammon and practically all of the other characters, gulls and knaves alike, prove helpless. This ending, though, is controversial; many readers who quite properly look for social and moral purposes in a Jonsonian comedy are disturbed because Lovewit collaborates with Face in the final act and wins both Dame Pliant and the cozeners' accumulated self. The problem is compounded, it seems, by the fact that Face shares the benefits of Lovewit's success, and even Dol and Subtle escape any real punishment.[17]

These problems begin to resolve themselves, I think, if *The Alchemist* is seen not only as an attack upon greed and dishonesty, but as a mockery of the dream that a man can magically transform himself or the world in accordance with his private desires. If Jonson's aim, as I have argued, is to

17. Several of the most significant discussions of this issue are the following: John Enck, *Jonson and the Comic Truth* (Madison, Wis., 1957), pp. 159–168; Alan C. Dessen, "*The Alchemist*: Jonson's 'Estates' Play," *RenD*, VII (1964), 46–50; Jonas Barish, "Feasting and Judging in Jonsonian Comedy," *RenD*, N.S. V (1972), 25–28. My own position is consistent with that of Judd Arnold in "Lovewit's Triumph and the Jonsonian Morality: A Reading of *The Alchemist*," *Criticism*, XI (1969), 151–166. "Lovewit's Triumph" and Arnold's subsequent *A Grace Peculiar: Ben Jonson's Cavalier Heroes* (University Park, Pa., 1972) provide a survey of criticism and a detailed discussion of this problem.

mock his characters' pretensions and to expose their Faustian impulses as prideful self-delusions, then Lovewit quite logically appears on the scene as a man whose clear-sightedness, good nature, and common sense contrast sharply with the credulity and wild imagination of Mammon or the Puritans. Lovewit is not perfect, but at least he suffers from no delusions. He has wit enough to take advantage of what chance provides him, but he would hardly attempt to control Fortune herself, as Dapper wished to do. He is secure in his station as proper master of his household, and when Face tries to persuade him that the unusual occurrences at his home are "illusions" or are caused by "some spirit o' the aire" (V.iii.66), he dismisses the notion rather quickly and demands the plain truth. He does not force Dol, Face, and Subtle into prison, but he does at least require them to give up their costumes and assumed personalities. Face, in particular, reassumes his proper identity as Jeremy the Butler and is allowed by an indulgent master to remain in service. As Judd Arnold has pointed out, Lovewit is a self-possessed and intellectually superior aristocrat, a member of that class of persons whom Jonson most desired to please.[18] He is indeed not the sort of character one would create if one's purpose were to reform the knaves and gulls of the play, but if we realize that Jonson's aim is simply to deflate his characters' illusions, we can see that Lovewit suits his purposes admirably well.

Deflating illusions, of course, is Jonson's typical comic business. In *The Alchemist* he has effectively turned his wit against those who had embarked upon a subjective quest for a vision of perfection and for the power to make that vision an objective reality. The accuracy of his analysis of portions of Renaissance history is startling. As I mentioned at the outset of this essay, we are just now beginning to understand fully some of the implications of Renaissance magic which Jonson, judging from *The Alchemist*, perceived with exceptional clarity. Renaissance man as artist/ magician had found within himself a world of perfect form, and his ultimate aim—whether as magus, statesman, sculptor, or poet—was to embody that form in physical reality. The Hermetic alchemist thus believed he could perfect the *species* of all created things, and as alchemy blends into millenarianism we encounter the assertion that the magus can bring back the Golden Age, the lost prelapsarian world. When magic becomes a metaphor for poetry it embodies the belief that the world can be

18. "Lovewit's Triumph" and *A Grace Peculiar*, esp. pp. 1–9, 55–61.

idealized in a realm of poetic symbols: the artist's prophetic vision becomes the Golden World of art. When Jonson attacks occultism in *The Alchemist* he is questioning all of these things. He is saying that our own limitations and those of the world around us are something we must learn to live with.

In the changing currents of thought of the seventeenth century, occultism was a key issue, and Jonson's response to the occult tradition points clearly toward the solutions to Renaissance problems which subsequent writers will find sensible. His successors in the neoclassical tradition, seeking to restrain uncontrolled individualism, will reject all forms of Platonism and ally themselves with the new Baconian science which imposes strict limits upon the individual's powers of cognition even as it promises new knowledge through discipline and cooperative effort.[19] In fact one might argue that the butts of satiric attack in Jonson's plays and in neoclassical satire in general are the victims of Bacon's Idols, particularly the Idol of the Cave. Ben Jonson's ridicule of magical or Puritan enthusiasm and his willingness to limit his own art to the treatment of the practical affairs of the world of men and manners are what set him apart from most of his immediate predecessors and contemporaries and make him the acknowledged founder of a new movement. Like Pope, Swift, or Samuel Johnson in the next century, all of whom ridiculed occultism at some point in their major works, Jonson has no sympathy for the romantic longing for the absolute which leaves us wavering between exultation and despair and which characterizes so much of Renaissance literature. He regards the subjective quest for perfection as self-centered escapism, the belief that man can totally reform the world as a mere jest. In fact he does not even regard the disillusionment of the romanticist as tragic—that would bring *The Alchemist* quite close to *Dr. Faustus*—but as merely comical. He willingly reduces his vision of human stature. His art is not often as captivating as that of Marlowe or Shakespeare, because it is not meant to be. Its value is of another order. Its purpose is to convince us that what is really important is not an imaginary vision of infinite potential, but the concrete possibilities of the here and now.

19. See Joseph Mazzeo's suggestive chapter on Bacon in *Renaissance and Revolution: Backgrounds to Seventeenth-Century English Literature* (New York, 1965) and Donald J. Greene's discussion of the relationship between empirical science and the neoclassicists' sense of limit in "Augustinianism and Empiricism: A Note on Eighteenth-Century English Intellectual History," *ECS*, I (1967), 33–68.

# Crowd and Public in Bartholomew Fair

## LEO SALINGAR

Now, good people, pay attention, if you really like plain speaking. For now the poet feels impelled to reproach the spectators.

*The Wasps*

PROBABLY NO ENGLISH DRAMATIST has created the impression of a crowd upon the stage as vividly as Ben Jonson in *Bartholomew Fair*. There is a score of speaking parts, besides supers, calling for the audience's attention, in the midst of noise, smell, brawling, and confusion; and in contrast to his previous comedies, Jonson has not provided a master intrigue or a pair of master manipulators to impose an evident cohesion on the plot. Instead, we are to be shown at least half a dozen different characters or groups of characters—Littlewit and his party, Cokes and his party, Winwife and Quarlous, Overdo, the people of the Fair, Troubleall, the Watch—each of them pursuing their separate aims or interests at the Fair, and pursuing them, what is more, without any drive of consistency. It is true that Littlewit's desire to have his puppet play shown and his maneuvering to witness it form a constant factor in the total action; but this wish is not announced until the end of Act I, and does not govern the general action of the play until Act V. Similarly, Cokes is constant in his

141

desire to see the sights; but then Cokes is a scatterbrain, the quintessential sucker, incapable of resisting each successive distraction, still less of planning realistically to influence anybody else. The denizens of the Fair—Ursla, Knockem and Edgworth, and their associates, and Leatherhead and Joan Trash—are also consistent in their desire to exploit their visitors, but they are opportunists by nature, and their professional purpose breaks up, in dramatic terms, into separate coney-catching tricks and combinations, similar but not cumulative; they have tactics, as it were, but no dramatic strategy. As against them, Overdo and Busy wish persistently to expose the Fair or denounce it, but the targets of their officiousness are chosen at random; while Quarlous, the gentleman gamester, the only character whose role approaches that of the skillful intriguers in Jonson's earlier plays, also changes his objectives, and only emerges as an active intriguer in the second half of the play. No one, in effect, pursues the same specific goal for long, or continuously shares a goal with any other character.

Moreover, as Richard Levin points out in his lucid and influential analysis, a central motif in the action is the way the little parties of visitors to the Fair disintegrate when they get there and then reassemble in unexpected groupings—Grace, for example, escaping from Cokes's party to marry Winwife, Littlewit's widowed mother-in-law falling to Quarlous, and Littlewit's wife and Cokes's married sister fluttering together into Knockem's care as potential "birds o' the game." The general effect of organized confusion, or "controlled complexity" as Richard Levin calls it,[1] resembles a kermess by Bruegel; with the difference that in a Bruegel painting there may be a common activity, a dance or a wedding feast, to consolidate the composition, whereas Jonson, until the end, eschews any such focus. Toward the end of each act, he clusters a number of his actors together: for Overdo's oration at the close of Act II, for Nightingale's ballad and then Busy's assault on the gingerbread basket in Act III, in Act IV for the game of "vapours" and then for the scuffle at the stocks, and in the last act for the puppet play. But the cast is not the same from one such episode to another, the participants in each are at cross-purposes, whether as doers or observers; and until the puppet play, which is no more, after all, than a sideshow, brings nearly all of the actors to the same part of the Fair, these gathering points of the action are more like happenings than

---

1. "The Structure of *Bartholomew Fair*," *PMLA*, LXXX (1965), 172–179.

revels. In the play as a whole, the characters converge and affect each other because of an annual commercial attraction, the Fair; but they affect one another chiefly by contiguity, covertly or haphazardly, without any mark of collective order. Although it is a holiday occasion, they are not a community but a crowd.

The play would require an amazingly retentive spectator to summarize the plot. In performance, however, the confusion is not merely appropriate to the fairground setting but a source, as Jonson twice promises, of "delight." [2] It is orchestrated; it has a rhythm and pattern, in the use of different areas of the stage, in the introduction of alternating character groups and alternating types of motive, and in the sequences of the action. Beneath the surface disorder, there is an ebb and flow.

In attempting to describe this process in more detail, it will be helpful to take advantage of Professor R. B. Parker's likely conjectures about the staging of the first production of the play, at the Hope. [3] Briefly, he envisages two tents or booths, stage right and stage left, and the stocks midway between them, probably front-stage. If that was the arrangement, the tent at stage right could have been used, he points out, as the setting for Littlewit's house and later for the puppet show, the product of Littlewit's brain; stage left, in the traditional location for Hell-mouth, would be Ursla's pig booth; and the open central area of the stage could be used for the pitch of the toyman and the gingerbread woman, and the miscellaneous comings and goings of the Fair. If so, there would be a spatial rhythm in the action. Act I concentrates on the "house" at stage right; the middle acts divide attention between the central stage and stage left, with a strong emphasis on Ursla's booth in Act II, more fluid movement in Act III, and staccato interchange in Act IV between the unlocalized mid-stage, the booth and the stocks; while Act V swivels attention toward stage right again.

Such an arrangement would make for an orderly, quasi-cinematic pattern. But Jonson both reinforces and complicates the pattern by the way he handles his characters. The Stage-keeper who comes on first in the Induction prepares the audience right away for "he that should begin the

2. *Bartholomew Fair*, in *Ben Jonson*, ed. C. H. Herford and Percy and Evelyn Simpson, 11 vol. (Oxford, 1925–1952), Prologue 12; Induction, 83. All quotations from *Bartholomew Fair* are taken from this edition, which is hereafter cited as H & S.

3. "The Themes and Staging of *Bartholomew Fair*," *UTQ*, XXXIX (1970), 293–309.

play, Master Littlewit, the Proctor"; so that, although Littlewit does not follow "instantly," as promised, there is no surprise when he enters in soliloquy at the start of Act I. But each act thereafter begins with a speaker new, or virtually new, to the play: Justice Overdo, then Captain Whit, Troubleall, and finally Leatherhead, "translated" from toyman to puppeteer. None of them offers the audience a clear expository statement to begin with, but each of them launches into an exclamation or the like, with a promise of significant incoherence. "A pretty conceit, and worth the finding!" says Littlewit; "I ha' such luck to spinne out these fine things still, and like a Silke-worme, out of my selfe": words arousing curiosity instead of providing information, but already hinting at qualities to be important in the play, the speaker's self-centeredness and naïve self-satisfaction. Overdo soliloquizes in a similar manner, dramatizing himself for an audience of one:

Well, in Justice name, and the Kings; and for the commonwealth! defie all the world, *Adam Overdoo*, for a disguise.

This is not the first time the main audience have heard of this speaker, but the first time that they realize that he has a striking part in the play. The third act opens with a minor character, but a new topic—the speaker upbraiding the Watch—and a fresh accent, Captain Whit's stage Irish:

Nay, tish all gone now! dish tish phen tou vilt not be phitin call, Master Offisher!

Then Jonson reverses his procedure for an act opening, by reintroducing the Watch, but this time with a new and weird-looking interlocutor, Troubleall, whose first words are arresting, not for their content, but for their manner of enunciation: "My Masters, I doe make no doubt, but you are officers." And the last act begins with a recall of Littlewit's opening speech, together with a promise of fresh noise:

Well, Lucke and Saint *Bartholomew*; out with the signe of our inuention, in the name of *Wit*, and do you beat the Drum, the while.

                                                        (V.i. 1–3)

Each of these opening lines discloses a separate humor or seems to impart a new direction to the plot. And yet each of them harks back to the idea of "judgement," which had been the key word in the Induction—either judgment in "conceit" or judgment by law. This procedure sketches out the general movement of the plot, which appears to advance in zigzags, only to return, by a roundabout route, toward the point of departure.

According to Richard Levin, the key to the pattern in the plot is the deferred meeting and simultaneous "rearrangement" of the two parties accompanying Cokes and Littlewit to the Fair, together with the discomfiture of their respective censors, Wasp and Busy, and the more formidable general censor, Overdo. Winwife and Quarlous stand apart as wits, "understanding and judging," rather than tricking, the gulls. The motive forces at work are "Luck and Saint Bartholomew." And the people of the Fair, who remain unchanged at the end, are only incidental to the plot. While this analysis goes a long way, it is open to several objections, the chief of which is that it does not point to any reason within the play itself why the reshuffling of the two parties of visitors should be so important. Though each of these visitors carries his or her special interest, not one of them is given enough prominence by the dramatist to make his fortunes seem to the audience a primary concern. Nor does Levin's analysis explain why the outstanding funny scenes should be devoted to the enemies of the Fair, or why Justice Overdo (who has no family connection with the Littlewits) should take the dominant part among them. Again, while Luck, or Fortune, is a regular agent in Elizabethan comedies, there are different ways of representing its workings, and Jonson hints in the Induction that his way will not include marvelous coincidences such as those in *The Tempest* and *The Winter's Tale*. The luck of the Fair is partly gambler's luck (Quarlous is a "gamester"), but chiefly the natural- or mechanical-seeming result of collisions among the members of a crowd; except that these collisions, in turn, resolve themselves into a pattern of human appetites and errors.

Besides the grouping of the characters within the Littlewit and Cokes parties, three other groupings among the characters and their motives seem significant to the plot. Previously, Jonson had grouped his comic figures chiefly as cheats or gulls, or as humorists or wits. Here, the division between cheats and gulls corresponds to that between the people of the Fair and most of their customers or visitors (including their self-appointed inspector, the Justice in disguise). It is true that the people of the Fair have no egregious master plan like Subtle and Face, and that they remain unpunished and apparently unchanged at the end; nevertheless, they have a vested interest in catering, or seeming to cater, for their customers' pleasure, and this vested interest is essential, not incidental, to the play. Secondly, in this play Jonson's usual distinction between humorists and wits follows a particular line, that of attitudes toward the pleasures of the Fair, ranging from the enthusiasm of Cokes and Littlewit at one extreme to the intolerance of Wasp, Busy, and Overdo at the other, Grace and the two gentleman-wits standing somewhere between. The initial movement of the plot takes rise from this matching of attitudes between Littlewit and Cokes. And thirdly, there is a distinction between the characters as actors, creatures of impulse, and the characters as observers.

This third distinction is not entirely new in Jonson's comedy, of course, nor is it a rigid one, but in this play it takes on a special importance, because the visitors go to the Fair in the capacity of spectators even more than customers: Cokes at first says he wants "to shew Mistris *Grace* my Fayre" (I.v.65), and Littlewit proposes that Win should "long" to eat pig as a ruse to enable them to "see" the "sights" in the Fair, particularly his own puppet play (I.v.148; III.vi.4). All the visitors, and the Fair people themselves, are alternately observers of a sort and impulsive actors, and sometimes both together. While Quarlous, for example, is first mainly an observer of others and then mainly an impulsive plotter on his own account, the special humor of Littlewit and of Overdo is to imagine that they are "apprehending" conceits or "detecting" "enormities;" and the closing scenes, concerning the puppet show, indicate that witnessing can be also a mode of acting, an expression of character. By this time it is clear that the assembly of people at the Fair constitute not only a crowd but a public. This links the actors on the stage with the real spectators in the Hope, who had found themselves the principal subjects, if not exactly the heroes, of Jonson's Induction. As the plot unfolds, the motive forces behind it are first the opposition between admirers and opponents of the Fair and the clash between the people of the Fair and their visitors, and finally, the transition from observing to acting. All three themes are intertwined, however, and the last is present from the outset.

The first phase of the play, to the end of Act II, scene iv, is relatively static and expository, showing the intending visitors to the Fair and the sources of friction between them, and then Ursla and her confederates under the squint-eyed watch of Overdo. The second phase begins, and the

action starts to quicken, with the entry of Winwife and Quarlous, who are
at once engaged in a squabble with Knockem and Ursla, with the result
that the termagant scalds herself with her own pan. Ursla in this scene has
been described as the emblematized spirit of Discord in the play,[4] but the
first concern she voices is not fighting but custom, and it is clearly the
gentlemen who begin the verbal aggression; at this point they consider
themselves in the Fair but not of it (II.v.25 ff.). And their initiative is
followed by Overdo's oration on "the fruits of bottle-ale and tobacco," an
oration designed, with the Justice's crazy logic, to protect the "lamb" he
has singled out, Edgworth the "civil" cutpurse—who takes the occasion of
the small crowd that gathers to rob Cokes, the orator's natural *protégé*,
while, in reward for his interference, it is Overdo who gets beaten. After
the scenes introducing the Watch, who missed the rumpus, and showing
Littlewit's party pushing into the pig booth, this phase of the action is
brought to a close in Overdo's part-overheard soliloquy (III.iii) in which
he professes to examine the lessons of his experience and cheerfully adjures
himself to persist in his chosen course:

To see what bad euents may peepe out o' the taile of good purposes! the care I had
of that ciuil yong man, I tooke fancy to this morning (and haue not left it yet)
drew me to that exhortation, which drew the company, indeede, which drew the
cutpurse; which drew the money; which drew my brother *Cokes* his losse; which
drew on *Wasp's* anger; which drew on my beating: a pretty gradation! And they
shall ha' it i' their dish, i' faith, at night for fruit: I loue to be merry at my table.

(III.iii.13–21)


This part of the soliloquy illustrates the Justice's Littlewit-like (or
Polonius-like) complacency with his own figures of speech, but it also
illuminates, by caricature, the play's indecorous and arsy-versy logic of
"events," which Overdo both sees and does not see; and it points forward
to the supper promised at the end. Altogether, the soliloquy marks a
resting point in the action, a partial gathering of the threads; Winwife
and Quarlous, who are also present on the stage, cap it with a brief
interchange in the choric manner of Mitis and Cordatus, in *Every Man Out*:

    —What does he talke to himselfe, and act so seriously? poor foole!
    —No matter what. Here's fresher argument, intend that.

(III.iii.42–45)

---

4. See Jackson I. Cope, "*Bartholomew Fair* as Blasphemy," *RenD*, VIII (1965), 141–146.

This "fresher argument" is the reentry of Cokes and his party and Bartholomew's enthusiastic purchases, which lead to a new phase in the action, virtually a counteroffensive by the people of the Fair. Now that Cokes is back on stage, Nightingale has the audience he wants for one of his ballads. And in one way the ballad scene (III.v) follows exactly the pattern that Overdo has just sagaciously discerned: in effect, the ballad, A *Caveat against Cutpurses*, follows the line of his own declamation against ale and tobacco; Edgworth picks Cokes's purse again; and again it is Overdo who gets the blame. But this time the incident has been planned by Edgworth and Nightingale, as a professional maneuver (and also in response to Cokes's challenge to the unknown cutpurse). And after a countersortie in the next scene (Busy's attack on the toys and gingerbread), the people of the Fair resume their offensive in Act IV (against Wasp, Win, and Mrs. Overdo).

The ballad episode marks a decisive turn. It prompts Wasp to snatch back the box holding the marriage license from his charge, and it causes Wasp, Cokes, and Mrs. Overdo to hustle Adam Overdo away toward the stocks—thus beginning the breakup of Cokes's party by leaving Grace on the stage with Winwife and Quarlous. Above all, it converts Quarlous from an observer into an intriguer, since, having seen Edgworth cut the purse, he decides to enlist him against Wasp; and although at first he seems to intend no more than a biting practical joke, the humiliation of a "serious ass" (III.v.265), his plans gather momentum as he goes along.

The climax of confusion is reached in Act IV. Through most of Acts II and III the presence of Leatherhead and Trash on the stage has provided a sort of continuity to the scene, but by the end of Act III they have decamped, and in the course of Act IV the stage is several times left empty, as if to emphasize the even more jerky movement of the plot, to and fro between mid-stage, pig booth, and stocks. To add to the confusion, Overdo's forgotten victim, Troubleall, appears as a zany *persona ex machina*. But on the other hand, Quarlous's inventiveness begins to work toward a settlement. By using Edgworth and his partners, who trap Wasp into the game of "vapours," he causes "the date" of Wasp's "authority" to end, as well as gaining possession of the license; by disguising himself as Troubleall, he is enabled to cheat Overdo out of his control over Grace; and by attracting Mrs. Purecraft, in his character of madman, he frustrates Busy's matrimonial hopes. It is true that he too is made to look foolish at the end of the "vapours" game, that he loses Grace to Winwife, and that in the end he silently swallows his initial diatribe against widow hunting. Nevertheless, his "madcap" opportunism rounds off the pattern of events constituted by petty roguery, officious misjudgment, and luck, and he stands out as the most authoritative opponent of the opponents of the Fair and the most successful "discoverer" in the cast.

This does not mean, on the other hand, that Quarlous becomes Jonson's spokesman, or sums up the themes and ideas latent in the play. When he tells the magistrate, "remember you are but *Adam*, Flesh, and blood! you haue your frailty, forget your other name of Overdoo" (V.vi.96–98), he delivers a satisfying reproof, but leaves untouched the questions raised about the values of the Fair as such. In the "disputation" over the puppet show, for example, the decisive point had been precisely that the puppets were not flesh and blood. In any case, Quarlous had been off stage during the puppet show and the "disputation."

The argument of the play, considered as thematic idea, is not exactly the same as its "argument," considered as a pattern of events. As a spectacle, *Bartholomew Fair* exhibits Londoners in a crowd and glances at topical abuses. Many of the abuses were well-known targets for satire or complaint—false measures, the wiles of the "civil cutpurse *searchant*," tobacco, drunkenness and the proliferation of tippling houses (a particular concern of the mid-Jacobean years),[5] prostitution, the offense of "swaggering" or "roaring," the defects of Justices of the Peace and of the watch, wardship, the miseducation of young heirs, superstitious recourse to fortune-tellers,[6] and "the petulant ways" of "your land's Faction," which Jonson singles out in his Prologue addressed to the king; and in addition, there is noise, a symptom of metropolitan overcrowding to which the poet was specially sensitive. But his tone here is ironic gaiety rather than an earnest spirit of satiric correction. The very miscellaneity of these abuses is

5. On Jacobean concern over alehouses, see Joan R. Kent, "Attitudes of Members of the House of Commons to the Regulation of 'Personal Conduct' in late Elizabethan and early Stuart England," *Bulletin of the Institute of Historical Research*, XLVI (1973), 41–71; cf. W. H. and O. C. Overall, eds., *Analytical Index in . . . Remembrancia . . . of the City of London, 1579–1664* (London, 1878), pp. 358–359, 540–545; E. A. Horsman, ed., *Bartholomew Fair* (London, 1960), pp. xviii–xix.

6. *Remembrancia*, p. 269 (letter from the Archbishop of Canterbury, November 1615).

appropriate to the spectacle of the Fair, but no one of them carries dramatic weight enough to give coherence to the whole. It has been maintained that the governing idea of the play is the ridicule of false authority, or else the lapse of authority in social life,[7] or else (with the court performance in mind) that the very "absence" of order within the play is meant to point toward an ideal order embodied in the audience, James and his court.[8] But the court, *ex hypothesi*, were absent from the Hope; and, while it is clear that pretensions to authority form an important component theme, they do not account (as Richard Levin's article brings out) for the meanders of the plot. Nor does Jonson suggest what established authority, legal, religious, or scholastic, could or should do to correct the follies on display; *Bartholomew Fair* is a comedy, not a morality.

Another significant but still marginal theme, related to the confusion over sources of authority indicated in the play, is the commercialization of social life, including the commercialization of values for the landed gentry increasingly settling in the capital. This was indeed a focal subject for Jacobean comedy, especially as it concerned the educated gentry, often magistrates or potential magistrates, and the Inns of Court men, who formed the nucleus of "the judicious" in the playhouses, or what Jonson in the Induction calls "the Commission of Wit."[9] Like his earlier comedies, *Bartholomew Fair* illustrates the disorderly mixture of social standards in London, and the pretensions and aggressive self-assertion that go with it; "vapours" here are in large part the same as the "gentleman-like monster" of "humours" in his previous plays. And "wit" was crucial, on the Jacobean stage, to the portrayal of the gentleman in London, expressing his response, in words and action, to a world where his inherited standards were slipping away. From this point of view, Winwife and Quarlous share a good deal with such resourceful gentlemen of leisure as Witgood in *A Trick to Catch the Old One*, or the heroes of Fletcher's *Wit without Money*. In spite of this, however, it cannot be said that their wit shows to the same

---

7. E.g. by Jonas A. Barish, *Ben Jonson and the Language of Prose Comedy* (Cambridge, Mass., 1960), pp. 225–239; Alan C. Dessen, *Jonson's Moral Comedy* (Evanston, Ill., 1971), pp. 148–166.

8. William Blissett, "Your Majesty Is Welcome to a Fair," in *The Elizabethan Theatre*, IV, ed. G. R. Hibbard (Waterloo, Ont., 1974), p. 100.

9. Cf. Jean Jacquot, "Le Répertoire des compagnies d' enfants à Londres (1600–1610)," in *Dramaturgie et Société . . . aux XVI<sup>e</sup> et XVII<sup>e</sup> siècles*, ed. Jean Jacquot (Paris, 1968), p. 740; Alexander Leggatt, *Citizen Comedy in the Age of Shakespeare* (Toronto, 1973), p. 13.

advantage, or governs the plot to the same extent, as that of Truewit and his friends in *The Silent Woman*.[10] And, conversely, it cannot be said that the economic aspect of the Fair takes up Jonson's interest to the same extent as the business transactions in *The Devil is an Ass*. It is noticeable, for instance, that he virtually ignores the cloth trading and the sale of horses that were still important at Smithfield,[11] except for the drunken northern clothier who figures briefly in the "vapours" game, and the veterinary blarney of the horse courser, Knockem, which is merely a coloring for his dramatic role as roarer and pimp.

The Fair Jonson presents on the stage is a place of commercial entertainment; his comedy is the spectacle of a spectacle, with a dominant interest in those who go to see the sights. The Induction dwells on the relations between author and spectators; the cast is distributed between those who profit from, those who are lured by, those who can tolerate, and those who denounce extravagantly the pleasures of the Fair; and the action is introduced by a disquisition on poetic wit, turns on a street ballad, and culminates in a puppet show. In short, the underlying theme is London society considered as a literary or theatrical public. The expression "the public," in its literary sense, meaning society at large conceived of as the market for books and plays, was not formulated until the generation after Jonson.[12] But *Bartholomew Fair* hinges upon an effort to assemble and clarify the materials for such a concept, undertaken by the most wholeheartedly professional of Jacobean writers.

Jonson belonged to a generation of dramatists, humanists by formation, who were obliged to adapt themselves to the novel but already changing conditions of a commercial theater. To write English poetry in conformity with Renaissance principles was a comparatively untried ambition; to acquire fame, or even part of a living, by writing for the plaudits of chance assemblies in playhouses was more unfamiliar still. "Shame," wrote the university satirist at the very beginning of Jonson's career,

> that the Muses should be bought and sold,
> For euery peasants Brasse, on each scaffold.[13]

10. See Barish, pp. 189–195.

11. Henry Morley, *Memoirs of Bartholomew Fair* (London, 1857), pp. 150–151.

12. See Erich Auerbach, "'La Cour et la Ville'" (1951), in *Scenes from the Drama of European Literature* (Gloucester, Mass., 1959), pp. 133–179.

13. Joseph Hall, *Virgidemiarum*, I.iii.57–58, in *The Poems of Joseph Hall*, ed. A. Davenport (Liverpool, 1949).

In those conditions, who was qualified to write, and what was his proper scope? Who was qualified to judge him, and how should he be judged? Even, who were his ultimate paymasters, and what did they really want? Ever since Marlowe's haughty dismissal of "such conceits as clownage keeps in pay" and Greene's unhappy protest against exploitation by the players, these and similar questions must have pressed hard upon the eager or reluctant recruits to the new profession of writing for the stage.

Consciously or not, the Elizabethans reverted to the Aristophanic practice of discussing or alluding to their profession in the course of their plays. In the public theaters, Shakespeare was the first to do so. He was specially concerned with the rapport between actors and audience, ideally a national audience with courtly patrons at their head—though he makes Hamlet wryly note that the latter might well include a Polonius, expecting "a jig or a tale of bawdry, or he sleeps." Shakespeare's younger contemporaries, Jonson among them, were relatively more dependent on London and more affected by the changing atmosphere of the turn of the century: satire and censorship, personal rivalries, vocal if not published criticism. They used inductions or prologues, and even prefaces added to the printed texts of their plays, in order to educate, repress, conciliate, or at the least, describe the unpredictable responses of their mixed auditories. Marston, for instance, told the audience of the Blackfriars, about 1604:

> the highest grace we pray
> Is, you'll not tax until you judge our play.
> Think, and then speak: 'tis rashness, and not wit,
> To speak what is in passion, and not judgment, fit.
>
> (*The Dutch Courtesan*)

In the Induction to *The Malcontent* at the Globe, Webster makes Burbage ask, speaking in his own person, "Why should not we enjoy the ancient freedom of poesy? No, sir, such vices as stand not accountable to law, should be cured as men heal tetters, by casting ink upon them." These statements sound like replies to possibly influential, as well as captious, patrons; other playwrights emphasize the leveling-down effect of the playhouse, where (as Dekker explains to his Gull, or initiate in London gallantry)

your Stinkard has the selfe same libertie to be there in his Tobacco-Fumes, which your sweet Courtier hath: and . . . your Car-man and Tinker claime as strong a voice in their suffrage, and sit to give judgment on the plaies life and death, as well as the prowdest *Momus* among the tribe of *Critick*.

The theater, in short, is the "Royal Exchange" for poets, where their "Muses" have become "Merchants."[14] And some of the consequences of this state of affairs are described by Dekker and Middleton in the epilogue to their *Roaring Girl* (at the Fortune, ca. 1608), where they compare their task to that of the painter who ruined his portrait by altering it, feature by feature, in the vain hope of satisfying every prospective buyer:

> And thus,
> If we to every brain that's humorous
> Should fashion scenes, we, with the painter, shall,
> In striving to please all, please none at all.

Like Marston, they assume that every individual criticism is likely to be "humorous," capricious, ungrounded on common principles. With the benefit of historical hindsight, we may congratulate Shakespeare's contemporaries on the golden opportunity they enjoyed in writing at the same time for the groundlings and the judicious; but the challenge must have seemed as much daunting as invigorating to the men on the job.

Jonson was more engaged than any other in critical exhortation and reproof, from his pioneering *Every Man out of his Humour* onward; and his view of the writer's condition was more fully articulated and complex than that of anyone else. At first he mainly emphasizes the principles on which he claims appreciation; but then increasingly he examines those factors in the reception of his work that affect or hinder appreciation. Briefly, they are competition, patronage, censorship or interference, and popular taste; and his achievement as a critic or theorist of drama was partly to draw these together into something like a coherent system. In the 1607 preface to *Volpone*, addressed to the two Universities, he refers to attacks or dangers from several sides at once. In order to reassert "the dignity of poet," he hits out both at the "license" of vulgarians who degrade "stage-poetry" and at the malice—which he had good reason to fear—of "invading interpreters" with access to highly placed patrons. But at the same time he concedes some reason to "those severe and wise patriots" who

14. *The Gull's Hornbook*, 1609, chap. 6, in *The Elizabethan Stage* IV, ed. E. K. Chambers (Oxford, 1923), pp. 365–366, spelling modernized.

would like to turn the clock back or retrench the liberty of the stage, and he points out that he has met their case in part by so arranging the "catastrophe" of the play as "to put the snaffle in their mouths, that cry out, We never punish vice in our interludes"—though this means incurring "censure" from academic purists. Between poetasters, informers, statesmen, classicists, and puritans, the dramatist has a difficult course to steer, precisely because the would-be censors of the stage have some legitimate cause for complaint. In the preface "To the Reader," attached to the 1612 edition of *The Alchemist*, Jonson goes to the root of the problem as he sees it: the alliance between bad writing and popular taste. The uninstructed reader is bound to be "cozened" by plays, because

now, the concupiscence of jigs, and dances so reigneth, as to run away from nature, and be afraid of her, is the only point of art that tickles the spectators;

and the source of the cheat is to be found in "the multitude, through their excellent [*supreme*] vice of judgement":

For they commend writers, as they do fencers or wrestlers; who if they come in robustuously, and put for it with a great deal of violence, are received for the braver fellows. . . . For it is only the disease of the unskilful, to think rude things greater than polished; or scattered more numerous than composed.

Sensationalism and aimless bustle, then, are the typical vices of mind displayed on the popular stage. And in turn they constitute, in effect, the basic motivation of the characters in *Bartholomew Fair*.

In opposition to such vices, the Induction to the *Fair* urges settled individual judgments. Confronting a typical audience in a public playhouse, Jonson now surveys their inclinations more comprehensively (but also more genially) than before. He takes account of their variety, "the favouring and judicious" as well as "the curious and envious"; and he touches on what he sees as ignorant approval as well as wrongheaded opposition to the stage—the "concupiscence of jigs and dances" (again) as well as prudish suspicion of "profaneness"; the stock responses of those stick-in-the-mud stage fans who have not changed since "Master Tarlton's time" or the days of "*Jeronimo* or *Andronicus*" as well as the industrious perversity of any lurking "state-decipherer, or politic picklock of the scene." His method is an ironic conflation of opposites. The Stage-keeper says the "master-poet" has been too obstinate; the Book-holder, too indulgent. The groundlings in the Hope become "the grounded judgements here," and the hidebound admirer of *The Spanish Tragedy* "shall pass unexcepted at here as a man whose judgement shews it . . . hath stood still," since, "next to truth, a confirmed error does well." And, in the pose of an honest tradesman, the author concedes to every paying spectator his "free-will of censure," exactly "to the value of his place—provided always his place get not above his wit." The further conditions of the bargain are "that every man here exercise his own judgement, and not censure by contagion, or upon trust, . . . as also that he be fixed and settled in his censure" (Induc. 100–101); above all, that he should show sufficient self-respect to measure trifles at their right proportion—

else you will make him [the author] justly suspect that he that is so loth to look on a baby or an hobby-horse here, would be glad to take up a commodity of them, at any laughter or loss, in another place.

(Induc. 162–165)

The stage is precisely the place where trivialities can (ideally) be exhibited for what they are, without arousing either "concupiscence" or indignation. Failure to perceive this is, at bottom, failure in self-respect. Or, as the court Prologue states it, the play is presented

for your sport, without particular wrong,
Or just complaint of any private man
Who of himself or shall think well or can.

(ll. 8–10)

There is still a hint of irony here, a challenge to the spectator to think well of himself—if he can; but the main statement is close to Jonson's statement of his fundamental moral viewpoint in *Discoveries*: "I know no disease of the *Soul*, but *Ignorance*; not of the Arts, and Sciences, but of itself." [15] What the Prologue and Induction to *Bartholomew Fair* propose as the solid ground for "censure" of the play, favorable or not, is personal "judgement" stemming from and confirming self-knowledge. And it is not accidental that references to censorious objectors and such phrases as "the

15. H & S, VIII, 588, l. 801, spelling modernized.

Commission of Wit" in the Induction suggest judgment of a legal kind as well as the expression of taste; as Jonson saw it, the institutional status of the theater and its literary quality were interdependent. Would-be censors and confirmed spectators formed a continuous public.

The Induction is a miniature play, in the style of prologues to the *commedia erudita*, bridging the gap, or blurring the distinction, between the reality of the spectators and the fiction of the stage. "The poet" and "his man, Master Brome, behind the arras" stand on the same plane as the legendary Kindheart and Master Tarlton and the pretended Stage-keeper and Book-holder of the company and "Master Littlewit," who is said to be mending his stocking—an actor described by the name of his part. The pretended "argument" of the Induction-as-play is the question of what the audience are to expect or not expect—predictably, a factor in the performance itself. There is a similar sleight of hand with reality and fiction in the scenes leading to the puppet show, as when Littlewit explains that he has made *Hero and Leander* "a little easy, and modern for the times"; or when Cokes, having identified one of the puppets with the leading player in the real company ("Which is your Burbage now? . . . Your best actor. Your Field?"), identifies the puppet Leander in turn with one of his "fairings," his "fiddle-stick" (V.iii.85–137); or when Leatherhead, as puppet master, sagely counsels the poet not to "breed too great an expectation" of the show among his friends—"that's the onely hurter of these things" (V.iv.13–14). And these ironic variations on themes from the Induction begin to round off the play proper, which is an extension of the same group of ideas.

Littlewit and Cokes, who lead their respective parties to the Fair, are complementary to one another, as rhymester of puppet plays and archetypal "favourer of the quality," and are likewise complementary in other ways to the Fair people who cater for them and also to minds like Busy and Overdo, as enemies of the Fair. A similar want of the "judgement" designated in the Induction operates in or for them all. Littlewit opens the play proper with his pun about the license: "Bartholomew upon Bartholomew! There's the device!"—which turns out to be exact in the heraldic sense, if childish as a conceit. And his self-appreciation a moment later prepares an intellectual position for Overdo to occupy (as well as another for Mooncalf, by Ursla's fire):

When a quirk, or a *quiblin* does scape thee, and thou dost not watch, and apprehend it, and bring it afore the constable of conceit: (there now, I speak *quib* too) let 'hem carry thee out o' the Archdeacon's Court, into his Kitchin, and make a *Jack* of thee, in stead of a *John*. (There I am againe, la!)

(I.i.13–18)

Littlewit's "apprehension" of "quirks" prepares the way for the disguised magistrate's "detection" of "enormities," and similarly his account of his home-bred wit prepares the way for Busy's "inspiration" and Knockem's "vapours";

A poxe o' these pretenders to wit! your *Three Cranes, Miter,* and *Mermaid* men! . . . . But gi' mee the man, can start up a *Justice* of *Wit* out of six-shillings beare, and give the law to all the Poets and Poet-suckers i' towne.

(I.i.33–40)

Though he is an amiable ass, his "ambitious wit" (as Quarlous calls it) is essential to the satiric scheme of the plot. And his "apprehension" shows its true colors at the Fair. Not only does he lose his wife, but he lends Cokes the money to watch his own puppet play, and then fails to see it himself.

If Littlewit and Cokes together represent the upholders of the shows at the Fair, Busy and Overdo are their complementary opposites. The puppet show and the like are indeed "enormities," but they are incapable of seeing why. Busy's marvelously self-hypnotic verbiage is a magnified version of his intended son-in-law's "quibs"; "Good Banbury-vapours," in Knockem's condescending appraisal. But (as C. H. Herford remarked),[16] he is no Tartuffe; and his final "confutation" by the puppets is no head-on satiric retort to the Puritan case against the stage. It merely shows that he cannot observe what is in front of him, or tell the difference between puppets and players. It is consistent that in the end he should "become a beholder" with the rest (V.v.116); in part, the implication is that his noisy and irrelevant objections merely serve to sustain the real abuses in plays.

Overdo is both a more complex and, within his limits, a more formidable figure. Unlike Busy, he has genuine authority, as far as it goes; and in part he is the contemporary type of an upstart and irresponsible Justice of

16. H & S, II, 144.

the Peace.[17] But in his language, with its mixture of complacent pedantry and pulpit clichés, he is allied both to Littlewit and—in spite of surface opposition—to Busy.[18] And, however, "parantory," "severe," and "angry" he may have been on the bench (IV.i.70–78), his role on the stage is a caricature of that of the disguised Duke in *Measure for Measure*—to pretend to observe others, while forgetting to know himself. After declaring that he has come to inspect the Fair in disguise, so as to avoid having to rely upon the evidence of "other men's ears" and "other men's eyes" (II.i.29–30), he promptly turns to the amiable Mooncalf for information about the characters at the Fair; and when he comes to deliver his diatribe against ale and tobacco, he picks up his medical warnings from Knockem (II.iii.20; II.vi.13). He is essentially literary and dramatic "judgement" (or misjudgment) in action, rather than a representative of the law. In spite of his professed familiarity with "my Quintus Horace," he is a foe to poetry, in the line of old Knowell, in *Every Man in his Humour*; with a special naïveté that makes him susceptible to the crudest junk if it carries a surface message that he approves. He suspects Nightingale "of a terrible taint, poetry" (III.v.6), but he stays to hear his ballad against cutpurses—(which must be Jonson's riposte to the Autolycus scenes in *The Winter's Tale*)—precisely because the ballad "doth discover enormity" (III.v.112); and, because he stays to "mark it more," he finds himself in the stocks. As the observer who willfully fails to observe, he is both a representative of those civic magistrates who tried to restrict or suppress the acting of plays and the outstanding negative example in the comedy of the principle of exercising one's own judgment.

Wasp is related to Overdo and Busy less by any pretense of ideology than by temperament. His name suggests a probable source of suggestions for Ben Jonson—the Aristophanic comedy about Philocleon and the other irascible jurymen who cling to the shadow of power through formal legal authority because they do not possess the substance; (as a "friend of Cleon," the old man is, by inference, an enemy of the poet at first as well). Like Philocleon, he has a passion to contradict; and like him, he tumbles

17. Cf. John Bond, in the House of Commons in 1601: "Who almost are not grieved at the luxuriant authority of Justices of Peace? . . . For magistrates are men, and men have alwayes attending on them two ministers, *libido* and *iracundia*. Men of this nature do subjugate the free subject"; quoted in Kent, p. 52.

18. See Barish, pp. 209–213.

over into riotous misbehavior once his show of authority is taken away. As his name suggests, he exhibits in an extreme form the aimless restlessness that agitates Overdo and Busy—which is not very different from the qualities he so scornfully diagnoses in Bartholomew's mind:

He that had the meanes to travel your head, now, should meet finer sights then any are i' the Fayre; and make a finer voyage on't; to see it all hung with cockle-shels, pebbles, fine wheat-strawes, and here and there a chicken's feather and a cobweb.

> (I.v.93–97)

This is perhaps the most striking statement in the play about the psychological qualities that link its humorists together; and its jerky vehemence characterizes Wasp himself almost as much as Cokes. As Quarlous has said, a few minutes earlier, "it's cross and pile" between master and man. When Jonson wants to voice a considered judgment about Bartholomew, he delivers it in a different tone:

Talke of him to have a soule? 'heart, if hee have any more then a thing given him instead of salt, onely to keepe him from stinking, I'le be hang'd afore my time, presently.

> (IV.ii.54–56)

This more judicial observer is the "civil cutpurse," Edgworth, who has just helped to strip Cokes of his cloak and sword. No doubt the cutpurse as such was an indispensable figure in a gallery of comic portraits representing the world of the Jacobean playhouses in general. But it is one of Jonson's sharper ironies that he is the only character on the stage self-respecting and dispassionately observant enough to ask whether the prime enthusiast for street ballads and puppet shows can have such a thing as a soul.

# The Boys from Ephesus:
# Farce, Freedom, and Limit in
# The Widow's Tears

## LEE BLISS

P ERHAPS BECAUSE it challenges many scholarly preconceptions, Chapman's best comedy, *The Widow's Tears*, has been considerably neglected. The play poses fundamental generic problems as well as formidable threats to theories of Chapman's development as dramatist and as philosophic moralist. Disturbingly, the play even seems to challenge critics' private moral beliefs: disgust with the play's subject matter and cynicism often turns attempts at critical analysis into either condemnation of the playwright himself or excuses for this isolated lapse from his usually high moral standards. Recent emphasis on *The Widow's Tears*'s own, internal, problems (rather than, or at least prior to, its problematic place in Chapman's literary development) has provided more interesting analyses, but also surprisingly irreconcilable conclusions about the moral status of the main characters, about the degree, and even the object, of the play's satire, and about the dramatist's relation to his play's outspoken amorality.

Central to these critical problems is Chapman's witty and cynical Tharsalio, whose dual roles dominate the play: he is both actor (instigator of both plots as well as principal intriguer) and observer (satiric commentator

on everyone, including himself). The play's action seems to validate Tharsalio's reductionist views of human nature, yet such total cynicism would
be unique in Chapman; hence critics still feel morally obligated to take
sides, to judge Tharsalio and through him Chapman. Analysis becomes
simplified: one must only decide whether Tharsalio is Chapman's "hero"
and spokesman, or his anti-hero and his satire's object.[1] In either approach, the play becomes didactic and lifeless, a cynical exposure of universal and permanent human hypocrisy or a vitriolic attack on the fallen
world's perversion of human possibilities, aptly symbolized by the mate-
rialist Tharsalio. Both approaches assume a satiric, rather than a comic,
play and a consistently bitter tone culminating in Act V's grotesque tomb
scenes.

To ignore the important component of "comic vivacity" and exuberant
farce, or to discuss it as "beneath" Chapman's usual high seriousness, is to
overlook the source of the play's theatrical effectiveness.[2] Such self-
imposed restrictions inhibit our full response to the play as well as to
Chapman's generic daring. Neither Tharsalio's intrigues nor his cynical
observations can be abstracted from his function within the play's

---

1. In "The Widow's Tears and the Other Chapman" (HLQ, XXIII [1960], 321–338),
Samuel Schoenbaum sees Tharsalio as Chapman's spokesman; hence "his vision, terrible as
it may appear, is also Chapman's vision," and "it is not Tharsalio but his detractors who
are ultimately discredited" (pp. 334–335). Henry Weidner, however, disagrees. Since
Chapman nowhere else upholds "Machiavellian or even atheistic doctrines," Weidner
posits an external system of ideals which "by implication" condemns the cynic, who
represents "everything Chapman denounces," and suggests that his triumph is really
Chapman's "satiric commentary on the fallen world and one of its chief disciples"; see
"Homer and the Fallen World: Focus of Satire in George Chapman's The Widow's Tears,"
JEGP, LXII (1963), 519. Albert Tricomi varies this dichotomy: Tharsalio is "Chapman's
true-seeing anti-hero" and, though Tharsalio is satirized in the early acts, the fact that he
successfully "revels in the corruption he uncovers" indicates the sad "deterioration of
Chapman's ideal of heroic reform"; see "The Social Disorder of Chapman's The Widow's
Tears," JEGP, LXXII (1973), 350.

2. In "Chapman and an Aspect of Modern Criticism" (RenD, VIII [1965], 153–179),
Thelma Herring effectively answers Weidner's argument and offers a balanced view which
tries to account for the play's humor. Chapman is concerned, in good comic fashion, with
unmasking "pretensions to a superhuman virtue" rather than with a decadent or fallen
world, and the chief objects of his satire are "the two women—and (as has been less
commonly noted) Lysander" (pp. 157 and 160). In contrast, others find the play dominated by its satiric vision—in Schoenbaum's words, a "mirthless comedy" (p. 336).

tragicomic structure; to do so makes the play a poorly constructed philosophic vehicle by an enraged dramatist who had momentarily lost control of theatrical necessities.[3] Chapman's venture into Jacobean tragicomedy is disturbing, but its unsatisfying lack of resolution stems from identifiable manipulations of a genre—its form and structure of feeling—which Chapman shares with contemporary experimenters. Like Jonson and the Shakespeare of the problem comedies, Chapman has pushed "comedy" to its limit and consciously created our dissatisfaction with the generic "happy ending"; the experimental form, as much as its content, produces the satiric effects. More careful study of Chapman's generic manipulations in *The Widow's Tears*—his distinctive sequential plot structure as well as the stock materials from which he fashioned his story—may uncover the causes of this comedy's disturbing, bifurcated effects and, perhaps, Chapman's handling of his pivotal character, Tharsalio.

Part of what I take to be critical misunderstanding stems from a tendency to see the play as all of a piece throughout: the wooing of Eudora, technically the subplot, appears to be a simple preparation for the main event, Lysander's "parallel" test of his own Cynthia. Both plots then serve as a continuous series exposing female inconstancy and lust, Chapman's variation on a theme as old as Petronius. This view is inadequate: it endorses the characters' own facile assumption of the two plots' similarity, but fails to account for the care with which Chapman's structure creates the play's dynamic tensions. Rather, the apparent parallelism glosses a fundamental disjunction of subject and form, and Chapman's sequential plotting forces us, finally, to recognize and define this disjunction in moral terms. Thus instead of developing his plots concurrently, allowing the characters and themes of the subplot to comment satirically on the main plot's action by juxtaposition (as in, for example, *Measure for Measure*), Chapman lulls us into one frame of mind, appropriate to the generic treatment of his subplot; he then uses the subplot as false preparation for the Petronian story. With his characters' own assumption of logical and moral continuity, Chapman even delays our recognition of dissonance.

3. Marilyn L. Williamson, too, sees Tharsalio as a figure within a comic structure, hence determined by that structure's needs. In elaborately excusing Tharsalio's harshness, however, she ultimately softens him—and the play—beyond recognition; see "Matter of More Mirth," in *RenP* (1956), pp. 34–41.

Indeed, if we add the final scenes of the Governor and the Watch, *The Widow's Tears* contains three distinct sections, each of which criticizes or modifies our response to the preceding mode.[4]

Chapman's first mode is farcical comedy. Though the setting is Cyprus and the characters elevated in rank, the story is basically a city comedy plot in which an impoverished younger son seeks to recoup his own and his family's fortunes by a wealthy marriage;[5] obstacles to Tharsalio's success include his lower social status but derive largely from the attractive young widow's vow of perpetual mourning. To judge such a plot by the standards of romantic comedy (to say nothing of nondramatic criteria, such as contemporary attitudes toward Degree or widows' remarriage) seems beside the point, unless one condemns the whole genre as a distasteful violation of dramatic and social propriety. City comedy characteristically emphasizes witty and amoral cunning; standards of efficiency replace those of morality, and the spoils belong to the cunning and the bold.[6] City comedy's humor depends upon our (perhaps) shocked delight in a world which refuses to exalt, even to recognize, human fulfillment of those social and personal ideals to which we pay such eager lip service. Virtuous claims invariably prove hypocritical; plots revolve around sex and business, and successful action can only be based on the "true," unfeigned passions—greed and lust. Of course, Chapman goes out of his way to make his plots, at least superficially, both socially and morally acceptable, and I will return to these softening techniques. At present, I wish to explore further the fundamental psychological appeal of the farcical first plot and the ways Chapman ensures our acceptance of its inverted norms.

City comedy's appeal is at base that of farce—regressive. Like dreams and fantasies, farce expresses and thus satisfies the childish ego's amoral

4. Interestingly, Richard Levin does not discuss *The Widow's Tears* in *The Multiple Plot in English Renaissance Drama* (Chicago, 1971). Levin is concerned with the predominant multiple-plot structure—alternating scenes—and, although his chapter on "Three-Level Hierarchies" remarks on a number of clownish third "half-plots," his moral and social ranking of plots seems unhelpful for Chapman's play.

5. Herring notes both that "there is a Middletonian realism in Tharsalio's pursuit of a profitable marriage" and that "indelicate though his methods are, Tharsalio is *not* presented as an ineligible suitor" (p. 159).

6. See Alexander Leggatt, *Citizen Comedy in the Age of Shakespeare* (Toronto, 1973), pp. 58 ff.

desire for total gratification. From Aristophanic Old Comedy to the twentieth-century Marx Brothers, farce gives acceptable, cathartic form to man's basic, unextinguished, acquisitive and aggressive drives and allows him to laugh at, to desecrate, his culture's primary ideals: harmonious family relationships and disinterested, even self-sacrificing, social behavior.[7] Like tendentious wit in Freud's analysis, farce allows us to circumvent encultured values and inhibitions in order to tap once more basic sources of pleasure, to free psychic energy which had been bound to the maintenance of inhibitions;[8] it provides a circumscribed, permissible area in which forbidden impulses can be enjoyed and lived out vicariously.[9] The liberating laughter of the Tharsalio-Eudora plot can temporar-

7. Eric Bentley likens farce to dreams, for both show "the disguised fulfillment of repressed wishes" and satisfyingly desecrate our "household gods"; see Bentley's introduction to *'Let's Get a Divorce!' and Other Plays* (New York, 1958), esp. p. x. Bentley's discussion stems, of course, from Freud's chapter on jokes, dreams, and the unconscious in *Jokes and their Relation to the Unconscious* (1905), in *The Standard Edition of the Complete Psychological Works of Sigmund Freud* (hereafter referred to as *SE*), trans. James Strachey, Anna Freud, Alix Strachey, and Alan Tyson, 24 vols. (1960; rpt. London, 1973), VIII, 159–180. Philip Rieff, in *Freud: The Mind of the Moralist* (1959; rev. ed. Garden City, N.Y., 1961), discusses both internal and external effects: "Joking, like dreams, represents an overthrow of the mind's order and integrity. On the other hand, Freud emphasized the socially subversive tendency of joking—the significance of wit as a rebellion against authority, and of jokes as themselves an unmasking of public morality" (p. 384).

8. See Freud's chapters on "The Purposes of Jokes" and "The Mechanism of Pleasure and the Psychogenesis of Jokes" in *Jokes and their Relation to the Unconscious*, pp. 90–139. For further development of Freud's ideas, consult Ernst Kris's chapter, "Ego Development and the Comic," in *Psychoanalytic Explorations in Art* (1952; rpt. New York, 1964), pp. 204–216; see also Bentley's introduction, cited above, on the "function of 'farcical' fantasies" as "compensation": "one is permitted the outrage but is spared the consequences" (p. xiii).

9. Institutionalized opportunities for such release, social safety valves, offer a carefully demarcated and contained topsy-turvydom in which participants may flout traditional sexual and pacifist mores, social or religious hierarchies, and even freely attack the authorities who daily safeguard these restrictions. Particularly helpful in understanding this comic catharsis are the initial chapters in C. L. Barber's *Shakespeare's Festive Comedy: A Study of Dramatic Form and Its Relation to Social Custom* (1959; rpt. Princeton, N.J., 1972), and Erich Segal's *Roman Laughter: The Comedy of Plautus* (Cambridge, Mass., 1968). Jacob Levine, in his introduction to *Motivation in Humor* (New York, 1969), notes that both Freud and Kris find humor unable to "overcome strong dysphoric emotions"; a playful, festive attitude is crucial to enable the listener to share "an invitation to common aggression and regression" (pp. 17–18).

ily explode taboos on sexual, economic, and familial aggression because Chapman adheres to farce's requirement: an outrage which successfully inverts society's most cherished values (i.e., those values the audience dutifully brings to the theater) without arousing the guilt which usually accompanies private self-indulgence in aggression.

To succeed, then, farce must insulate its topsy-turvy world from the normal consequences of such shocking, asocial behavior: we must laugh at the banana peel's victim without worrying that he will break his neck; we must be assured that the practical joke's object will not suffer as we would suffer. The appeal is to a world free of civilized moral restraints, where the ego can "rightfully" (i.e., guiltlessly) possess whatever it can win by craft or force. Such a world is marked by egoistic competition and aggression, and this exuberant delight in man's inhumanity to man also suggests farce's closeness to tragedy (when, seen through another lens, aggression entails frightening consequences), rather than to romantic comedy.[10] In the Cynthia-Lysander plot Chapman exploits the tragic possibilities of such unsoftened aggression in order to puncture our earlier sense of festive release.

Release is the keynote of the first plot. With his first words, Tharsalio introduces a chaotic social order in which ego reigns supreme. What might have been a satiric complaint for Blind Fortune's worldly rule becomes instead the comic overreacher's occasion for complete moral inversion. Blind Confidence replaces "weak Fortune" as the only "friend to worth," since her worship may ensure satisfaction of those desires chance refuses to provide (I.i.1ff.).[11] Gazing into his own mirror, Tharsalio chooses a narcissistic, subjective reality as the only one he will acknowl-

---

10. On the aggressive, asocial behavior which began in physical beatings (notable in Roman comedy and its sixteenth-century imitators) and was slowly transformed, under repression's demands, into wit, see Erich Segal's comments on "comic *hubris*" in "Marlowe's *Schadenfreude*: Barabas as Comic Hero," in *Veins of Humor*, ed. Harry Levin (Cambridge, Mass., 1972), pp. 69–91. On farce's relation to tragedy, Bentley's words are suggestive: "Farce confronts the cruder kinds of man's strength, all of which he misuses. Man, says farce, may or may not be one of the more intelligent animals; he is certainly an animal, and . . . one of the chief uses to which he puts his intelligence, such as it is, is to think aggression when he is not committing it" (p. xix).

11. All citations from Chapman's *The Widow's Tears* will be to Akihiro Yamada's edition for the Revels Plays (London, 1975).

edge; deifying egoism, he also renounces passivity (waiting for Fortune to provide advancement's occasion) in favor of aggressive, unrestrained pursuit of his private goals. Tharsalio rejects both the ideal of virtuous action for its own sake and the moralist's pursuit of social reform; putting aside the rules in order to pursue pleasure and profit, Tharsalio invites us to join him. His verbal excess—soon publicly proclaimed in his outrageous answers to Lysander and Cynthia and physically realized in his actions at Eudora's palace—mirrors the exuberant unreality and indulgent behavior characteristic of privileged, festive occasions on and off the stage.[12] We laugh at Tharsalio's childish monomania, but delight in his social blasphemy as well as his vitality. Chapman need only guarantee that we too may safely treat life as a game, at least temporarily, for us to accept Tharsalio and through him find vicarious freedom. Chapman does so by supporting Tharsalio's outrageous behavior with farce's traditional distancing techniques: exaggerated unreality of situation accompanied by dehumanization and stereotyping of character.

Tharsalio's triumphant self-assurance reduces others to minor actors in his drama, to be distinguished by their parts (male/female, hindrance or object of pursuit) rather than by human individuality. Though social behavior may vary by rank and gender, all are reducible to the same few primitive instincts: "a woman" (or, "you wives"—I.i.99) is a woman, whether she be Cynthia, Eudora, or Arsace. Indeed, to the true narcissist, others are not "people"—of the same status and individuality as the self—and hence require no real consideration. Their significance is limited to their impingement on the egoist's own desires—as extensions of himself, as objects to be pursued and possessed, as obstacles to fulfillment which need to be denied, circumvented, or destroyed. In the opening scene's exposition of the wooing plan, Tharsalio's attitude to his own blood relations suggests this simplified, childish outlook and the antagonisms which fuel his behavior. He envies Lysander's easy life and resents the trick of birth by which Lysander "gulled me of the land that my spirits and parts were indeed born to" (I.i.46–47); Lysander can *afford* to be pompously cautious and moralistic, and Tharsalio pointedly tells

12. On Plautine verbal excess and its relation to festivity, see Segal, p. 39; some pertinent remarks on Shakespeare's "great feast of languages" and wit's extravagance may be found in Barber, pp. 95–113.

him so. The fact of brotherhood does not alter Tharsalio's reflexive urge to hurt those who mock him. Yet we glimpse more than Tharsalio's underlying indiscriminate aggressiveness; his witty self-possession, and the apparently ruthless honesty with which he initially admits his share in the elemental emotions which rule human behavior, both contrast favorably with the smug self-righteousness of Lysander and Cynthia. Indeed, Lysander too enters "with a glass in his hand" and soon reveals himself to be as egocentric, though not as honest, as his brother. Such qualities— especially in a man whose prudent counsel threatens our fun—encourage us both to enjoy Tharsalio's outspoken freedom from cant and to adopt his point of view.[13]

The ego's depersonalization of others is, of course, even more obvious (and acceptable) outside the family ranks. In *The Widow's Tears*, as so often in city comedy, economic rather than amatory terms define the prospective bride. Although Tharsalio once speaks of "love" to Eudora (I.ii.87), to others he unemotionally terms the wooing a "business" whose success procures a rich "jewel worth the wearing" (I.i.60–61). Elsewhere, his stated motives reveal more distinctively Tharsalian characteristics. He resents the condescension of the wealthy and well-born (indeed, his brother's contempt as well as Eudora's) and spitefully wishes to prove his worth by humbling and humiliating the widow whom he once served as a page. He prays to Confidence that the "rich and haughty Countess" (I.i.59) may be taught a lesson:

> that she, whose board
> I might not sit at, I may board a-bed
> And under bring, who bore so high her head.
>
> (I.i.178–180)

The successful wooing of Eudora will also teach his smug brother a lesson and make Tharsalio socially and economically superior. Since Lysander had mocked Tharsalio's "insatiate spirit of aspiring" (III.i.34), part of the younger brother's revenge consists of forcing an exchange of places: when Tharsalio throws off his shabby cloak and brags about "my ushers and

---

13. Herring notes that Cynthia and Eudora both function as *alazon* figures in a plot which calls for their exposure; Lysander, too, needs to be cured of his "excess"—egoism (pp. 158 and 162).

chief servants" and "my women," he asks Lysander, "Good brother, do not you envy my fortunate achievement?" (III.i.76–77, 86).[14] Others' envy is necessary to complete the ego's triumph.

Tharsalio's other motive for wooing Eudora embraces his family's welfare: "Alas, brother, our house is decayed, and my honest ambition to restore it" (III.i.49–50). Indeed, Tharsalio uses his anxiety for "the ancient inheritance of our family" to rationalize instigating Lysander's test of Cynthia (II.iii.75–85). Yet Tharsalio's concern aims, in both plots, to advance an extension of himself, his nephew Hylus whose

> sweet face,
> Which all the city says is so like me,
> Like me shall be preferred.
>
> (I.i.160–162)

Tharsalio prefers his own image. The brothers' antagonistic egoism further questions—perhaps negates—the socially commendable goal of family advancement. Lysander cannot forbear taunting his younger brother, and Tharsalio immediately retaliates. Spite rules both brothers: in order to revenge his wounded pride, to pay "veny for veny" (I.iii.132), Tharsalio sacrifices his sister and destroys his brother's happiness as well as his illusions. Instead of advancing his family, Tharsalio in some sense destroys it.

Tharsalio's attitude toward others protects him from caring. His depersonalization also resembles the farceur's, and Chapman's initial support of Tharsalio's view allows us guiltlessly to enjoy the adventurer's assault on culture's two-dimensional representatives. Tharsalio refuses to believe that rank or public statements of one's own virtue can elevate one's nature (I.i.80–96), and we revel in his blasphemy and share his desire to bring the mighty low. As we have seen, Lysander's and Cynthia's smug mockery and complacent claims to purity beg for comic exposure; they set themselves on the same superhuman pedestal as Eudora, and the expectations raised by the first plot demand that we, with Tharsalio, treat all such

---

14. Yamada follows the quarto's punctuation here, a period. In its context, the line seems to me to demand an interrogative reading, and I note that a similar interpretation prevails in Dodsley and, more recently, in Ethel M. Smeak's edition for the Regents Renaissance Drama series.

claims equally. Moreover, Cynthia's self-righteous condemnation of her "sister" marks her own share in Lysander's self-delusion (III.i.120–125): he uses her protestations and fame as his flattering mirror, and Cynthia finds herself flattered by her role. In the wooing plot particularly, Chapman obligingly provides Tharsalio with ludicrously stereotyped fops and a sketchily characterized widow whose indignant unapproachability and assumption that her social position ensures her virtue encourage our appropriately comic distance from her humiliation. Indeed, the actual wooing is the most traditionally farcial portion of the first plot: the dialogue is exaggeratedly and outrageously aggressive and sexual; both Tomasin and Rebus are physically buffeted by Tharsalio; and though initially tossed in a blanket himself, Tharsalio returns literally to storm Eudora's bedchamber, sword in hand.

We delight in the wooing's element of sheer adolescent playfulness. Further, the fact that Rebus, scorned even by Eudora's servants, is a patently unacceptable suitor also satisfies our social conscience: we need not feel guilty for our moral holiday. Despite Tharsalio's egoistic motives, Chapman contrives that this demonstration of female inconstancy in fact shatters suffocating hypocrisy and actually improves Eudora's situation. Tharsalio's trick allows Eudora to cut through self-deception and adherence to life-denying social mores; she gains a knowledge of herself—of human needs beyond the false differentia of rank—and an intelligent, vital husband who, in the play's terms, has rightfully "won" her from the lifeless (indeed, venereally diseased) manikins offered by polite society. Tharsalio offers his own (sexual) merits, not borrowed social honors. In a surprisingly uncynical speech to Lysander, Tharsalio himself defends Eudora's conduct and suggests the unnaturalness of those social expectations he has exploded, since they condemn a young and vital woman to death-in-life simply because one man has died (III.i.162–168). Tharsalio's witty reductionism here affords a clearer perspective on the natural comic rhythm his act upholds: in the mirror terms he had used earlier, just as he hopes to supplant the loss of one man in the young widow's life, so Nature's concern with life and gender will supply another to succeed him (I.i.124–129).

Nor does Tharsalio reduce all to animal fact; powerful sexual attraction may be necessary to overcome Eudora's self-delusion, but Tharsalio assumes a natural qualitative judgment will govern her choice: only he, or "another man of my making and mettle," will win her bed and hand (I.i.126). Finally, not only is Tharsalio on the side of life, vitality, boldness, wit, youth, and marriage—the winning side in any comic wooing plot—but he is further provided with an acceptable pedigree. Although a good deal of shock over Tharsalio's violation of Degree is expressed, both within the play and by its critics, his eligibility is defended by his brother and Lycus (I.ii.25–34) as well as by Tharsalio himself. Indeed, if Hylus in his guise as the oracular Hymen speaks truth, Tharsalio can claim equality by birth if not fortune: these nuptials readvance a family

> Noble and princely, and restore this palace
> To that name that six hundred summers since
> Was in possession of this bridegroom's ancestors,
> The ancient and most virtue-famed Lysandri.
>
> (III.ii.100–103)

Eudora may be forced from her pedestal to the dusty arena where mere "Contentment is the end of all worldly beings," but Chapman ensures that her physical satisfaction is completed within the social and religious sacrament of marriage and with a not unworthy object (II.ii.127–128).

That such softening reinterpretations of Tharsalio's assault on the widow's virtue and fortune seem to contradict earlier statements of motive should not convict Chapman either of dramatic confusion or of a belated attempt to rescue his self-seeking protagonist from villainy. The sequence of egotistic, socially blasphemous aggression later made morally acceptable by comedy's traditional sanctions is, I think, carefully calculated. Chapman chooses consecutive plot development, and in his own preparatory first plot he allows us to have our cake and eat it too. We enjoy vicariously Tharsalio's attack on social pieties about widows' conduct, female quasi-divinity, and the virtues assumed by rank. The psychological dynamics of wit ensure that we side with the rebellious hero while we laugh at society's conventions; and since wit represents repressed physical assault, it is not surprising that Tharsalio's humor prepares us to enjoy the liberated physical aggression of the wooing itself. What wit offers the individual, Chapman's dramatic techniques—the depersonalization and stereotyping which distance us from his characters—offer us: in Freud's definition, wit guards the ego from reality and protects it from having to expend pity on others.[15] Chapman allows us thoroughly to enjoy our vicarious rebellion and then, even as the main plot advances, reassures us of the harmlessness of our impulses.

Tharsalio's personal triumph and the vindication of his apparently destructive opinions thus entail neither general nor individual sacrifice; he proves a socially desirable, as well as cunning, husband. At the wedding masque which concludes the first plot, Eudora appears a satisfied bride, and Laodice has already fallen in love with the youth her stepfather intends her to marry. This masque scene provides a necessary temporal transition between Lysander's departure (III.i.) and Lycus's reappearance in IV.i to learn about Cynthia's mourning, but it also allows Chapman to round off his first plot guiltlessly by setting its narcissistic aggression in an approving social framework. The reminder is necessary, for the scene which discloses Tharsalio's success (III.i) also sets in motion Lysander's plan.

To encourage our easy transfer of expectations and sympathies in the second test, Chapman purposefully blurs fundamental distinctions and emphasizes apparent continuities. Cynthia's hyperbolic condemnation of Eudora ("O stain to womanhood!"—III.i.123) and reiterated protestations of her own marble constancy automatically nominate her for Eudora's newly vacated role. Lysander accepts his brother's challenge to repeat Tharsalio's experiment. There will be a second trial of a woman, the "pattern of [her] sex" (III.i.121), who promises her husband a love whose strength and constancy will outlast his death. Chapman also underlines similarities between the two experimenters: the Lysandri's response to challenge seems to run "in a blood" (I.i.168), as does so much else in the play. Both seek egoistic self-confirmation in their relations with others. Both regard the business at hand as a game, a battle of wits matching masculine craft and perseverance against feminine endurance, and the wager of Act III seems only a tangible confirmation of the spirit in which Tharsalio pursued the first plot's prize. Such an attitude emphasizes

15. In the classic summary of Freud's differentiation: "The pleasure of wit originates from an economy of expenditure in inhibition, that of the comic from an economy of expenditure in thought and that of humor from an economy of expenditure in emotion" (this formulation from Kris, p. 204). *The Widow's Tears* does not require such close discriminations: very simply, what I have termed "wit" lifts the inhibitions on infantile sexual and aggressive behavior and spares us that compassionate fellow-feeling demanded of civilized adults.

*situation*—at the expense of individual personalities—and the techniques by which to manipulate that challenging situation and thus win the game. Indeed, Lysander shows some of his brother's wit in the elaborate device whereby the living husband might check his own widow's faith. Both employ playlets which are at base practical jokes (Arsace's warning; the husband's death and burial); such ruses are designed to fool and, when revealed, to humiliate their victims. Both facilitate their deception's success by conquering the victim's servants as prelude to the mistress (Argus and Ero).

Chapman thus encourages his audience to share his characters' blindness by suggesting the identity of the experimenters as well as the trials themselves. His dramatic structure, too, seems to promise us continued comic distancing and hence a safe transfer of our expectations to the second plot. Tharsalio has functioned as an ultimately benevolent manipulator and unmasker in his assault on Eudora, and he apparently maintains that office when instigating his brother's imitation, though now the unmasker steps aside so that his device may economically cure two self-deluded fools. At this level, however, Tharsalio's apparent self-knowledge and honesty are not matched by his successor;[16] Lysander shares only his brother's aggressive egoism and must learn to accept his own, as well as his wife's, identity as "Poor naked sinners" (III.i.97). Lysander and Cynthia have both been characterized as "high i' th' instep," and we expect them to receive their comic comeuppance. Superficially, then, Chapman *seems* to offer us a second plot which will both attain this socially commendable (hence justified) goal and provide further occasions for the same liberating laughter we so enjoyed in the first trick.

Yet, though the name of the game remains the same, the major participants fail—or refuse—to see that the game itself, as well as the stakes for which it is played, has changed. As early as I.ii Tharsalio had spitefully switched the terms of the comparison so as to taunt his brother: widows' constancy becomes identical with wives' fidelity under a more general category—unrestrained female lust. The brothers' shared "confidence" confers the right to doubt the sincerity of their victims' protestations; indeed, the threat to self-love makes it psychologically necessary that the

16. See I.i.53–54 and 71 for Tharsalio's at least initial willingness to endure failure's mockery.

women conform to theory and submit to the tester's personal charms. Though Tharsalio repeatedly insists that both women cannot but submit to the libidinous cravings which rule their sex, it is more surprising to find his brother adopting the same moral imperatives. Lysander cannot forgo personally testing Cynthia, and his first rebuff serves only to fire his determination: "All these attractions take no hold of her; / No, not to take refection; 't *must* not be thus" (IV.ii.162–163; italics mine). In the excitement of the immediate challenge to his wit and virility (and the heady freedom his disguise offers?), Lysander overlooks the fact that imitating his brother's successful conquest will cost him far more than the chariot and horses; "winning the game" here means that everyone, except Tharsalio, loses.

The second test cannot end happily in marriage, for it is the marriage relationship itself which is on trial. Lysander's shortsighted imitation of his stubborn brother will be particularly disastrous because, as Lycus has pointed out, his personal and social identity is bound up with his marriage and his wife's famed loyalty (II.iii.49–58). Indeed, in his obsession with immediate concerns (setting up the conditions for trial), Lysander has even ensured that his folly will be made public: win or lose, he must finally explain his return from the dead. That Lysander's practical joke also disrupts Cyprus, through his "soldier's" dereliction of duty, only compounds our sense of the confused (and potentially disastrous) effects of foolish egoism.

Chapman thus paradoxically suggests that we join his characters in again concentrating on surface and technique—the exuberantly unrealistic situation, stereotyped characters, and emphasis on trivia crucial to the farceur's success—while he simultaneously destroys the framework which secured our enjoyment of farce's materials. The situation's fantasticality, usually matched by or reflected in linguistic excess and self-dramatization, is now pushed to extremes. The impertinent wooing at the widow's palace finds it grotesque parallel in the eight-penny soldier's invasion of the dead husband's tomb; hyperbolic promises of sexual fulfillment are reduced to mere food and wine; the bridal bed becomes the dead husband's casket. The wooer's verbal response is extreme, but no longer vivacious or witty. Cynthia will prove either partaker of Eudora's "foul shame" or heir to a "bright purity" which "disdain'st . . . to feed / Upon the base food of gross elements" (IV.ii.181–184); should his flattering mirror crack, Lysander vows to "split her weasand" (III.i.227). The new setting, hinting crucified bodies and grieving parents instead of palace finery and posturing fops, suits the changed mood which underlies Lysander's elaborate charade. Lysander, like Tharsalio, enjoys theatrical effects—witness the energy devoted to the elaborate surface of Lycus's tale, the staged funeral, and the soldier's disguise; but now concentration on the game's superficial features violates the player's fundamental responsibilities. Not only does Lysander fail in his duty to support and protect his wife; he insists on himself destroying her.

It is this depersonalization of even their closest relationships, fruit of the brothers' absolutism, which Chapman emphasizes through the moderate, humane Lycus. This servant-confidant's credibility as balanced observer and trustworthy advisor has been established early: he accurately assessed Lysander's strained dependence on his wife's renowned loyalty (II.iii.50–58); he tactfully tried to persuade Lysander to expect no more from his wife than is humanly possible, whatever her extravagant promises (II.i.58–76). More prominent in the second test, Lycus provides a new view of the wager, since he alone sees it in that wider social context where the brothers' attitudes cannot control the real consequences of their theatrical actions. Though Tharsalio may think his brother foolishly eccentric (and thus merely an easy mark for Tharsalio's revenge), Lycus's dissuasions insist on both the cruelty and the unnaturalness in Lysander's stubborn intentions:

Would any heart of adamant, for satisfaction of an ungrounded humour, rack a poor lady's innocency as you intend to do? It was a strange curiosity in that Emperor that ripped his mother's womb to see the place he lay in.

(III.i.1–4)

Lycus alone sees in Cynthia a suffering human being who does not deserve, whatever her shortcomings, to be a tortured puppet in someone else's private fantasy of self-justification.[17]

17. In *The Theater and the Dream: From Metaphor to Form in Renaissance Drama* (Baltimore, Md., 1973), Jackson I. Cope notes that the humane Lycus emphasizes "the cruelty and insensate nature of the test"; indeed, "from the beginning he warns against the danger and folly of confidence in its negative sense" (p. 63). Although Cope's approach and conclusions differ radically from my own, we both stress Lycus's function as an important (albeit lonely) moral norm for this topsy-turvy world.

In the dialogue of IV.i, Chapman uses Lycus's compassion to enforce a new perspective on Tharsalio himself and on that depersonalization and detachment from reality which we had enthusiastically shared in the first acts. Tharsalio continues to treat life as a game and gaily enters into the theatrical realization of Lysander's fiction, the funeral show which will "countenance truth out" (III.i.205–206). Faced with the naked ego which demands Cynthia's reassurance, Tharsalio shrugs off this glimpse of imminent disaster and concentrates on immediate, trivial regards: to his brother's threat to kill his wife if she fails his test, Tharsalio merely replies, "Well, forget not your wager, a stately chariot with four brave horses of the Thracian breed, with all appurtenances" (III.i.228–230).

Chapman no longer allows such casual refusal of involvement to go unchallenged; he now recalls us from the moral disorientation which Tharsalio's subordination of others to his fantasy encouraged. In IV.i Lycus questions Tharsalio's certainty that Cynthia's sorrow is mere hypocritical "show" meant to astound Cyprus. Tharsalio insulates himself by assuming Cynthia to be as self-conscious an actor as he and Lycus have been: given her "cue to whimper," she will "perform it well for her husband's wager" (IV.i.63, 33–34). Gleefully, he cites Cynthia's overly zealous performance as proof of insincerity: aiming at expressions "new and stirring," she "like an overdoing actor, affects grossly, and is indeed so far forced from the life, that it bewrays itself to be altogether artificial" (IV.i.9, 105–108). Moreover, to Tharsalio all are protected by the fictional nature of the drama they enact: since Lysander lives, real compassion for the joke's (hypocritical) victim is doubly wasted. Lycus insists that the practical joke enjoys no privileged, dreamlike exemption from physical effects. In life's presentation of what the actor personates, "tears, sighs, swoonings" may be "badges of true sorrow," and mourning's refusal of sustenance may end in death. In taking all life as a play, a game of skill, Tharsalio has lost crucial distinctions; his cynicism is now answered by the compassion of a man who regrets trifling with real emotion: "I am sorry I ever set foot in 't" (IV.i.115).

Lycus's reply to Tharsalio's cynical detachment exposes a darker side of the egoist's self-absorption: refusal to acknowledge the changed circumstances of the second test suggests a principled withdrawal of emotion from all other people. True Confidence means that Tharsalio has become entirely self-referential and will (nay, must) sacrifice even his closest relatives to validate his own infallibility. Cloaking such naked aggression with a playful attitude now magnifies its unnaturalness; pursuing the ego's satisfaction in a world no longer defined by cardboard people can produce nightmares instead of dream's wish-fulfillment. Replying to Tharsalio's concentration on theatrical effectiveness, Lycus enforces the very distinctions Tharsalio refuses to make:

Perform it, call you it? You may jest; men hunt hares to death for their sports, but the poor beasts die in earnest: you wager of her passions for your pleasure, but she takes little pleasure in those earnest passions.

(IV.i.35–38)

In the very metaphor with which he criticizes Tharsalio's attitude, Lycus captures the results of such detachment and suggests its logical conclusion.

Substituting Confidence for all other beliefs requires that Tharsalio continue to discount both Cynthia's words and her action; she must be hypocritical in order to prove his narcissism justified. Cynthia's moral absolutism demands comic unmasking, but the impossible choices imposed by the second "test" preclude that benign release from self-deception which would parallel Eudora's healthy (and socially acceptable) solution. In using the widow of Ephesus story for his second plot, Chapman forces us to see such egoism's consequences in extreme form. To such a skeptic, death from starvation is Cynthia's only means of proving her sincerity; having entered the tomb with her husband's body, she cannot return without indicting herself. Tharsalio does, at Lycus's insistence, try to save Cynthia later—though only when both fear "she is past our cure" (V.i.13); but he has earlier clearly stated his willingness to pursue the test until she prove him correct: "My sister may turn Niobe for love; but till Niobe be turned to a marble, I'll not despair but she may prove a woman" (IV.i.135–137). Tharsalio believes in a sharper's world, where lack of substance is supplied by show; though initially framed as a test of constant widowhood, Cynthia's choice has become one of joining Tharsalio's world or turning marble.

That Lysander shares his brother's disbelief (and new equation of "prov-[ing] a woman" with proving human and desiring to live) is clear when he changes the "rules" and insists on testing his wife's grief himself. Indeed, he has completely dissociated himself from the situation for which he is responsible; he contemplates the tomb and wonders, "Shall she famish, then? / Will *men* . . . suffer thus / So bright an ornament to earth, tombed quick / In earth's dark bosom?" (IV.ii.11–14; italics mine). Though Lysander ultimately offers Cynthia sexual satisfaction, his initial "temptations" are the reasonable and appropriate persuasions by which men try to reconcile the bereaved to life: for the body, food; for the soul, the traditional consolations of philosophy (IV.ii.64–86). Paradoxically, though this extreme mourning should prove flattering and Lysander redeem her to the upper air, his insistence on her superhuman purity (all soul, "all immortality," above the "base food of gross elements"— IV.ii.184–185) requires her refusal of life itself without him to share it. Lysander cannot bear a simply human Cynthia, one whom Ero can make "turn to flesh and blood, / And learn to live as other mortals do" (IV.ii.176–177); Cynthia has lost Lysander's test as soon as she accepts food, and with it life.

Though the brothers' responses are of course diametrically opposed (Lysander's hatred, V.ii.34–45; Tharsalio's glee, V.i.23–24, 31–33), their demands on Cynthia have been the same. Only Lycus can see that the fact of frail mortality need not cancel utterly our belief in human sincerity or faith in any bonds: he "will not say but she may prove frail. / But this I'll say, if she should chance to break, / Her tears are true, though women's truths are weak" (IV.i.144–147). Indeed, if we adopt the brothers' implicit equation of womanhood with accepting one's mortal flesh and blood, we see not only the lesson both Cynthia and Lysander must learn at great cost, but also a wider and perhaps compensatory significance in Lycus's qualification. However subject to time and our mortal natures, human emotions can be deeply, sincerely true.

Lycus's moderate advice carries no weight within the play, however, nor can his humanity counterbalance the impression of folly, loss, and events out of control which dominates the play's second half. This objective spokesman's presence in fact heightens our sense that the swift-paced farce mechanism has become an infernal machine. Suddenly one person stands outside the game and questions its premises; yet even as Lycus breaks through the insulation which has shielded this world from moral judgment, the pace of events intensifies. By exposing both brothers' valuation of Cynthia and their detachment from others' suffering before—and hence, despite—Cynthia's "fall," Lycus forces us to see that attitudes, as well as events, are out of control. The nightmare world of the play's last acts rests on these attitudes, and it is through Lycus that Chapman ensures our distance from—and new distaste for—Tharsalio's world of naked aggression.

We may wish to transfer earlier allegiances and expectations to the second test, but Chapman makes it increasingly difficult to do so. The second story remains unsoftened by those factors which allowed Tharsalio's original aggression to bear beneficial social fruit. This game ends in a broken marriage which can be only superficially patched. Lysander wishes his wife dead (V.ii.22–23 and V.v.13); Cynthia joins the brothers' shameless world of Confidence and outfaces her husband's accusations. The final consequence of withdrawing love and care from even the closest relationships is the tawdry new world in which Cynthia must be "arm'd" against her husband (V.iii.166). The marriage union, comedy's goal, has become in practice a battlefield because neither partner can afford trust. Indeed, in this paranoid world of certain deceit and betrayal, intimate knowledge merely ensures the betrayer's success: Tharsalio easily retaliates for his brother's mockery (I.iii); Cynthia's weapon is simply her wifely knowledge of Lysander's weaknesses (V.iii.181–183).

The external results of unchained egoism have proved disastrous; more significantly, we see that the self-absorbed man becomes finally self-enclosed, a man dramatizing himself before mirrors. The Tharsalio who had seemed admirably supple and wittily imaginative when surrounded by comic plodders, now proves himself rigid and unable to adapt to people or emotions undreamt of in his philosophy. His initially gleeful reaction to Cynthia's lapse no longer seems "adequate." Though our sympathy for Cynthia and her husband may be limited, they have not remained the flat, depersonalized characters of I.i: the anguished disillusionment they suffer, though comically self-inflicted, is not as comfortably distanced as Eudora's faint qualms about admitting sexual interest. Moreover, since Tharsalio's solipsism can include others only so far as (like Hylus) they become extensions of himself and his honor, what "moral" reaction he feels is both tardy and misdirected. Cynthia has provided "unspeakable sweet" justification for his belief in inconstancy, yet a few lines later an irate Tharsalio shifts the blame (and his last spiteful practical joke) in order to punish the upstart soldier who would not be served except by "my poor sister" (V.i.55, 71).

That Chapman does not intend this world to be saved by self-serving wit is evident in his introduction of a last disorienting mood—the Governor and the Watch, burlesque versions of comedy's climactic unravelling.[18] This final return to buffoonery allows Chapman to conclude his divergent plots on the traditional, though perhaps now tarnished, comic note of marriage without losing the dramatic—and moral—tension he has been at pains to establish. This eruption of a new cast of characters recalls the first plot's most high-spirited moments (the farcical confrontations with Rebus & Co. and with Eudora's servants); it also expands the play's social setting and thus comments on the themes and attitudes which precede it. Appropriately, in a work so self-consciously concerned with show and its relation to inner worth, the play holds up a mirror to itself—a fun-house mirror whose distortions are both farcically stereotyped and disturbingly revelatory.

The strained, even hysterical, conclusion of Lysander's test is thus interspersed both with the more serious concerns of the soldiers who condemn public negligence and with the final, double-edged humor of the Governor's "justice." The first juxtaposition emphasizes the "inevitable" disasters resulting from an apparently tragic sequence of events: in the private realm, Lysander's hatred, blame-shifting, and final bitter self-discovery ("What have I done? / O, let me lie and grieve, and speak no more"—V.v.89–90); in the public realm, crimes against society which demand both Lysander's and Lycus's lives. Appropriately, the threatened deaths are safely, amusingly, improbable; yet this tragicomic complication is not lightly dismissed. Chapman's juxtaposition stresses the dangerously close relation between private and public attitudes: Lysander's criminal irresponsibility as soldier simply mirrors his private failure as husband. Just before Lysander's final confrontation with Cynthia, two soldiers discuss the principle violated by the new guard: the law punishing negligence is designed to enforce mutual care and responsibility within a community of potential egotists. The second soldier's defense, with a few changed words, would as easily indict Lysander's (and Tharsalio's) familial behavior: "Tis not the body the law respects, but the soldier's neglect, when the watch (the guard and safety of the city) is left abandoned to all hazards" (V.iv.18–20). Lysander's stubborn solipsism has led him to ne-

18. Herring sees a possible "parody of the conclusion of Measure for Measure in the final scene of The Widow's Tears" (p. 164).

glect *all* bonds, but this failure now seems a general—not comically unique—condition. Lycus's apparent murder of his "dearest friend" inspires the first soldier's description of the shattered community they are sworn to defend: a "topsy-turvy world, [in which] friendship and bosom-kindness are but made covers for mischief, means to compass ill. Near-allied trust is but a bridge for treason" (V.iv.33–35).

Though common sense might impel us to see Tharsalio and Lysander as individual mirrors, perhaps victims, of this general social disintegration, Chapman's dramatic sequence suggests the opposite: private attitudes and actions shape public morality. Those passions which the brothers have unleashed in themselves by dramatic "logic" produce the topsy-turvy Cyprus of Act V; Tharsalio's witty egoism seems to summon forth its debased imitation to preside over the domain of Confidence. Tharsalio tries to reassume his earlier satiric-commentator role for the play's final parade of fools, yet the Governor expounds, in inflated form, Tharsalio's own attitudes and thus exposes the archmanipulator's share in the general folly. This civic leader merely extends into the public realm Tharsalio's attempt to force others to justify his confident "knowledge." Because comically simplified and two-dimensional, the Governor's distortion reflects the essential childishness of believing in thought's omnipotence. His defense of blind justice echoes Tharsalio's, and then Lysander's, certainty that private disbelief in virtue constitutes knowledge and proof: "For my part, I am satisfied it is so; that's enough for thee. I had ever a sympathy in my mind against him" (V.v.193–195). Personal antipathy and the certainty that verbal claims must always cloak an opposite reality become "fact" and threaten life itself. In all the play's tests, the "satisfied" imagination has proved sufficient authority for condemnation and punishment. Chapman underlines the parallel between foolish governor and governing fool by reintroducing Argus: the shrewdly presumptuous underling who had recognized Tharsalio's ascendant qualities now migrates to the Governor's service.

The similarities are not fortuitous: the final hilarity depends upon this caricature of Tharsalio, this fool at whom we can—and must—laugh. If Tharsalio in the second plot has come to seem both rigid and strangely peripheral, inhumanly detached from the reality we observed as well as powerless to control what he had initiated, the Governor hilariously parodies the narcissist's ideal. His whim is law, and he legally defines reality to fit his desires. In his total detachment from the facts and people around him, he lacks even Tharsalio's spiteful commitment. Self-inflated, the Governor floats free of human limitations, a balloon only moored to our unsatisfying reality by the tenuous thread of His Altitude's favor. With the soldiers, Chapman touches upon the social consequences, and punishments, for such carelessness as we have witnessed; his most powerful effects, however, remain implicit in his completed dramatic structure and in the changed relationship between Tharsalio and us.

By subtly altering his plot materials and techniques, Chapman has exposed the game—Tharsalio's and, through vicarious release, ours—*as* game, riotously satisfying on the stage but disturbing when transferred to extratheatrical situations. The play's situations, of course, become increasingly farfetched and "theatrical." Yet Chapman refuses to allow us the narcissist's aesthetic overdistancing; he turns the preposterous widow of Ephesus story into a hinted "real" world too complicated and elusive to fulfill tamely the manipulator's wishes. Put differently, Chapman's consecutive plotting establishes a balanced structure in which a cynical hypothesis is tested twice, in apparently identical situations. In the world of city comedy, generic expectations match Tharsalio's beliefs: people are viewed with detachment; women (and sex) become objects in an intrigue game won by the smartest trickster. Since society approves the result and all apparently live happily with their ill-gotten gains, the form implicitly defends these standards; we can have our cake and eat it with relish. Chapman's second situation is not identical, however, In fact, it tests the validity of those attitudes and values on which the first, farcical world was predicated. We are lulled by the apparent continuation of farce's conventions and norms, then shocked. When the Governor reintroduces that stable farcical world of predictable stereotypes which precludes tragic consequences, Chapman can play his regained comic surface against both Lysander's and Cynthia's bitter disillusionment and his audience's guilty entrapment in Tharsalio's world of confident "show."

Chapman's refusal to provide a satisfying end, to synthesize comic surface and revealed anarchy, creates a dynamic tension between this buffoon *ex machina*, the situation he has been called to arbitrate, and us. We are distanced from the action, yet involved in it by our greater knowledge of events. Worse, our early identification with Tharsalio implicates us, too, in the debacle to which unleashed and actualized desires have led. We wish to claim a wider, more humane understanding of events and their significance, yet the play refuses a social solution (via the Governor) and offers only Tharsalio's cynical comfort: "So; brother, let your lips compound the strife, / And *think* you have the only constant wife" (V.v.316–317; italics mine). At the most literal level, of course, Tharsalio is right, for Chapman has introduced (with fine Tharsalian wit) his own variation on Petronius: technically, Cynthia remains "chaste," since Lysander has in fact cuckolded himself. Paradoxically, her infidelity is both real and, like the body she mourns, a "mere blandation, a *deceptio visus*" (V.v.148).

Such an escape clause, however, proves no more satisfying than the Governor's final exercise of justice. For true resolution the play's jesting finale substitutes the disquieting humor of accommodation—accommodation as the only way to live with the fact that we cannot make the world conform to our ego's desires.[19] *The Widow's Tears* thus refuses the full cathartic release of that aggression and dissatisfaction which the permissible outrage of farce first offered. Although Tharsalio remains unchanged throughout the play, our response to this boy eternal alters. Tharsalio is the vehicle of an exhilarating release; through him we gleefully realize our deepest desires. By implicating us briefly in Tharsalio's games, however, Chapman also forces us to recognize Tharsalio as an emblem of that freedom's necessary limits.

19. In a later essay, Freud calls humor "the triumph of narcissism, the victorious assertion of the ego's invulnerability," and a victory of the pleasure principle which requires a "rejection of the claims of reality"; see "Humour (1927)" in *SE*, XXI, 162–163. The "humorous" solution is offered by Tharsalio, however, not by Lysander. Neither the disillusioned husband nor the audience seems capable of adopting this triumphant assertion of subjectivity. Within the play's context, then, the final lines state the harsh necessity for open-eyed reconciliation to an unsatisfactory reality: "*think*" your wife "constant." Arnold Hauser, in his fascinating study of seventeenth-century sensibility, *Mannerism: The Crisis of the Renaissance and the Origin of Modern Art* (London, 1965), suggests that "Humour reconciles itself to the alienation which tragedy is unable to accept, but is no less dependent on alienation and, like tragedy, expresses the sense of life of a generation dominated by it" (p. 141); see also Hauser's illuminating chapter "Narcissism as the Psychology of Alienation."

# Massinger's Patriarchy: The Social Vision of A New Way to Pay Old Debts

## MICHAEL NEILL

An Houshold is as it were a little Commonwealth, by the good government where-
of, Gods glorie may be advantced, and the commonwealth which standeth of
severall families benefited.

John Dod and Robert Cleaver,
*A Godly Forme of Household Government*[1]

STRANGELY, since it is one of Massinger's few acknowledged successes
and the most frequently performed of his plays, *A New Way to Pay Old
Debts*, has received scant critical attention. The play's continuing popularity evidently depends on the powerful characterization of Sir Giles Overreach; but the scale of this villain-hero and the violence of his end have led
to uneasiness about the "melodramatic" quality of the action, and about
the moralization which accompanies it.[2] Moreover the tendency to read
the play simply as Jonsonian satire of an extortionate arriviste—an outsize

---

1. *A Godly Forme of Houshold Government* (London, 1638), sig. A7.
2. Philip Massinger, *A New Way to Pay Old Debts*, ed. T. W. Craik, The New
Mermaid ed. (London, 1964), pp. xii–xiii. All citations from *A New Way* are to this
edition, referred to henceforth as "Craik."

burlesque of Sir Giles Mompesson[3]—can make the love plot of Margaret
Overreach and Alworth seem an irrelevant exercise in Fletcherian pathos,
and the graver courtship of Lord Lovell and Lady Alworth a concession to
the courtly preciosity of the Phoenix audience.[4] Seen like this, *A New Way*
may appear not only structurally confused but morally objectionable—
expecially in its vindication of Welborne, whose only obvious "right" to
restoration of the fortune he has wantonly squandered is that indicated by
his name: the birthright he shares with the idealized "true gentry" of the
play. Coolly regarded, then, Welborne's "new way" is no more than a
usurpation of the Machiavellian stratagems of the new man, Overreach,
himself; and it is justifiable only by a kind of indulgent snobbery little
better than the time-serving deference of characters like Marrall and Tapwell:

> When he was rogue Welborne, no man would believe him,
> And then his information could not hurt us.
> But now he is right worshipful again,
> Who dares but doubt his testimony?
> . . . . . . . . . .
>              [He] has found out such a new way
> To pay his old debts, as 'tis very likely
> He shall be chronicl'd for it.

(IV.ii.13–29)

The lines are those of Tapwell, who respects no other chronicle than his
alehouse register "in chalk" (I.i.25–26); but there can be no doubt that
from Massinger's point of view the Welborne who offers his service to
"king, and country" at the end of the play, is already reenrolled in the
chronicles of honor. "True gentry," it would seem, for all its fine rhetoric
of "honor," report," and "chronicle," can survive only through the un-
scrupulous improvisation of the entrepreneur. To be "worshipful," to be
"worthy" in this world is to be "worth" enough to pay your debts—to be a
"good man" in Shylock's sense of the term.[5] And if that is truly the case,

---

3. See L. C. Knights, *Drama and Society in the Age of Jonson* (London, 1962), pp. 228–
229. Cf. also Patricia Thomson, "The Old Way and the New Way in Dekker and Massinger," *MLR*, LI (1956), 168–178.

4. See Craik, p. xiii, and Thomson, pp. 177–178.

5. *Merchant of Venice*, I.iii.11–15.

then the whole elaborately created world of manners, of polite decorum and nice social discriminations, by which the dramatist sets so much store, becomes a dishonest decoration on the surface of reality.

However, it appears to me that *A New Way* is at once more coherent in its dramatic structure and most consistent in its social vision than this reading would imply—even if there remain lurking contradictions that Massinger's comic catastrophe never satisfactorily resolves. Like *The Merchant of Venice*, with which it is often compared, *A New Way* is about the pangs of transition to a capitalistic, cash-nexus society; and like Shakespeare, Massinger takes a fundamentally conservative attitude toward that process, asserting the primacy of communal bonds over legal bondage, of social obligation over commercial debt, of love over the law.[6] *The Merchant*, however, founds its critique of bourgeois values upon a familiar Christian mythos—the opposition of the Old Law and the New—and in a reassuring comic paradox neutralizes its new man, the Machiavellian capitalist, by making him a representative of the Old Law, rendered obsolete by the sacrifice of Christ. The Jew-Devil Shylock "stands for" Law, Portia for Sacrifice.[7] Though Sir Giles Overreach is sometimes made to appear like yet another diabolic incarnation from the Moralities,[8] and though Massinger invokes scriptural analogues for his judgment of prodigal Welborne and the false servant Marrall, *A New Way* has no such thorough mythic foundation. Instead it appeals to a whole set of normative social assumptions which, although they were customarily justified by the Scriptures, are in fact peculiar to Massinger's own epoch.[9] Because they belong, in Peter Laslett's phrase, to "the world we have lost,"[10] they can make *A New Way* seem a less universal comedy than its predecessor; but they also make it considerably more vivid as a document of historical attitudes. Massinger brings alive, as perhaps none of his contemporaries

6. Cf. Knights, p. 233; and Thomson, p. 170.

7. *Merchant*, III.ii.57; IV.i.103, 142.

8. See for instance III.i.83, III.ii.120–122, IV.i. 149–157. He is not only Mammon, but in effect the true "spirit of lies" who has entered Marrall (III.ii.248). Cf. Knights, p. 232: "I do not think it is too much to say that he represents Avarice—one of the Seven Deadly Sins."

9. For detailed accounts of seventeenth-century patriarchal thinking, see Gordon J. Schochet, *Patriarchalism in Political Thought* (Oxford, 1975), and "Patriarchalism, Politics and Mass Attitudes in Stuart England," *Hist. Journ.*, XII (1969), 413–441.

10. Peter Laslett, *The World We Have Lost* (London, 1965).

can, the ingrained social beliefs that were to make Sir Robert Filmer's writings the handbook of a generation of Royalist gentry.

In the last big speech of the play, Welborne reminds us of the double nature of the "debts" that must be paid before the social order can be reestablished:

> there is something else
> Beside the repossession of my land,
> And payment of my debts, that I must practise.
> I had a reputation, but 'twas lost
> In my loose courses; and till I redeem it
> Some noble way, I am but half made up.
>
> (V.i.390–395)

The "making up" of his "worshipful" self is dependent on the "making up" of a moral obligation more powerful than any merely financial debt. The method of redemption he proposes is that of "service"—service to his king, fittingly discharged through his immediate social superior, Lord Lovell (ll. 396–400). The idea of service is a crucial one in the play: and one which is pointedly taken up in the epilogue, where Massinger play-fully sees himself as the servant of the audience, seeking his freedom by the "manumission" of their applause (ll. 403–404). He elaborates the conceit in his dedicatory epistle, by way of graceful compliment to the Earl of Caernarvon, whose protection he seeks to earn "in my service," recalling that "I was born a devoted servant, to the thrice noble family of your incomparable Lady," and hopefully subscribing himself "Your Hon-our's true servant." Massinger, though he came of minor gentry, was born into service in the sense that his father was steward to the household of Henry Herbert, Earl of Pembroke; and the dedication invites us to read *A New Way* as a tribute to the ideals he imbibed at Wilton—as itself a new way to pay a personal debt of honor.[11]

Even the element of topical satire in the play can be seen to accord with this complimentary purpose, since, as Patricia Thomson has pointed out, Mompesson, as Buckingham's protégé, was a natural enemy of the Her-berts. But Overreach's villainy, of course, touches only tangentially on Mompesson's malpractice. Mompesson is important to the dramatist's

11. Thomson, pp. 172–176.

imagination less as a venal monopolist than as the hideous type of an alarming social tendency. A contemporary comment on Mompesson, cited by L. C. Knights, may help to make this point clearer:

> Sir Giles Mompesson had fortune enough in the country to make him happy, if that sphere could have contained him, but the vulgar and universal error of satiety with present enjoyments, made him too big for a rustical condition, and when he came at court he was too little for that, so that some novelty must be taken up to set him in *aequilibrio* to the place he was in, no matter what it was, let it be never so pestilent and mischievous to others, he cared not, so he found benefit by it.[12]

Mompesson's crime amounted to a double violation of that principle of service on which the order of society was founded: he had betrayed the obligations of that office in which the king had placed him, and he had attempted to rise above that position in society to which God had called him. Overreach is an incarnation of that anarchic impulse which seemed to fuel Mompesson's corrupt ambition. In his brutal assault on the bonds of a society felt to subsist on an intricate hierarchical network of communal service and mutual obligation, he is the nightmare projection of emergent capitalism, the monstrous herald of that new social order whose perfection Marx was to describe:

> The bourgeoisie, wherever it has got the upper hand, has put an end to all feudal, patriarchal, idyllic relations. It has pitilessly torn asunder the motley feudal ties that bound man to his *natural superiors*, and has left remaining no other nexus between man and man than naked self-interest, than callous *cash-payment*. . . .
> The bourgeoisie has stripped of its halo every occupation hitherto honoured and looked up to. . . . It has converted the physician, the lawyer, the priest, the poet, the man of science, into its paid wage-labourers.
> The bourgeoisie has torn away from the family its sentimental veil, and has reduced the family relation to a mere money-relation.[13]

Overreach's household includes Marrall, Will-do, and Greedy—lawyer, priest, and justice—among its paid wage-laborers; and "family" for him—as his relations with his nephew, and ultimately with his daughter too, illustrate—simply denotes a nexus of money relationships: when Welborne has lost his money they are no longer kin.

12. Knights, p. 229 n.
13. *The Communist Manifesto*, quoted in Laslett, pp. 16–17.

In contrast to the vast and ruthlessly impersonal machine conceived by Marx, the social order imagined by most of Massinger's contemporaries was that of a large family ruled by a father-sovereign: each family was itself a commonwealth (a paternal monarchy) and the state a family of such petty commonwealths. The relationship was not merely one of analogy: for it was from the first family that the state itself had grown.[14] The hierarchic order of society was thus a natural part of the divinely ordained scheme of things. Whatever the philosophic limitations of such patriarchalist thought, it took immense strength, as Gordon Schochet has shown, from its close correspondence to the practical socialization of the vast majority of seventeenth-century Englishmen for whom the family, or household, was the focus of most activity: "some form of paternal authority was the only kind of status relationship with which most of these people were familiar. . . . childhood was not something which was eventually outgrown; rather, it was enlarged to include the whole of one's life."[15]

Sir Robert Filmer's *Patriarcha*, written in the 1640s, is only the best known of a series of works which adumbrated a patriarchal model of society. With his *Observations upon Aristotle's Politiques* (1652) it constitutes the latest and most systematic attempt to work out a set of ideas which were already among the commonplaces of social thought in Massinger's time. When King James wrote in *Basilikon Doron* that a prince should act toward his people "as their naturall father and kindly Master," he appealed implicitly to a whole context of commentary which made of the Fifth Commandment a scriptural justification for all authority.[16] Prominent contributions to this pious tradition include Bartholomew Batty's *The Christian mans Closet*, translated by William Lowth in 1581, and two immensely popular books by John Dod and Robert Cleaver, *A Godly Forme of Houshold Government* (1598) and *A Plaine and Familiar Exposition of the Ten Commandements* (1604).[17] Society, from the perspective of these patri-

14. Schochet, *Patriarchalism*, pp. 1, 55, 92–96. A classic statement of this position can be found in Hooker, *Ecclesiastical Polity*, I.x.4.

15. *Patriarchalism*, p. 15; cf. also p. 64, and "Patriarchalism . . . and Mass Attitudes," pp. 413–415, and W. H. Greenleaf, *Order, Empiricism and Politics* (London, 1964), pp. 88–89.

16. *Patriarchalism*, pp. 73 ff.

17. The *Exposition* went through eighteen printings by 1632, *Houshold Government* at least seven by 1630.

archalists, consists of a community of priestlike fathers and their families, natural autocracies modified only by a carefully ordained set of mutual duties and obligations. "Parentes are Gods vicars in earth," writes Batty in laying out "The Duetie of Children towardes their Parentes," and "All are understoode by the name Parents, under whose government wee live," including "Magistrates, Elders, Preachers, Maisters, Teachers, Tutors and such like."[18] Dod and Cleaver similarly warn children "that whatsoever they doe to their fathers and mothers . . . they doe it to God," and in the word *Father* "are contained all superiors in what place soever set above us." Thus the servant, too, is to remember that his master "stands in the place of Christ unto thee, being of his familie."[19] The principal duty of the *paterfamilias* is to ensure the fit ordering of his household, to enforce the proprieties of place: "there are two sorts in every perfect familie: 1. The Governors. 2. Those that must be ruled." If this sounds like a formula for domestic tyranny, Dod and Cleaver insist that "these two sorts have speciall duties belonging to them, the one towards the other," and that fathers must not act "as tyrants" but treat children and servants alike "lovingly and Christianly."[20] In laying out this "Godly Forme of Houshold Government" Dod and Cleaver are not simply elaborating a metaphor, for in their estimation "it is impossible for a man to understand how to governe the common-wealth, that doth not rule his owne house."[21] The connection must have seemed a natural one in a society where, as Schochet emphasizes, political identity was effectively itself a function of familial headship.[22]

For the lesser members of the domestic commonwealth "social identity was altogether vicarious. The family was represented to the larger community by its head . . . and those whom he commanded were 'subsumed' in his social life."[23] Constrictive as such a family looks from our point of view, it provided its members with a sense of secure identity, and gave to

18. Bartholomew Batty, *The Christian mans Closet*, trans. William Lowth (London, 1581), Q3^v-R1^v.

19. *Houshold Government*, Y4; *A Plaine and Familiar Exposition of the Ten Commandements* (London, 1618), p. 185.

20. *Houshold Government*, A8, V5–6, Z5–6.

21. *Houshold Government*, A8^v. Cf. also Bodin's description of the family as "the true image of a Commonweale," cited in Greenleaf, p. 128.

22. *Patriarchalism*, p. 66.

23. *Ibid.*, p. 26.

society at large a comfortably human scale whose threatened loss was understandably painful.[24] Massinger's play is in some sense about this threat: and the horror it evokes in the dramatist helps to explain the titanic stature of Overreach. If Sir Giles's colossal ambition seems somehow too large for the world of social comedy that is because, in Massinger's imagination, he represents those forces whose insurgence menaces the very possibility of such a world, of an order that is in any familiar sense "social" at all.[25] In the imagery of religious outrage with which this usurper is condemned, Massinger is appealing, like Dod and Cleaver before him, to the hallowed sanctions of patriarchalist ideology.

The very popularity of such treatises as Dod and Cleaver's in a period when traditional organic models of political organization were subject to an increasingly critical scrutiny is a testimony to the social insecurities that Massinger's play attempts to soothe. But patriarchalist writing itself reflects the pressures of Puritan dissent and the contractual theories with which such dissent was frequently associated. Michael Walzer has argued that the domestic commonwealth imagined by the Puritans Dod and Cleaver already has many features in common with the conjugal family that was to replace the traditional patriarchy. Their conception of the father's role is to some extent a legalistic one which emphasizes "office" and "duties" at the expense of the natural bonds of affection. Thus it tends to downgrade the historical bonding of kinship, and for the mutual obli-

---

24. Laslett, p. 21. "One Out of Many," the second section of V. S. Naipaul's novel, *In A Free State* (London, 1973), p. 37, gives an illuminating account of the trauma suffered by a man suddenly transferred from the anonymity of a communal culture to a contemporary individualist society. Santosh, the displaced Indian servant, recalls his master as "the man who adventured in the world for me . . . I experienced the world through him . . . I was content to be a small part of his presence."

25. Compare Cicero, *De officiis* 3.6–7:

for a man to take something from his neighbour and to profit by his neighbour's loss is more contrary to Nature than . . . anything else that can affect either our person or our property. For, in the first place, injustice is fatal to social life and fellowship between man and man. For, if we are so disposed that each, to gain some personal profit, will defraud or injure his neighbour, then those bonds of human society, which are most in accord with Nature's laws, must of necessity be broken . . . that is an absurd position which is taken by some people, who say that they will not rob a parent or a brother . . . but that their relation to the rest of their fellow-citizens is quite another thing. Such people contend in essence that they are bound to their fellow-citizens by no mutual obligations, social ties, or common interests. This attitude demolishes the whole structure of civil society.

Quoted from the Loeb edition, trans. Walter Miller (London, 1961), pp. 289–295.

gations of parent and child, master and servant, to substitute the absolute authority of a father confirmed in office by a divinely ordained contract.[26] In this autocratic commonwealth the nice distinctions of hierarchy which are native to the true patriarchal family are at a discount: where a household can be so simply divided into "The Governors" and "Those that must be ruled," even the basic distinction between children and servants is blurred.[27] Overreach's autocratic tyranny, in which daughter and servants alike are treated as legally contracted agents of the master's will, and where the bonds of legal debt take the place of kinship as the principal links in the social chain, is as much an embodiment of a familial as of a commercial "new way." Though the connection may be one that the dramatist himself has not fully grasped, *A New Way to Pay Old Debts* is in some sense a play about religion and the rise of capitalism; and it is a reflection of Massinger's bitter conservatism that an atheistic iconoclast should come to epitomize the Puritan Household Governor.

In accord with his social menace, Sir Giles Overreach is presented as no common, petty miser—which even Shylock finally is—but a figure of heroic stature. He is a commercial and domestic Tamburlaine, whose *virtù* invites the admiration of Lady Alworth's servants even as they denounce him for his griping extortion:

> FURNACE
> To have a usurer that starves himself,
> And wears a cloak of one-and-twenty years
> On a suit of fourteen groats, bought of the hangman,
> To grow rich, and then purchase, is too common:
> But this Sir Giles feeds high, keeps many servants,
> Who must at his command do any outrage;
> Rich in his habit; vast in his expenses;
> Yet he to admiration still increases
> In wealth, and lordships.
>
> (II.ii. 106–114)

The glamor of his conspicuous consumption links him with Jonsonian anti-heroes like Volpone, whose energetic delight in stratagem he explicitly echoes:

26. See Michael Walzer, *The Revolution of the Saints: A Study in the Origins of Radical Politics* (Cambridge, Mass., 1966), p. 186.

27. See Walzer, p. 190.

> I enjoy more true delight
> In my arrival to my wealth, these dark
> And crooked ways, than you shall e'er take pleasure
> In spending what my industry hath compass'd.
>
> (IV.i.135–138)[28]

But he is something larger and more terrifying than Jonson's vulpine magnifico: both "a lion, and a fox" (V.i.25), as Lady Alworth sees him—a figure who embodies the martial aspect of the Machiavellian tyrant as well as his politic cunning. It is in heroic terms that we are repeatedly asked to see his diabolic prowess—by Order, for instance:

> He frights men out of their estates,
> And breaks through all law-nets, made to curb ill men,
> As they were cobwebs. No man dares reprove him.
> Such a spirit to dare, and power to do, were never
> Lodg'd so unluckily.
>
> (II.ii.114–118)

—by Lord Lovell:

> I, that have liv'd a soldier,
> And stood the enemy's violent charge undaunted
> To hear this blasphemous beast am bath'd all over
> In a cold sweat: yet like a mountain he,
> Confirm'd in atheistical assertions,
> Is no more shaken, than Olympus is
> When angry Boreas loads his double head
> With sudden drifts of snow.
>
> (IV.i.150–157)

—and not least in his own vaunting hyberbole:

> LOVELL
> Are you not frighted with the imprecations,
> And curses, of whole families made wretched
> By your sinister practices?

28. Cf. *Volpone*, I.i.30–33:
> I glory
> More in the cunning purchase of my wealth,
> Than in the glad possession, since I gain
> No common way.

OVERREACH

                Yes, as rocks are
When foamy billows split themselves against
Their flinty ribs; or as the moon is mov'd,
When wolves with hunger pin'd, howl at her brightness.
I am of a solid temper, and like these
Steer on a constant course: with mine own sword
If call'd into the field, I can make that right,
Which fearful enemies murmur'd at as wrong.
        .   .   .   .   .   .   .   .   .   .

Nay, when my ears are pierc'd with widows' cries,
And undone orphans wash with tears my threshold;
I only think what 'tis to have my daughter
Right honourable.
                                    (IV.i.111–129)

"To have my daughter / Right honourable": the reiterated phrase becomes
a kind of transformed bathos, like Tamburlaine's "sweet fruition of an
earthly crown," Overreach's equivalent of riding in triumph through
Persepolis. While at one extreme such language may link him with the
mock-heroic bombast of Greedy, that "monarch . . . of the boil'd, the
roast, the bak'd" (III.ii.20–21) and pillager of Furnace's pastry fortifica-
tions (I.ii.25–47), at the other it invites comparison with Lovell's heroic
enterprise in the Low Countries; and the power struggle in which Sir
Giles is engaged is, the play suggests, of equal moment to that undertaken by his noble adversary. For Overreach is a "blasphemous beast"
not merely by virtue of those "atheistical assertions" which horrify Lovell,
but through his titanic struggle to subvert an order of society decreed by
God himself.

   Massinger builds his social argument on the contrasted arrangement of
four households or families. Temporarily excluded from this society is the
déclassé Welborne, once a "lord of acres," who has prodigally squandered
his estates and thus forfeited those titles ("Master Welborne," "your
worship") which defined his proper place in the social order. The principal
intrigue in the play is devoted to the restoration of this outcast to the
power and privileges which belong to his gentlemanly rank and more
specifically to his position as master of a great household. To fully understand the parameters of his situation and to sympathize with the
melancholy rage which it inspires in Welborne, one must be sensitive to

the nuances of social address by which the play sets so much store. Peter Laslett emphasizes the critical importance of the terminology of rank in this society:

The term gentleman marked the exact point at which the traditional social system divided up the population into two extremely unequal sections. About a twenty-fifth . . . belonged to the gentry and to those above them in the social hierarchy. This tiny minority owned most of the wealth, wielded the power and made all the decisions. . . . If you were not a gentleman, if you were not ordinarily called *"Master"* by the commoner folk, or *"Your Worship"*; if you, like nearly all the rest, had a Christian and a surname and nothing more; then you counted for little in the world outside your own household. . . . the labourers and husbandmen, the tailors, millers, drovers, watermen, masons, could become constables, parish clerks, churchwardens, ale-conners, even overseers of the poor . . . [But] they brought no personal weight to the modest offices which they could hold. As individuals they had no instituted, recognised power over other individuals, always excepting . . . those subsumed within their families. Directly they acquired such power, whether by the making of the inheriting of wealth, or by the painful acquisition of a little learning, then they became *worshipful* by that very fact. . . . To exercise power, then, to be free of the society of England, to count at all as an active agent in the record we call historical, you had to be a gentleman. . . . you had to hold one of those exceptional names in a parish register which bore a prefix or a suffix. . . . The commonest addition to a name . . . is *Mr*, for the word "Master," and *Mrs*, for the word "Mistress". . . . *Gent.* and *Esq.* are rare . . . as is the word *Dame*. . . . and *Knight* and *Baronet* are, of course, much rarer still. The reader with the whole population in his mind . . . will, of course, occasionally come across the titles *Lord* or *Lady*, and the ceremonious phrase 'The right Honourable the . . .' which was often used to introduce them.[29]

Plain Timothy Tapwell and Froth, his wife, belong to that overwhelming majority who are not "free of the society of England," who have no natural powers beyond the compass of their own household. From Welborne's point of view, Tapwell, as his former under-butler, is still a "slave," a "drudge," a servant still bound to his master by the patronage Welborne has given him (I.i. 17–28). Tapwell, on the other hand, sees himself very differently. Having acquired "a little stock" and "a small cottage" through frugal opportunism, he has duly "humbled" himself to marry Froth, and set up as an alehouse keeper, his own man (I.i.59–61). From this base he has risen to the point where he is "thought worthy to be

29. Laslett, pp. 26–27.

scavenger;" and from the humble post of parish rubbish-collector he confidently expects to climb to even more exalted office:

> to be overseer of the poor;
> Which if I do, on your petition Welborne,
> I may allow you thirteen pence a quarter,
> And you shall thank *my worship*.
>
> (I.i.68–71; italics added)

Tapwell, in fact, is a kind of low-life Overreach, his desire to become "worshipful" echoing Sir Giles's passion to have his daughter made "right honourable." He will have Welborne his petitioner as Sir Giles will have Margaret attended by whole trains of "errant knights" and Lady Downefalnes. For both men "office" denotes not the large Ciceronian concept but a narrow, functionally determined accession of personal power and prestige. Like Sir Giles, too, Tapwell professes a view of society which denies all traditional sanctions: it acknowledges no past, only a pragmatically organized present and a future of untrammeled aspiration.[30] Welborne's appeals to ancient right and to the debts imposed by past generosity are equally vacuous to a man like Tapwell—there is no chronicle of honor or register of benefits in his commonwealth:

> WELBORNE
> Is not thy house, and all thou hast my gift?
>
> TAPWELL
> I find it not in chalk, and Timothy Tapwell
> Does keep no other register.
> .   .   .   .   .   .   .   .
> What I *was* sir, it skills not;
> What you *are* is apparent.
>
> (I.i.24–30; italics added)

30. In effect Overreach and Tapwell propound a secularized version of that Puritan attitude to the past so pithily expressed by Rev. John Stockwood in a Paul's Cross sermon in 1578, when he urged men with "earnest minds" not to be "blinded with those vain shadows of fathers, times and customs" (quoted in Walzer, p. 187). The families to which they are committed are significantly narrow, conjugal families of the type whose emergence Walzer connects with Puritan mores: where a child of the true patriarchal family was tied to the past by the bonds of "the old kinship system, [and] committed in advance to the family allies and followers" (p. 189), the members of the conjugal family are bound by no such absolute allegiances.

His chalk register of debt is the equivalent of Sir Giles's parchment deeds; and both are presented, like Shylock's bond, as the emblems of a social vision which seeks to make the narrow scruple of commercial law the sole principle of human organization. For Tapwell, his fellow office-man, the constable, is the great Prince of this legalistic realm:

> There dwells, and within call, if it please your worship,
> A potent monarch, call'd the constable,
> That does command a citadel, call'd the stocks;
> Whose guards are certain files of rusty billmen.
>
> (I.i.12–15)

This sarcastic degradation of heroic language anticipates, in its heavy way, the cynical wit of the pun with which Sir Giles will deflate the pretensions of "errant" knighthood (II.i.79).

Tapwell can detail the story of that "man of worship, / Old Sir John Welborne, justice of peace, and *quorum*" and even recall the magnanimity of his housekeeping, but the whole report is swept away in a single contemptuous phrase: "but he dying" (I.i.30–37). Sir Giles (who has the current J.P., a jumped-up tailor's son, in his pocket) roundly confesses to Lovell, "I do contemn report myself, / As a mere sound" (IV.i.91–92). He is equally contemptuous of the obligations of friendship and the duties of office:

> 'tis enough I keep
> Greedy at my devotion: so he serve
> My purposes, let him hang, or damn, I care not.
> Friendship is but a word.
>
> (II.i.19–22)

And "Words," he insists, "are no substances" (III.ii.128)—they are empty ceremonious "forms" which disguise the fact that society is merely an arrangement of services rendered for cash. Given Overreach's philosophy, his desire to "Have all men sellers, / And I the only purchaser" (II.i.32–33) is nothing less than the longing for absolute tyranny. Dod and Cleaver's prescription for wise domestic government includes a warning against borrowing and usury: "Salomon saith, *The borrower is servant to the lender*: that is, beholding to him, and in his danger."[31] The

---

31. *Houshold Government*, F2, quoting Proverbs, 22:7.

chain of debt created by Overreach's lending is one which seeks to override the traditional obligations of society, and to replace the patriarchal hierarchy with a vicious commercial autarchy, governed by himself, the unfettered master of an anti-family of slaves. His own household, where officers of church and state are already thrown together in indiscriminate bondage with children and servants, is the model for this new tyranny, where the issue of his inveterate opponents, the "true gentry," will be forced "To kneel to mine, as bond-slaves (II.i.81–89).[32]

Set against the conspicuous consumption and cash-nexus relationships of Sir Giles's household is the ideal of liberal housekeeping embodied in the households of Welborne's dead father, of Lord Lovell, and most immediately of Lady Alworth. If the anarchic individualism and all-engrossing ambition of Sir Giles are emblematized in the names of Marrall and Greedy, the values of traditional society are suggested by those of the Alworth servants, Order and Watchall. Order, in particular, seldom misses an opportunity for sententious observation on the morality of true service and the hierarchical decorum for which he stands:[33]

> Sir, it is her will,
> Which we that are her servants ought to serve it,
> And not dispute.
>
> (I.iii.4–6)

> Set all things right, or as my name is Order,
> And by this staff of office that commands you;
> This chain, and double ruff, symbols of power;
> Whoever misses in his function,
> For one whole week makes forfeiture of his breakfast,
> And privilege in the wine-cellar.
>
> (I.ii.1–6)

32. Compare the autocratic leveling of the God imagined by Puritan "covenant theology": "Through the covenant men became the 'bondsmen' of God—not the children—and the image implied the voluntary recognition of an existing debt, a legal or commercial obligation. *God was the creditor of all men*" (Walzer, p. 168; italics mine). Overreach once again resembles a secular caricature of Puritan doctrine, the legal bonds by which he attempts to build a society of creditors constituting a kind of blasphemous social covenant.

33. Cf. *Exposition*, p. 218: "The master therefore (that the house may be well ordered) must let everyone know his place and calling. . . . The house might be enriched, every thing might be done in good order, and would fall out in their just and due compasse, where every one were diligent in his place."

The sturdy sense of place which informs Order's humor in this last speech contrasts with the ludicrously exaggerated deference of Marrall who addresses even Lady Alworth's waiting-man as "your worship" (II.ii. 132), and whose groveling before the reborn prodigal shows Massinger's gift for satiric farce at its best:

> MARRALL
>
> Then in my judgement sir, my simple judgement,
> (Still with your worship's favour) I could wish you
> A better habit, for this cannot be
> But much distasteful to the noble lady
> (I say no more) that loves you, for this morning
> To me (and I am but a swine to her)
> Before th' assurance of her wealth perfum'd you,
> You savour'd not of amber.
>
> WELBORNE
>
> I do now then?
>
> MARRALL
>
> This your batoon hath got a touch of it.
> [*Kisses the end of his cudgel*]
>
> (II.iii.20–28)

The caricature of courtly style with its self-deprecating parentheses and tactful circumlocutions culminates in a perfect frenzy of servility. Marrall explicitly seeks a "place" in return for his vassalage, "the lease of glebe land [fittingly] called Knave's-Acre." But for him service is merely enslavement, place merely hire and salary. Like Greedy, devastated by the prospect of losing "my dumpling . . . And butter'd toasts, and woodcocks" (III.ii.307–308), Marall finds his "worship" only too readily dispensable.

True service on the other hand, because of its function in a scheme of mutual obligation, implies self-respect, a solid conviction of one's own worth. Spelled out in this way the opposition may seem too pat; but it is given dramatic life in the easy condescension and unforced kindness that characterizes relationships in the Alworth household—in the indulgence with which the mistress treats the choleric outbursts of her cook, Furnace, the dignity of his office wounded by her failure to eat (I.ii); and in the comically touching affection between the servants and "Our late young

master" (I.ii and II.ii). The language in which young Alworth acknowledges their "service"—

> Your courtesies overwhelm me; I much grieve
> To part from such true friends, and yet find comfort.
>
> (II.ii.27–28)

—gracefully echoes the terms of his conversation with his own master,
Lord Lovell, and with his stepmother, and so places the relations of the
domestic "family" in living continuum with the more intimate connections of kinship.[34]

If Alworth is "young master" to his family servants, he himself owes
"service" to Lady Alworth and to Lord Lovell—to his stepmother as the
explicit incarnation of his father's patriarchal authority (I.ii.85–94), and
to Lovell as both ruler of his household and as a benevolent patriarch who
has been "more like a father to me than a master" (III.i.30). To Lovell is
given the crucial speech which defines the difference between the generous
housekeeping of "true gentry" and the domestic tyranny of the ambitious
arriviste:

> Nor am I of that harsh, and rugged temper
> As some great men are tax'd with, who imagine
> They part from the respect due to their honours,
> If they use not all such as follow 'em,
> Without distinction of their births, like slaves.
> I am not so condition'd; I can make
> A fitting difference between my foot-boy,
> And a gentleman, by want compell'd to serve me.
>
> (III.i.21–28)

Though Alworth is technically a "stipendiary," in the language of Welborne's prickly vanity (I.i.173), his relations with Lovell are governed by a
firm sense of mutual obligation—so that if Alworth's duty as a servant
requires that he yield his rights in Margaret to his master (III.i), Lovell in
turn must prove his paternal care by contriving their elopement from the
tyranny of Sir Giles.

34. Cf. Dekker's injunction in *The Seven Deadly Sins of London*: "Remember, O you rich
men, that your servants are your adopted children; they are naturalized into your blood,
and if you hurt theirs, you are guilty of letting your own" (quoted in Walzer, p. 189).

Overreach, by contrast, governs by treating even his own family as stipendiary slaves.[35] Since the only bonds he acknowledges are those of financial debt, he contemptuously denies his bankrupt nephew's kinship—"Thou art no blood of mine. Avaunt thou beggar!" (I.iii.40). By the same token once he recognizes new prospects of indebtedness he seeks Welborne's friendship with disarming candor, hailing him as "nephew" once again:

> We worldly men, when we see friends, and kinsmen,
> Past hope sunk in their fortunes, lend no hand
> To lift 'em up, but rather set our feet
> Upon their heads, to press'em to the bottom,
> And I must yield, with you I practis'd it.
> But now I see you in a way to rise,
> I can and will assist you.
>
> (III.iii.50–56)

He proposes to redeem Welborne's debts and send him "a *freeman* to the wealthy lady" (ll. 64–68; italics added): but the manumission is one which, as Welborne notes with urbane irony, only "Binds me still your servant" (l.70). The courtesies of speech are those of the traditional society, their meanings wantonly perverted:

> My deeds nephew
> Shall speak my love, what men report, I weigh not.
>
> (III.iii.75–76)

For honorable "deeds," the conventional subject of "report," Sir Giles in fact proposes to substitute the parchment deeds that will encompass the

---

35. Once again the contrast recalls the Puritan attack on traditional political thought: Overreach's tyranny with its indifference to "fitting difference" resembles the leveling despotism of the Calvinist God (Walzer, pp. 151–152), while Lovell asserts the Anglican doctrine of hierarchy, in which "men of different degrees in the body politic related to one another in terms not of command and obedience, but rather of authority and reverence. Hierarchy depended on mutual recognition of personal place" (Walzer, p. 159). General slavery is also the condition to which Luke, the pious "hypocrite" of *The City Madam* seeks to reduce his enemies, while the virtuous Lord Lacy and Sir John Frugal combine to restore a sense of fitting "distance 'twixt the city and the court" (V.iii.156), and to reinstate the proper ordering of Frugal's patriarchal family. Both orders have been undermined by the tyrannic ambition of Lady Frugal and her daughters.

final downfall of true gentry. Significantly, this exchange is immediately juxtaposed with a genuine manumission—Lovell's "discharge" of Alworth "from further service" (IV.i. 1–3)—which ends in the acknowledgment of a very different kind of debt, one which admits the primacy of honorable report:

> Let after-times report, and to you honour,
> How much I stand engag'd, for I want language
> To speak my debt.
>
> (IV.i.5–7)

It is the opposition we have met before, between Timothy Tapwell's register of chalk and the chronicles of ancient right and historic obligation—between the new morality of contract and the traditional morality of "benefits."

Sir Giles's relation with his daughter, significantly called to account as "The blest child of my industry, and wealth" (III.ii.53), is not qualitatively different from that with his nephew. For it is once again conceived in master/slave terms: Margaret owes him an absolute and peremptory duty (even to the point of prostituting herself to Lovell) and he owes her nothing in return except the promise of those honorable titles which serve to cocker up his own vanity. Shylock's wish to have his revolted daughter dead at his feet can still be read as the outrage of a distorted love; Overreach's attempt to kill Margaret is merely the calling-in of a debt— "thus I take the life / Which wretched I gave to thee" (V.i.292–293).[36] Shylock at least can suffer the pain of lost affection through the ring "I had . . . of Leah when I was a bachelor" (*Merchant of Venice*, III.i.111); Sir Giles's ring bonds him to no one, but becomes the instrument of his daughter's loss to Alworth. His corruption of family relationship to bond slavery includes his courtship of Lady Alworth—as it must have included the courtship of Mistress Welborne, Margaret's mother. It is finally a matter of indifference whether the Lady marries Welborne or himself: either match will put her fortune in his power. Set against the business

---

36. In his claim to the power of life and death over his child Overreach has the authority not only of Puritan divines like Perkins but of the Anglican convocation of 1606 (Walzer, pp. 185–191). Margaret, on the other hand, might appeal to the more liberal ethic of Seneca's *De beneficiis* 2.29 ff. which sharply contests the view that mere begetting is a benefit which no child can ever adequately repay.

contract of the two marriages which Overreach attempts to contrive, is the "solemn contract" (V.i.66) undertaken by the ideal couples of the play—a contract hedged about by nicely balanced mutual obligations of "honour," "service," and "duty" (IV.i and III, V.i).

The ending of the play vindicates, as it is bound to do, the traditional bonds of service, housekeeping, and the patriarchal family. Marriage unites the ideal households of the true gentry and establishes young Alworth as master of his own; while Welborne, his financial and moral debts discharged, sets out to redeem his honor under Lord Lovell in "service" to the supreme patriarchy, "my king, and country" (V.i.398–399). The subverters of patriarchal order, on the other hand, are made to feel the hopeless isolation of their position. Marall, the epitome of perverted service and false friendship, is somewhat smugly dismissed by Welborne to take his own place, stripped of office, among the masterless outcasts of this society:

> You are a rascal, he that dares be false
> To a master, though unjust, will ne'er be true
> To any other: look not for reward,
> Or favour from me,
> .    .    .    .    .    .
> I will take order
> Your practice shall be silenc'd.
>
> (V.i.338–344)

If "This is the haven / False servants still arrive at" (ll.349–350), the fate of false masters is even more desperate. Overreach, who hurls from the stage seeking "servants / And friends to second me" (ll.312–313), finds only revolted slaves. Forced to confront the ironic truth of his own aphorism, "Friendship is but a word," he is left to the maniacal self-assertion of despair:

> Why, is not the whole world
> Included in my self? to what use then
> Are friends, and servants? say there were a squadron
> Of pikes, lin'd through with shot, when I am mounted,
> Upon my injuries, shall I fear to charge 'em?
> .    .    .    .    .    .    .    .    .    .
> no, spite of fate,
> I will be forc'd to hell like to myself.
>
> (V.i.355–371)

If this speech seems to recall *Richard III*, the echo is fitting and perhaps deliberate, since Overreach has come to embody that same anarchic principle of self-love that Shakespeare incarnates in Richard of Gloucester. The forms and bonds of communal society, which for Overreach were vacuous nothings, prove immutably solid, while his own omnipotent bond becomes literally "nothing," "void" (ll. 289, 323), showing (through Marrall's ingenuity) "neither wax, nor words" (l. 186).[37] By the same token the chronicles of honor, which in Overreach's eyes were so much historical dust, prove indestructible, while his own "deed" turns to dust before his eyes:

> What prodigy is this, what subtle devil
> Hath raz'd out the inscription, the wax
> Turn'd into dust! the rest of my deeds whole,
> As when they were deliver'd! and this only
> Made nothing.
>
> (V.i.190–194)

Like Shylock, Sir Giles appeals to law, threatening the power of "statute" and "a hempen circle"—but the whole episode is like a parable of Dod and Cleaver's "justice" that *"vertue, that yeeldeth to every man his owne"*:

the riches gotten by ill meanes, have a heavie destinie uttered against them: *The gathering of riches by a deceitfull tongue is vanity, tossed to and fro of them that seeke death.*

And Sir Giles's fate is an ample illustration of the doom reserved for the merciless man:

*He that stoppeth his eare at the crying of the poore, he shall also cry, and not be heard.*[38]

Overreach's repudiation of society leaves him to the punishment of his own consuming egotism, "myself alone," without servants, friends, or even kin—a man without a family.[39]

---

37. Compare the conclusion to which Luke is ironically brought in *The City Madam*: "I care not where I go; what's done with words / Cannot be undone" (V.iii.147–148).

38. *Houshold Government*, E3–E3ᵛ, quoting Proverbs 21:6 and 13.

39. Here once again Overreach's individualism turns him into a kind of monstrous inversion of the alienated Puritan saint as Walzer describes him—the wanderer, cut off from family and kin, a self-chosen "masterless man" turning his back on the cries of his wife and children in his remorseless quest for salvation.

The last irony of his situation, of course, is that he has been a man trying to make a family, a dynasty of "right honourable" descendants. For all his bitter scorn for the "forms" of the hereditary order, for the hollowness of "word," "name," and "title," Sir Giles is nevertheless mesmerized by these same forms. The obsession renders him incapable of living consistently by his ruthlessly economic analysis of society. The unrecognized paradox of his desire to have his daughter made "right honourable" is what finally blinds him to Lovell's stratagem and lures him into a pit of his own digging. He is ultimately destroyed by the same monstrous fury of self-contradiction which drives him to threaten honorable revenge against the man he hopes his daughter will seduce:

> Do I wear a sword for fashion? or is this arm
> Shrunk up? or wither'd? does there live a man
> Of that large list I have encounter'd with,
> Can truly say I e'er gave inch of ground,
> Not purchas'd with his blood, that did oppose me?
> Forsake thee when the thing is done? he dares not.
> Give me but proof, he has enjoy'd thy person,
> Though all his captains, echoes to his will,
> Stood arm'd by his side to justify the wrong,
> And he himself in the head of his bold troop,
> Spite of his lordship, and his colonelship,
> Or the judge's favour, I will make him render
> A bloody and a strict accompt, and force him
> By marrying thee, to cure thy wounded honour.
>
>                                     (III.ii.140–153)

Marall's intervention '("Sir, the man of honour's come," l. 154) points up the absurd irony: the gestures, the rhetoric are those of the code he is seeking to subvert; they acknowledge debts and accounts of a kind he professes not to countenance; and they are echoed with savage pathos in the berserk frenzy of his final speech:

> I'll through the battalia, and that routed,
> I'll fall to execution.
> [*Flourishing his sword unsheathed*]
>             Ha! A am feeble:
> Some undone widow sits upon mine arm,
> And takes away the use of't; and my sword

>Glu'd to my scabbard, with wrong'd orphans' tears,
>Will not be drawn.
>
>                                        (V.i.360–365)

The disproportion between the ranting heroics of Overreach's defiance and the domestic ordinariness of the situations which provoke it is not an arbitrary comic device: it is the expression of that fatal confusion of purpose on which his life is wrecked. Sir Giles is an instinctive revolutionary whose vision is fatally constricted by the values of the society against which he is in revolt.[40]

But the confusion is not his alone: it also infects his maker. For all the consistency with which Massinger attempts to construct his patriarchal arguments, ambiguities remain in his own stance. Some of these appear in the characterization of his villain: the sense of unbalance which has worried critics of the play has much to do with the overplus of energy and dramatic life in Sir Giles—as though a part of Massinger identified with his violent iconoclasm. And something of the same subversive impulse may be felt in the treatment of Marrall. The psychological penetration with which Massinger uncovers the source of his peculiarly vicious symbiosis of envy and subservience surely springs from the dramatist's own early experience among the upper servants of a great household. The hysterical fury with which Marrall announces his own revolt reveals a sense of deep violation that helps to account for the other revolutionary currents in the play:

>OVERREACH
>Mine own varlet
>Rebel against me?

40. Ironically, he makes the same foolish confusion as is fostered by Lady Frugal: Milliscent flatters her mistress's pride with the hope

>to see
>A country knight's son and heir walk bare before you
>When you are a countess,

while she herself expects to "take the upper hand of a squire's wife, through justice" (*City Madam*, I.i.71–77). Luke Frugal similarly promises to revive "the memory / Of the Roman matrons who kept captive queens / To be their handmaids" (*City Madam*, III.ii. 162–164). Massinger's revolutionaries (like the Commonwealth leaders after them) can still conceive of social change only within the framework of what Andrew Sharp has called "heraldic definition." See Andrew Sharp, "Edward Waterhouse's View of Social Change in Seventeenth Century England," *Past and Present*, LXII (1974), 27–46.

MARRALL
    Yes, and uncase you too.
The idiot; the patch; the slave; the booby;
The property fit only to be beaten
For your morning exercise; your football, or
Th' unprofitable lump of flesh; your drudge
Can now anatomize you, and lay open
All your black plots; and level with the earth
Your hill of pride; and with these gabions guarded,
Unload my great artillery, and shake,
Nay pulverize the walls you think defend you.

(V.i.213–223)[41]

Yet the levelers of the play can make no common cause: Marrall's revolt is merely against Sir Giles, and both are simply individualist anarchs. It was not until Congreve brought the two together in the character of the Double-Dealer, Maskwell, who combines something of Overreach's iconoclastic energy with Marrall's humiliated bitterness, that the English stage could produce a genuinely revolutionary comedy. Congreve, significantly, came from a social background very similar to Massinger's; but he wrote with two revolutions behind him—and even Maskwell had to be destroyed in the end.

A further uneasy ambiguity involves the problem of Overreach's own patriarchial authority; and this may be partly a function of Massinger's attempt to combine Jonsonian satire with a romantic comedy more immediately appealing to the Phoenix audience. The conventions of satire require that Marrall be thoroughly punished for his revolt; the conventions of comic romance require that Margaret be rewarded for hers. Massinger the conservative satirist is forced to argue that even the worst masters deserve to be obeyed, even while Massinger the romancer is vindicating the overthrow of tyrannical fathers. A sincere patriarchalist can hardly have it both ways, since the authority of fathers and masters is one and indivisible. But both ways are the way Massinger likes to have it: in *The Roman Actor*, for instance, a similar dilemma is resolved by a pious,

---

41. Compare Greedy's marvelous comical iconoclasm when Lovell offers his hand:

This is a lord, and some think this a favour;
But I had rather have my hand in a dumpling.

(III.ii.165–166)

but fundamentally evasive, appeal to legitimacy. The First Tribune acknowledges that Domitian was a tyrant who deserved his end, but warns his assassins that

> he was our prince,
> However wicked; and, in you, 'tis murder,
> Which whosoe'er succeeds him will revenge.
>                              (*Roman Actor*, V.ii.77–79)

Moralists like Dod and Cleaver had insisted on the limits to patriarchial authority, especially in the matter of forced marriages:

This is a most unnaturall and cruell part, for parents to sell their children for gaine and lucre, and to marrie them when they list, without the good liking of their children, and so bring them into bondage . . . especially in this matter of greatest moment and value of all other worldly things whatsoever, let them . . . beware they turn not their fatherly jurisdiction and governement, into a tyrannicall sourenesse and waywardnesse, letting their will go for a law. . . . the rule of parents over their children, ought to resemble the government of good Princes toward their subjects: that is to say, it must bee milde, gentle, and easie to be borne.[42]

But children are granted no right of revolt against such bondage—"whatsoever they doe to their fathers and mothers . . . they doe it to God"—and those who marry without their parents' consent incur "the curse of God."[43] Batty similarly insists that even foolish and crabbed parents must be obeyed, and inveighs against the impiety of "private spousages and secret contractes . . . enterprised and taken in hand without the consent of Parentes."[44] Most patriarchial writing, however, ad-

---

42. *Houshold Government*, V5ᵛ–V7. Walzer, pp. 193–196, notes the way in which the Puritan insistence on voluntary marriage tended to "subtly . . . undermine" the authority of parents which they ostensibly maintained.

43. *Houshold Government*, Y4–Z1.

44. Batty, S4ᵛ,Bb4. Cf. George Wither's *Fidelia* in which the poet inveighs against parental tyranny:

> For though the will of our Creator binds
> Each child to learn and know his parents' minds,
> Yet sure am I so just a deity
> Commandeth nothing against piety.
>                              (Quoted in Walzer, p. 194)

For a thoroughgoing patriarchalist like Filmer, on the other hand, no such qualification of

mits an escape clause, and it is one which Massinger gratefully seizes upon. The child's final duty, after all, is to his Father in Heaven; and thus resistance becomes possible to parents or magistrates who command "wicked and ungodly things." "Wee must obey God rather than man," says Batty: "Honour thou thy father, so that he doth not separate thee from thy true father."[45] From the moment Sir Giles orders Margaret to prostitute herself to Lovell, and she identifies the projected match as founded on "devilish doctrine" (III.ii.122), from the moment too at which Lovell, in confirmation, castigates the blasphemer's "atheistical assertions" (IV.i.154), we are meant to see that Overreach's government undermines the very foundations of patriarchal authority. No longer to be regarded as a natural father, he has become simply what Alworth called him, "Mammon in Sir Giles Overreach" (III.i.83).

The invocation of this Morality abstraction exactly anticipates the device by which Massinger seeks to bolster the uncertain ordering of his conclusion. That stroke of divine vengeance which suddenly paralyzes Overreach's sword arm—reminiscent of the astonishing coup by which D'Amville is made to dash out his own brains in the denouement of *The Atheist's Tragedy*—invites us to review the whole action in theological terms:

> Here is a precedent to teach wicked men
> That when they leave religion, and turn atheists
> Their own abilities leave them.
>
> (V.i.379–381)

In the light of this comfortable moralization a quasi-allegorical scheme begins to emerge by which the whole conclusion is seen to hang on three familiar parables. Most obviously Welborne's redemption from his life of prodigal abandon recalls the forgiveness accorded to another repentant prodigal in Christ's parable. Hungry and in rags in the opening scene,

---

authority is possible. Filmer maintained: "1. That there is no form of government, but monarchy only. 2. That there is no monarchy but paternal. 3. That there is no paternal monarchy, but absolute, or arbitrary. 4. That there is no such thing as an aristocracy or democracy. 5. That there is no such form of government as a tyranny. 6. That the people are not born free by nature" (quoted in Schochet, *Patriarchalism in Political Thought*, p. 115).

45. Batty, S3$^v$–S4$^v$.

Welborne is the very image of the starving prodigal in Luke; Lady Alworth kills the fatted calf in the feasting which marks his readmission to the patriarchal society, while Sir Giles, that "scourge of prodigals" is ironically cozened into sharing the biblical father's role:

But the father said to his servants, Bring forth the best robe, and put *it* on him; and put a ring on his hand, and shoes on *his* feet.
Luke 15:22

Overreach similarly commands Marrall

> go to my nephew;
> See all his debts discharg'd, and help his worship
> To fit on his rich suit.
> (IV.i.33–35)

"This my son was dead, and is alive again; he was lost and is found" (Luke 15:24); and Overreach, however hypocritically, acknowledges a similar resurrection of the nephew whose kinship he has once denied. At the same time the envy and astonishment of the elder brother at the restoration of his wastrel sibling is echoed in the baffled indignation of both Marrall and Overreach at Welborne's sudden elevation. Finally, Welborne's offer of "service" to Lovell and his king at the end of the play is a transposition of the prodigal's penitence:

I will arise and go to my father, and say unto him, Father, I have sinned against heaven, and before thee, And am no more worthy to be called thy son: make me as one of thy hired servants.
(Luke 15:18–19)

The identification of "Mammon in Sir Giles Overreach" links the fable in turn to the parable which immediately follows the Prodigal Son in Luke—the Unjust Steward, a parable about the payment of debts and the morality of true service, which precisely anticipates the play's judgment of Marrall:

If therefore ye have not been faithful in the unrighteous mammon, who will commit to your trust the true *riches*?
And if ye have not been faithful in that which is another man's, who shall give you that which is your own?

No servant can serve two masters: for either he will hate the one, and love the other; or else he will hold to the one, and despise the other. Ye cannot serve God and mammon.

(Luke 16:11–13)

"I must grant / " Lady Alworth has reflected, as though with this passage in mind, "Riches well got to be a useful servant, / But a bad master" (IV.i. 187–189). Sir Giles's own fate more loosely paraphrases the last of the parables in this series, that of Dives and Lazarus. The Overreach described by Furnace who "feeds high, keeps many servants . . . [is] rich in his habit; vast in his expenses" (II.ii. 110–112) recalls that "rich man, which was clothed in purple and fine linen, and fared sumptuously every day" (Luke 16:19), spurning the beggar Welborne as Dives spurns the beggar Lazarus; and his desperate fate at the end of the play is equally suggestive. As Sir Giles is carried off to "some dark room" in Bedlam, his daughter reaches out to him—"O my dear father!" (V.i. 378)—but between them, as between Dives and Lazarus, "there is a great gulf fixed:" Overreach, tormented by "furies, with steel whips / To scourge my ulcerous soul" (ll. 368–369) is already in hell.

In the end this invocation of a theological scheme is a kind of cheat designed to silence the awkward questions the play has raised. Who, finally, are the innovators in this social upheaval: the old gentry who contrive a deceitful "new ways" to pay their "old debts," or Overreach, the proponent of contract and statute law? In *The Merchant of Venice* such questions are preempted by the triumphant appeal from Old Law to New which is implicit in the play's whole mythic structure: the Jonsonian realism of Massinger's satire forbids so nearly consistent a solution. Furthermore, the play's very conservatism has a revolutionary potential: Overreach, in many ways, is less a usurper than a legitimate patriarch who has tyrannically abused his powers and who accordingly is deposed. In the light of this we may remember that Coleridge thought Massinger "a decided whig,"[46] and that some dozen years after *A New Way* the dramatist's views on Charles's personal rule were to attract the indignation and censorship of the king himself.[47] Overreach's deposition, though carried out in the name of the old hierarchic order, has awkward contrac-

---

46. Quoted in John Danby, *Elizabethan and Jacobean Poets* (London, 1965), p. 184.
47. See Andrew Gurr, *The Shakespearean Stage* (Cambridge, Eng., 1970), p. 55.

tual implications—implications of a kind which would be spelled out in the trial and execution of the royal patriarch, Charles I.

Outwardly, however, the social vision of the play remains impeccably conservative: once again the rigid and indiscriminate operation of law—the new way—is mitigated by the equity of communal obligation—the old debts. The patriarchal hierarchy is conceived not simply as a ladder of authority, but also as a family circle—a circle bound by Seneca's decorum of giving, receiving, and returning.[48] The symbol for that bonding, here as in *The Merchant*, is the ring. The ring with which Overreach unwittingly secures his daughter's marriage to young Alworth completes with benign irony a Senecan circle of obligation, by returning to Alworth the lands unjustly taken from his father. Another such circle, broken by the ingratitude of Tapwell and the unkindness of Overreach, is knit up in the restoration of Welborne—a restoration brought about through Lady Alworth's acknowledgment of obligations and determination to "redeem" what's past (I.iii.118–119). In the last analysis the play's "new way" (for all its witty duplicity) is an old way, the way of a vanishing society—new only by virtue of its unsatisfactory appeal to New Testament values against the Old (ironically epitomized in the "new man" Overreach). However harmonious the circles contrived in this old new way, they cannot, even in comic fantasy, contain those turbulent spirits whose rise would break the circle forever. Whatever was restored in 1660, it did not include an intact patriarchal ideology. The literature of the Restoration from *Aureng-Zebe* to *Abasalom and Achitophel*, from *Venice Preserved* to *Love for Love*, is full of failing patriarchs, enfeebled, corrupt, and ridiculous by turns. It contemplates a world where, in Otway's words, "the foundation's lost of common good" and that "dissolves all former bonds of service."[49]

48. Seneca, *De beneficiis* I.3.2–5.
49. *Venice Preserved*, ed. Malcolm Kelsall, Regents Renaissance Drama Series (Lincoln, Nebr., 1969), I.i.201, 211.

# Notes on Contributors

LEE BLISS, Assistant Professor of English at the University of California, Santa Barbara, has published essays on Shakespeare and Webster.

RICHARD BRUCHER is Assistant Professor of English at the University of Maine at Orono. He has an article on *Hamlet* and *The Revenger's Tragedy* awaiting publication, and he is writing a book on witty and ritualistic violence in Elizabethan and Jacobean tragedy.

MAURICE CHARNEY is Distinguished Professor of English at Rutgers University. His most recent book is entitled *Comedy High and Low*. He is presently engaged in editing a collection of essays, *Shakespearean Comedy: Theory and Traditions*, for the *New York Literary Forum*; a book on Joe Orton; and a book on Shakespeare in relation to his fellow dramatists.

HOWARD C. COLE, Associate Professor of English at the University of Illinois (Urbana), is the author of *A Quest of Inquirie: Some Contexts of Tudor Literature* (1973) and several articles on Shakespearean comedy and its backgrounds. He is presently completing a study of the *All's Well* story from Boccaccio to Florio.

NANCY S. LEONARD is Assistant Professor of English at Bard College and the author of recent articles on Sir Thomas Wyatt's poetry and on Shakespeare's problem comedies.

JOHN S. MEBANE is Assistant Professor of English at Troy State University, Dothan, Alabama. He is currently at work on a book entitled *Renaissance Magic and English Renaissance Drama*.

MICHAEL NEILL is Senior Lecturer in English at the University of Auckland, New Zealand. He is the author of a number of articles on Shakespeare and his contemporaries. He is currently working on the social politics of Restoration comedy and coediting an edition of Marston.

LEO SALINGAR is a Fellow of Trinity College and Lecturer in English at Cambridge. His most recent work includes a book, *Shakespeare and the Traditions of Comedy* (1974), and an article on "Comic Form in Ben Jonson: Volpone and the Philosopher's Stone," in *English Drama: Forms and Development*, edited by Marie Axton and Raymond Williams.

FRANK WHIGHAM is an Assistant Professor of English and European Studies at Claremont Graduate School. He is currently writing a book on courtesy and ideology in Renaissance England.